William R. McIntyre
Paladin of the Common Law

This is the first biography of a justice of the Supreme Court of Canada to appear since the entrenchment of the Canadian Charter of Rights and Freedoms in 1982. McIntyre played a key role at a critical time in Canadian constitutional history, as the Bench sought to give the new Charter life and legal authority.

Using archival resources, interviews with contemporaries, and legal sources, W.H. McConnell traces McIntyre's personal evolution from defending the Charter as a workable counterpoint to established common law principles, to gradual disenchantment with its overuse, by many of his colleagues and the lower courts, for developing social policy. In retrospect McIntyre's reservations have been prophetic: the "interventionist" trend has given rise to considerable criticism of the court by legal professionals, the media, and the Canadian public. He remained, however, a staunch proponent of freedom of expression and, in the *Andrews* case, framed the pivotal definition of "equality rights" in section 15 of the Charter that is still prevalently applied in Canadian courts.

McConnell is persuasive in connecting McIntyre's restrained approach to Charter jurisprudence, especially its relation to governmental legislation, with his upbringing in Moose Jaw during the Depression and his early career at the Bar. This is an original contribution to our understanding both of an important judge and an important era in Canadian legal history.

W.H. MCCONNELL is professor emeritus of law at the University of Saskatchewan.

The Hon. W.R. McIntyre
Justice of the Supreme Court, 1979-89

WILLIAM R. McINTYRE
Paladin of the Common Law

W.H. McConnell

PUBLISHED FOR CARLETON UNIVERSITY
BY McGILL-QUEEN'S UNIVERSITY PRESS,
MONTREAL & KINGSTON, LONDON, ITHACA

Copyright © Carleton University Press, 2000

ISBN 0-88629-341-3

Printed and bound in Canada

Canadian Cataloguing in Publication Data

McConnell, W. H. (William Howard), 1930-
    William R. McIntyre : paladin of the common law

Includes bibliographical references and index.
ISBN 0-88629-341-3

    1. McIntyre, William R. 2. Canada. Supreme Court—
Biography. 3. Judges—Canada—Biography. I. Title.

KE8248.M35M33 1999   347.71'03534   C99-901491-9

Interior: Lynn's Desktop Publishing
Cover: BCumming Designs

McGill-Queen's University Press acknowledges the financial support of the Government of Canada through the Book Publishing Industry Development Program (BPIDP) for our publishing activities. We also acknowledge the support of the Canada Council for the Arts for our publishing program.

CONTENTS

	Preface	*vii*
I	Early Influences: Education and Wartime	*1*
II	Practice in Victoria	*21*
III	A Judge in British Columbia	*37*
IV	The Supreme Court of Canada	*63*
V	McIntyre's Constitutional and Quasi-Constitutional Decisions	*99*
VI	Criminal and Other Decisions	*153*
VII	The Charter of Rights and Freedoms	*185*
VIII	The Summing Up	*215*
	Bibliography	*237*
	Index	*243*

PREFACE

For the common lawyer and constitutionalist, William McIntyre's judicial career elucidates an important time of transition in Canadian legal history. The decade that McIntyre spent on the Supreme Court of Canada (1979-89) was divided equally into a phase of mainly "common law" adjudication followed by another compassing the inaugural years of interpreting the new Canadian Charter of Rights and Freedoms. Although the Charter was entrenched in the Canadian Constitution in 1982, Charter appeals to the Supreme Court only began arriving from lower courts for final disposition about two years later.

After some 20 years of legal practice in Victoria, McIntyre was appointed to the British Columbia Supreme Court in 1967 and to the provincial Court of Appeal in 1973. Of the three tribunals on which he has sat he was fondest, he said, of the B.C. Supreme Court. As the superior court of general jurisdiction in this province and an historic descendent of the English court of King's Bench, it was this forum where McIntyre felt most fulfilled in his vocation. Here, on a gradual case by case basis, the principles of common law were elaborated in litigation involving contracts, torts, property, and criminal law. Here was where the real law was pronounced in legal disputes between subject and subject and in causes prosecuted by the Crown, and where the right to liberty and procedural fairness was most clearly enunciated. Appellate courts, like the Supreme Court of Canada, were essentially courts of error which affirmed or reversed decisions by trial courts of original jurisdiction.

As an admirer of the common law, McIntyre initially saw no incompatibility between its principles and those of the new Charter. Except in specific areas such as language guarantees, almost all of the principles of the Charter were traceable to common law antecedents. They were not all present in earlier times, of course, but had developed gradually over centuries. The distinction between the common law and the Charter was that the latter, through constitutional entrenchment, was hierarchically superior to statute and common law and prevailed over them in case of conflict.

When the Supreme Court of Canada embarked on its inaugural interpretations of the Charter under the leadership of Chief Justice Brian Dickson, McIntyre attempted to construe the Charter consistently with common law principles. As time passed, however, he was disappointed by the propensity of a majority of his colleagues to invoke Charter norms in a broad fashion that undermined the texture of the common law and framed social policy. He regarded the latter tendency as an essential abrogation of legislative prerogative. Perhaps the most far-reaching manifestation of this trend occurred once the court began to "read in" provisions deemed to be missing from statutes. That McIntyre was never an enemy of the Charter, however, is amply demonstrated by his creative formulation of the test for "equality rights" in section 15, in the *Andrews* case, a very important contribution to Charter jurisprudence. His growing disenchantment with Charter interpretation did not impair friendships with Justice Antonio Lamer (as he then was), and Madam Justice Bertha Wilson, who deeply disagreed with his approach to the Charter but remain among his closest friends.

This examination of McIntyre's life, opinions, and legal craftsmanship endeavours to show how one important jurist, at a pivotal time in Canadian legal history, assessed the advantages and disadvantages of the new legal order.

Jennie Strickland's meticulous editing of the text and her advice on style, syntax, and substance was invaluable. To her, and to Dr. John Flood of Carleton University Press, I am deeply indebted. I also want to thank Douglas Campbell for his assistance with an earlier version of the manuscript.

Mr. Justice William McIntyre was tireless in answering queries and suggesting further sources for research during my 1996-97 sabbatical year in Vancouver, when this work was being prepared. Other members of the McIntyre family, Dr. Barbara McIntyre, Dr. Hugh McIntyre, and Mr. Justice McIntyre's children, John S. McIntyre and Elizabeth Diamond, provided useful information, as did Elizabeth's husband Tony Diamond. Among McIntyre's Supreme Court colleagues, I was kindly granted interviews by former Chief Justice Brian Dickson, Chief Justice Antonio Lamer, and Madam Justice Bertha Wilson. Mr. Justice G.V. La Forest supplied helpful information by letter. Mr. Justice D.M.M. Goldie of the British Columbia Court of

Appeal; McIntyre's former law partner, Mr. Justice Lloyd McKenzie of the British Columbia Supreme Court; Mr. Justice M.A. "Sandy" MacPherson of the Saskatchewan Court of Queen's Bench; Mr. Justice William Grant of the Nova Scotia Supreme Court; the Honourable Allan E. Blakeney, QC, and the Honourable Marc Lalonde, QC, Harry Rankin, QC, Carol Fogal, Ray Bryant, and Edward Cantell of the British Columbia bar, all gave helpful interviews. George MacMinn, QC, clerk of the B.C. Legislative Assembly, who appeared in criminal prosecutions in Victoria as McIntyre's junior, and David Ricardo Williams, QC, an authority on legal history who appeared against McIntyre in court, and later pled before him when he sat on the provincial bench, were both most helpful. Bill MacKay and Glenn Wright of the RCMP Centennial Museum, Regina, supplied useful archival material.

Among my academic colleagues, Professor Alan C. Cairns read the whole manuscript and made invaluable comments, and Professor Emeritus Douglas A. Schmeiser gave useful counsel on specific points of constitutional law, as did Professor Stephen A. Scott of McGill University. Professor Len Findlay provided material on Dr. Carlyle King, one of McIntyre's teachers at the University of Saskatchewan. I am also indebted to Dean Kent Roach and Professor Ron Fritz. Dr. Maryla Waters, a legal historian of the University of Victoria was very helpful, as was Dr. George F. Curtis, a Saskatchewan law alumnus and founding dean of the U.B.C. law school, both of whom I interviewed. Reverend J.A. Davidson and his wife Marian, who knew McIntyre as a university student, provided a valuable interview.

Invaluable assistance was afforded by three Saskatchewan law students, Carla Crozier, Mark Franko and James Fyfe, and research resources were provided by Ken Whiteway, law librarian, and the staffs of the University of Saskatchewan and University of British Columbia law libraries, the British Columbia Provincial Archives in Victoria, and the historical section of the Vancouver Public Library.

For any errors that remain, I am alone responsible.

I am especially thankful for generous funding supplied by the University of Saskatchewan Publication Fund, administered by Dr. Michael E. Corcoran, Vice President (Research), and from the Legal Endowment Fund, made available by Saskatchewan Law Dean and now University President, R. Peter MacKinnon, QC.

Warm thanks go to Mandy Hill of Saskatoon and Judith Sommerfeld of Vancouver for their excellent and painstaking preparation of the manuscript, to my generous hosts in Vancouver during my sabbatical year, Hugh and Georgia Humphries, whose commodious residence on West 10th Avenue provided an excellent base for meditation and research, and also to my Saskatoon hosts, John and Johanna Lucas.

I

EARLY INFLUENCES:
EDUCATION AND WARTIME SERVICE

WILLIAM ROGERS MCINTYRE was born in Lachine, Quebec, on March 15, 1918, third of the six children of Charles Sidney McIntyre and Pauline May Sifton, and the only child to be born outside of Moose Jaw, Saskatchewan. His parents were native Ontarians but had joined the westward migration to the prairie provinces that began at the turn of the century, and the family had been firmly ensconced in the Canadian West for more than a decade by the time William was born. His father settled into a solid position with the Prairie City Oil Company and later with its successor companies, North Star and Shell Oil, where he would work all his life. William's lineage on his father's side was a mixture of Scottish and English, on his mother's, Irish Protestant. Her ancestors, the Siftons, had preceded her husband's, the McIntyres, in settling and farming the area and also had better success, but the agricultural society in which this couple grew up demanded strength of character and personal sacrifice of all its members, and this pioneering heritage left its stamp on their children.

The children's professional lives testify to this spirit. The eldest, Hugh, became a successful surgeon in Moose Jaw. William's older sister Barbara taught school in Saskatchewan and St. Louis, Missouri. She obtained her PhD in Speech at the University of Pittsburgh and taught there for 16 years before taking academic positions at Northwestern and the University of Victoria. Of William's two younger sisters, Jean became a nurse. She took specialized training in England and Montreal and went on to work in the public health services of Saskatchewan and British Columbia. Eleanor served in the women's division of the RCAF during World War II. She later specialized in physiotherapy and worked at the Montreal General Hospital. Jack, the youngest, studied medicine at the University of Saskatchewan and McGill after completing military service. He did postgraduate work in obstetrics and gynecology in Boston before entering practice in Maine and later, Baton Rouge, Louisiana.

Children generally began work at a much younger age than they do now, and higher education was less accessible. In all, Sidney had only four years of elementary schooling, which in Ontario was then called "First Book." After the death of his mother, Justice McIntyre found among her possessions his father's entrance certificate, which enabled the recipient to enter high school; he later obtained his high school certificate through home study. Despite his meagre formal education, Sidney was an avid reader throughout his life and was keenly interested in politics and current events. A good conversationalist with a well-stocked mind, he resolved to provide his children with the educational opportunities he had lacked. Indeed, this was a common goal of both parents. Whenever any of the children became despondent about school, their father would say, "The cheapest thing in the world is muscle." His love of education was manifest in a peculiarly Scottish trait. When, as frequently happened, he became incensed at what he thought was a wrong-headed argument proposed by a minister or other University-trained man, he would always hear them out — this was an educated man speaking, and for that reason his opinions should not be interrupted or simply brushed off.

As Sidney became responsible for the sale, storage, and distribution of his company's petroleum products through southwestern Saskatchewan, Pauline was left for long periods to nurture, preserve and protect the family on her own. She was a gentle woman who also possessed great inner strength. Her children would not realize until they had grown up, the burden that their mother had borne throughout their childhood. In her youth she had been a brilliant student. She and her sister were awarded gold medals upon graduating from high school. Economic circumstances made a university career impossible, but she never lost her keen interest in ideas. Pauline and Sidney resolved that their children would have the educational advantages they had been forced to forego.

The family attended church but as a boy, McIntyre found it difficult to listen through the long sermons and didactic Sunday School sessions. In retrospect he is happy he went, although he came away with little affinity for the dogmatic aspects of religion. Like many others brought up in a churchgoing atmosphere, he retained a predilection for the ethics or morality of religion even when the more doctrinal aspects had ceased to persuade. The McIntyre home was a happy one where the lively energies of childhood were not constrained. William's daughter Elizabeth considers her father to be a Christian Agnostic. He had a respect for religion and worked hard in a disciplined way. "He toiled," she said, "like an 'intellectual Jesuit,' concentrating on how to make the most compelling legal argument possible in a given case." Her father regards the early religious influence more simply. He does not regret it, but cannot honestly say it made much difference in his attitudes to life. He can scarcely recall, in fact, having attended religious services since the last time the army paraded him to church during World War II.

The McIntyre home was an intellectually lively place, where politics and other subjects, as Barbara recalls, were often discussed around the dinner table. The family was far from uniform in its political views. McIntyre remembers that his father's brother was a confirmed Liberal, while his father was a Tory, and remained so until he became disillusioned with the dismal economic performance of the Conservative Anderson government in Saskatchewan (1929-34) and became a Liberal. At the time McIntyre regarded his father's abandonment of Conservatism as a form of apostasy, but he later became a Liberal himself. His earlier disapproval largely stemmed from the fact that Liberals had formed every government in Saskatchewan from 1905, when it achieved provincehood, until 1929. McIntyre's mother came from a strong Liberal tradition, but in 1957 she succumbed to Diefenbaker's oratory and voted Conservative. Sid was sad when he learned of his wife's change of heart.

McIntyre remembers the Moose Jaw of his youth as a thriving, booming, active town that served as the divisional point for the CPR, which connected with the Soo line from Chicago. The town had an exceptional public library for a community of its size, and gifted teachers in its schools. Among local industries were the Robin Hood flour mill and Swift's packers. With the onset of the Great Depression in 1929, however, economic stagnation retarded population growth, with the result that Moose Jaw had roughly the same population in 1941, when McIntyre left university to join the army, as in September 1923, his first day at elementary school. The removal of the major part of the CPR's operations and other industrial underpinnings from Moose Jaw after World War II reduced the economic base of the town and limited its prosperity.

Despite hard times, McIntyre ranks the Central Collegiate of his day as an outstanding secondary school, an evaluation concurred in by fellow alumnus Dr. George F. Curtis, the founding Dean of the University of British Columbia law school, who was 12 years older than McIntyre and had attended the Collegiate earlier. McIntyre also lauds the efforts of the University of Saskatchewan to make university education more accessible to residents of the province in the midst of economic depression. Where high schools had appropriate faculties, as in Moose Jaw or Regina, first-year university courses were offered locally, with professors from the university travelling to Moose Jaw to give lectures in some courses while high school teachers conducted others. Final exams were set and marked by the University, and those who passed them received credit for an entire first-year course. Accordingly, McIntyre finished his first year of university in Moose Jaw in 1936-37 and started second-year Arts in Saskatoon in 1937-38, which then enabled him to enter law school (after two years in Arts) the following year. He was enrolled in the combined Arts-Law program, which allowed a student to obtain degrees in both Arts and Law by taking certain additional courses in five years rather than six.

McIntyre remembers the terrible devastation caused in Saskatchewan by natural disasters and their economic consequences in the dozen years or so after the onset of the Great Depression. "In 1929," he recalls, "I was 11 years old. By the time I was 12 or 13, I had resolved not to spend my life in Saskatchewan." People were wondering whether these terrible conditions were ever going to end. "My memory is just of a brownish-grey landscape with the air full of dust. I remember going to Victoria during the war; and there was no dust in the clear Victoria air. To me wind and dust were the same thing. It was only later that I realized Victoria was windy enough — but it did not seem so to one from the prairies in those days." The Saskatchewan of that era was a land of drought, rust, grasshoppers, and dust storms. The year 1928 produced the biggest grain crop in the province's history and prices were also very good, but this was followed by the great crop failure of 1929 and a decade or more of unremitting natural disaster. The social and psychological consequences of the Depression in Saskatchewan were formidable.

Because of his father's contacts in the oil industry, McIntyre was able to earn money during summer vacations working in a bulk oil warehouse and driving trucks for the North Star and Texaco oil companies. In 1937, when the effects of Depression and drought were at their worst, he was driving a truck from Moose Jaw to a town called McCord, two or three miles from the U.S. border. "That was on the 22nd of June; I remember the date," he says, and I didn't see anything green. I saw only one or two animals in an area once known for its livestock. That was the year they took much of the livestock out of Saskatchewan; there wasn't enough feed. I remember talking to M.A. MacPherson, who was Provincial Secretary and Treasurer in the Anderson government from 1929 to 1934. If I remember correctly he figures the whole revenue of the Province of Saskatchewan was only $17 million; that was what they took in, not counting grants from Ottawa.

I was travelling along a road towards Brownlee, Saskatchewan one day. The wind got up and the dust started blowing. Finally, I couldn't see the radiator cap on the hood of the truck from my place in the cab. I had to stop, put on all the lights, and work my way around the side of the truck to see how much space I had in order to get off the road. I kept my hand on the truck so I would know where it was. I stayed there until the wind abated.

I remember driving into clouds of grasshoppers. They would come so fast it was just like rain or hail falling on the rooftop. My arm would rest on the side of the open window and it would be hit by flying grasshoppers. One would get painful bruises at times. Whenever I stopped at a farm or a prairie town, chickens and turkeys would come and pick all the dead grasshoppers off the truck for food. One good thing about grasshoppers was that there were lots of good turkeys and chickens later! It was a place of utter discouragement and I hadn't the slightest intention of ever returning. It was visceral.

World War II broke out in September 1939, when McIntyre was in his second year of law school. The following year was also the year of the first good wheat crop in ten years. "We knew at the university we were going to be in the war. I remember the Dean of the law school saying to us boys that there would be lots of war for us and there should be no hurry. One of the most moving things about the first year of the war was that father and mother wanted me to stay on, the Dean wanted me to stay on, and most of the class did stay on."

On a monthly wage of $50.00 for driving a truck, Bill was able to save enough money to support his university studies. He recalls that the tuition when he commenced study in Arts and Science in Saskatoon was $60.00 per year, and that by the time he started law it had increased to $90.00, a modest sum by today's standards. He was able to live in residence at St. Andrews College for $7.00 per week for room and board. The small University of Saskatchewan of that day had about sixteen hundred students when he entered in the late 1930s and eighteen hundred when he left, about one-tenth the current enrolment.

The teachers he remembers best from his pre-law studies in Saskatoon were Dr. Carlyle King,[1] in English, and Dr. George Britnell, in Economics. In two courses, English 41 and 51, the former introduced a wide array of authors and insisted on good grammar and syntax in all written work. "Professor King had a slight hesitancy in his speech and was not a strong-looking personality," McIntyre recalls, "but he was a very impressive lecturer who improved our comprehension of literature and our writing style by having us write shorter critiques, which he criticized." King was a political radical. He was a pacifist, a socialist, and an anti-imperialist, and belonged to the wing of the Cooperative Commonwealth Federation (CCF) led by J.S. Woodsworth, which opposed Canada's entry into the war. McIntyre was impressed by many of the political ideals expounded by King in his classes but considered the CCF an impractical instrument for implementing such ideals. Social justice would be achieved incrementally and gradually rather than overnight, through some utopian vision. While McIntyre was never an ardent political partisan, he was inclined to support the Liberal Party as the best vehicle to achieve practical reform.

The small but dynamic law school to which McIntyre came in the later thirties had no permanent housing of its own on the Saskatoon campus. For a time after the inception of the three year LL.B. program in 1912, lectures were held downtown in buildings adjacent to local law firms where students articled at the same time. Downtown lawyers actually complemented the small permanent law faculty by serving as sessional lecturers. Classes were later moved to the administration building on campus. In McIntyre's time, the classrooms and the law faculty were situated in Qu'Appelle Hall, which doubled as a student residence. It was only in 1967-68, during Dean Otto E. Lang's time, that the College of Law acquired its permanent home in the Arts-Commerce complex. McIntyre considers that the University of Saskatchewan had, at that time, as good a law faculty as any he has since encountered in other law schools. He recalls that while there were only three full-time professors and never more than 47 law students during the years he attended, every class and every lecture was virtually a seminar because of the small enrolment. The professors worked constantly in the library with the students and were always accessible for consultation. To anyone of sceptical disposition, he cites, *inter alia*, the great success of local law graduates in the practice of public law.

Among earlier graduates of the law school, Wilber R. Jackett and Elmer A. Driedger both served as Deputy Ministers of Justice in Ottawa. Jackett was also President of the Exchequer Court and inaugural Chief Justice of the Federal Court of Canada, which succeeded it in 1970-71, while Driedger was the virtual draftsman of John Diefenbaker's Canadian Bill of Rights and the writer of legal textbooks still in use.[2] A large number of able colleagues in the Department of Justice were also alumni of the Saskatchewan law school, including David Mundell, Edward Mile, T.M. Anderson, and later, E.A. Tollefson and Barry Strayer, who helped to draft the Charter of Rights and Freedoms before he became a judge on the Federal Court. Mundell was also Chief Counsel to the Attorney General of Ontario, and E. Russell Hopkins was law clerk to the Senate. Two graduates from the 1950s, Otto Lang and Ray Hnatyshyn, both served as Ministers of Justice in the federal cabinet and, of course, McIntyre and W.Z. Estey served concurrently in the 1980s on the nine-member Supreme Court of Canada.

It would certainly be a rarity for smaller law schools to have two sitting members on the nation's final appellate court at the same time. The distinguished Canadian historian P.B. Waite has referred to the disproportionate employment of Saskatchewan law graduates in the federal public service in the context of the Quebec-Ottawa dispute in the 1950s over federal grants to universities:

> St. Laurent feared in 1951 that federal grants to universities would provoke a new quarrel with Duplessis. He would rather have raised tax rental payments in order to allow the provinces to support their own universities better. Pickersgill may have persuaded St. Laurent to the contrary. He argued that the high mobility of university graduates encouraged politicians in, say, Saskatchewan to ask why Saskatchewan farmers should pay taxes to help educate lawyers in Saskatoon when the lawyers so subsidized ended up working in Ottawa for the Department of Justice? It was a palpable hit. St. Laurent knew that half the department's lawyers for some odd reason came from the University of Saskatchewan. In fact, the largest consumer in Canada of university graduates of all kinds was the federal government itself. St. Laurent announced the government's determination on June 19, 1951; effective for the academic year 1951-52, it would support universities on the basis suggested earlier by Pickersgill. Even Duplessis accepted it, at least for the first year.[3]

It should also be mentioned that a 1919 graduate of the Saskatchewan law faculty, John Diefenbaker, served as Prime Minister of Canada

(1957-63), and one of his classmates, Emmett M. Hall, served for a decade (1963-73) on the Supreme Court of Canada, while a more recent law graduate, Ray Hnatyshyn, was appointed Governor General of Canada in 1990.

M.A. "Sandy" MacPherson, who attended the law school a year or so earlier than McIntyre, describes its law faculty as adequate if not ample. He could recall few, if any, case books used by students or law professors in that era. The faculty would post case lists on the bulletin board and the students would read them in law reports. Students would also consult treatises but refer only infrequently to legal periodicals. At that time there were fewer such periodicals, and the library did not subscribe to as many as it did later. MacPherson had graduated from Dalhousie with a B.A. in 1936, enjoying particularly the classes in government given by R. MacGregor Dawson, the doyen of Canadian political scientists. After one year at Dalhousie law school, he returned to his home in Saskatchewan for financial reasons to complete his law course. He considered that a student could get an excellent grounding in the fundamentals of law at either Saskatchewan or Dalhousie. However, he ranked Dean Vincent MacDonald of Dalhousie as the best all-round law teacher in his experience.

Such opinions are bound to be subjective. Dean George Curtis, who attended the law school in Saskatoon earlier, and who later attended Oxford as a Rhodes Scholar and taught at Dalhousie as well as the University of British Columbia, would rank Dean Arthur Moxon of Saskatchewan as his outstanding teacher and a prime influence on his choice of law teaching as a profession: "A great influence was Arthur Moxon, my Dean at Saskatchewan. He was, of course, a superb teacher. In fact, I think I can say, that this does no discredit to anyone else, I think he was by far the greatest teacher I've every heard in law and that's bound to influence one. It set up an ideal picture. I thought, what a wonderful, wonderful occupation."[4] Curtis referred also to Moxon's very deep knowledge of the law — his scholarship — and his style, wit, humanity, and great integrity.[5] Of course, the field of selection was scantier at that time than it is now. Three full-time professors assisted by a number of part-time sessional lecturers from the practising profession was often the complement at a Canadian law school: Moxon, Cronkite, and Corry in Saskatchewan; MacDonald, Willis, and Curtis at Dalhousie; Ryan, McAllister, and La Forest at the University of New Brunswick.

When Dean Harry Arthurs of Osgoode Hall deplored the lack of intellectual rigour in the teaching of law in former times, he singled out the law school in Saskatchewan as a significant exception. The small prairie institution emphasized jurisprudence and legal theory. According to McIntyre, that was Dean Cronkite's emphasis during the period when he attended law school. During his long tenure as Dean (1929-61), in fact, Cronkite taught jurisprudence to generations of law students. A visiting group of students from Manitoba once asked Cronkite where his law students would get practical training — how, for instance, would they learn to search a title? Pondering for a moment, the Dean responded that after solving the first problem, finding the address of the Registry Office, they would have to go through the stages of a title search mechanically, perhaps occasionally asking the help of the registrar of titles if there was a problem. The Dean was fond of citing a statement given by his Harvard mentor in law Dean Roscoe Pound. Pound had said that if one student studied cases and statutes exclusively and the other jurisprudence for an equal amount of time, the latter student would have the superior legal education. McIntyre recalled that Cronkite used to say that the civil law was an exercise in developing principles that would apply to all cases, while the common law would seek a principle for each case. A homely example would be the different methods employed by a common law lawyer and a civil law lawyer in training a dog. The civil law lawyer would develop an ideal notion of what a dog should be and then seek to train the dog to conform to his idea. The common law lawyer would acquire any old dog, then kick him if he didn't behave.

Cronkite was a product of the Harvard "paper chase" and adept at teaching by the Socratic method. The method often engenders mystification, particularly among the uninitiated. It assumes that the law is in a state of flux and that it is impossible, often, to declare what it is. Nothing is finally decided. The professor, for example, could take two or more conflicting currents of case law and ask students to explore their implications, without ever telling them what the law is. The emphasis is on the reasoning process rather than the result. Sometimes a tentative result would be hazarded subject to possible modification later. Eventually the students would develop improved reasoning powers and self-confidence and discover either what the law on a disputed point was or why it was impossible to say what it was. The less able students often experienced frustration and self-doubt in attempting to cope with such a challenging approach.

Dean Curtis remembers that when he was studying law at Saskatoon in the 1920s, Cronkite would admonish his students concerning the Christmas examinations, "These are trial exams. They don't count at all, but don't underestimate them; don't be complacent, they're not easy." Curtis recalled that he had struggled valiantly with Cronkite's mid-term torts examination. Cronkite had told his students, "There's a way to answer law exams," without, however, telling them what that way was. Early in the new year, Curtis saw Cronkite pull a paper from the Christmas pile and begin to read it out loud (of course, he recognized it immediately) — "He threw it down and uttered the sweetest words I've ever heard in my life: 'That's the right way to answer a law exam!'" Curtis remained grateful to Cronkite for his praise, which he took as encouragement to persevere in his law studies. Later, in the early 1930s, as a Saskatchewan Rhodes Scholar at Oxford, he and Ronald Martland (who held the Alberta scholarship), obtained "double firsts" in law and jurisprudence.[6]

McIntyre was most influenced by Cronkite's course in jurisprudence, which ranged over centuries of Western legal thought from Plato and Aquinas to Hobbes and Mill, and in the contemporary era dealt with Holmes, Frank, Pound, and Canada's Caesar Wright. He invited his students to explore the underlying assumptions of statutes, judgments, and legal procedures. Influenced by Pound's sociological jurisprudence, he looked upon law not as an autonomous discipline, but as a subject that could benefit from insights from other areas of knowledge. The questions asked were often the perennial ones that each new generation would have to struggle with and to which it would have to propose its own tentative answers. McIntyre acquired his lifelong interest in philosophy in Cronkite's class. He had in his library a two-volume edition of Kant's *Critique of Pure Reason*, and has puzzled over the years concerning the difficult propositions advanced in that work. He considers the Categorical Imperative to be a sound if unattainable standard, one which is essentially the same as that articulated in the Sermon of the Mount, "Do unto others ...". He considers that an interest in theoretical questions rooted in principle differentiates a good law student (or lawyer) from a legal mechanic.

McIntyre recalled that no student got a very high mark or a very low one in Cronkite's jurisprudence examination. The examination questions were real tests of reasoning ability: for example, define "thing" in a legal sense. They dealt essentially with generalities, with points of view rather than points of law. Such a pedagogical approach, according to McIntyre, emphasized the distinction between education and training. In the academic component, broad questions could be asked the answers to which were grounded in principle. The training component, involving the drafting of pleadings and the drawing of wills, or the mastery of evidence and rules of procedure, could come later — perhaps in expanded phases of post law-school training, where practitioners adept in the practice of law could build on the principles instilled in the more academic phase. The excellent value of his legal education in Saskatoon, he considered, resided in the fact that good teachers were provocatively raising basic issues of principle. The critical pattern of thought so developed remained with the best law students for a lifetime.

Another subject Dean Cronkite taught, McIntyre recalled, was constitutional law. In the realm of constitutionalism, the church and the feudal system had a tremendous influence on the law of both continental Europe and England. While separated from the continent physically, England had a history that was similarly bloody, violent, and filled with domestic upheaval. Through all the tumult, the English were able to develop a sensible constitutional base, taming the monarchy as an integral element of an increasingly autonomous Parliament, but at the same time preserving it as a kind of unifying force ideally above party or faction. Evolution rather than revolution was the hallmark of England constitutionalism.

By constitutional convention, the sovereign, who earlier had ruled by arbitrary fiat, now ruled almost exclusively on the advice of his ministry. In Canada, the institutional format developed in England was incorporated, with modifications, into the Canadian parliamentary system with such distinctive additions as the division of powers between the federal government and the provinces, the Canadian Bill of Rights, and the Canadian Charter of Rights of Freedoms. Such theoretical matters assumed great practical importance when McIntyre, from the vantage of the Supreme Court, considered the constitutional validity of Prime Minister Trudeau's initiative to patriate the Constitution.

In addition to Cronkite, those permanently on faculty in McIntyre's time were Ernie F. Whitmore, who taught property and equity, and E. Russell Hopkins, a former Rhodes Scholar and distant relative of McIntyre's who taught contracts, legal history, and statutes. Hopkins (who replaced Corry) later joined the Department of External Affairs, winding up as law clerk to the Senate. As a student at the University of Saskatchewan he had written a variety show, a precursor of the Legal Follies that have become an annual event. He also authored a valuable commentary on the Canadian Constitution as it had developed in the century following Confederation.[7]

McIntyre remembers somewhat ruefully his experience in the compulsory first-year moot court, in which a faculty member would set a legal problem and serve as judge, with one student arguing against another. In one such case, Dean Cronkite had set a problem on assault, with William Grayson facing McIntyre. The Dean sat inscrutably through the presentations, then finally commented: "These presentations have been so ingenuous that they are almost ingenious. If you submitted such arguments to an actual court, you would be thrown out."

A unique test in McIntyre's time that is no longer administered was the dreaded comprehensive examination. The assumption of the test was that although for pedagogical purposes law was divided into discrete topics, there were actually many interrelationships, overlaps, and areas requiring reconciliation in a more integrated body of legal doctrine. The test sought to evaluate how competently the student could perceive linkages in law as a totality and broader systemic problems. It was given at mid-term in the third year, with students writing in the law library and having access to all library books. They started the examination at 9:00 a.m. and continued for as long as they wanted: there was no time limit. Having heretofore proceeded analytically, on a subject-by-subject basis, students were required to proceed by synthesis to allow their professors to find out what they knew about law as a whole. McIntyre reflected that the questions were fair but that the students considered the examination particularly gruelling.

Although he later acquired a reputation on the bench for taciturnity, even inscrutability, on informal occasions McIntyre had an excellent sense of humour, sometimes manifested in practical jokes. One of McIntyre's close friends and associates at law school was Bud Estey (known in later years as W.Z. Estey), who became a leading counsel in Ontario and sat with McIntyre on the Supreme Court of Canada during the 1980s. Estey and McIntyre once played a prank that is still remembered by their classmates. When the pair were not invited to a Sadie Hawkin's Day dance being held at the women's residence in Saskatchewan Hall, Estey procured a quarantine sign for measles from a nearby house and, on the evening of the dance, affixed it to the front door of the residence. "We waited and waited and as time for the dance neared, taxis began to arrive to take the young ladies out to pick up their dates and go to the dance. By this time, confusion reigned. The ladies were clustered around in all their finery asking taxis to wait while they discovered who was ill. The dance was greatly delayed and it may be said that Estey and I considered that a fair response to the unbelievable neglect of any young lady to invite us." The law school was notorious at this time for frequent clandestine crap games, in which law students and even some professors participated. Players took the screen from the window in the back room where the games were played, and used it as a table, in order to muffle the sound of the rolling dice.

Ordinarily McIntyre would have graduated with the class of 1941, but in addition to passing all the individual law examinations (which he did), students were required to achieve an overall weighted average in order to receive the degree, and he lacked sufficient credits to attain the average. In his last year at university, with all the disturbance of wartime and other activities, McIntyre had neglected his studies. He did not do as well as expected on some of his exams. Consequently, on his return from war service in 1946 he had to write special exams to improve his weighted average, a feat that he accomplished easily. In hindsight, one may say that McIntyre's difficulty with his exams in 1941 was totally out of character with his overall abilities. An omnivorous reader who handled the English language with elegance he was clearly a superior student.

When McIntyre returned for his final year of law studies in 1940, the Canadian government had introduced a requirement that persons in his category serve thirty days in home defense. He fulfilled his commitment as part of the Canadian Officers Training Corps contingent at the University of Saskatchewan, and joined the active force for overseas service in May 1941. He began training in the infantry, but toward the end of his final year a request came through for artillery cadets, and he elected to transfer to the artillery. One problem was that he always hated mathematics, a subject he scrupulously avoided at university. "When I got into the field artillery," he said, "it was necessary for me to learn some trigonometry. I went to work and within a few days I realized it wasn't that difficult. I didn't have much difficulty at all."

McIntyre served overseas with the Third Field Regiment, First Divisional Artillery, Seventy-Seventh Field Battery, which was a militia unit mobilized in Moose Jaw at the beginning of the war. "There were many boys I'd gone to school with," he recalls. "It was a real homecoming. We were theoretically in an operational role as the first line of defence on the south coast. But at that time, there was not much danger of a German invasion." By this time, he was a first lieutenant with two pips. He served with the Third Field Regiment in the U.K., largely in the south of England, until the spring of 1943. The First Canadian Division was then concentrated in Scotland and re-equipped in preparation for the Sicilian invasion, which commenced on July 10, 1943. The Regiment suffered many casualties in Sicily. The First Division was then engaged in the Italian campaign ending 1943 with the taking or Ortona, a small Adriatic port. As an experienced officer, McIntyre was sent back to England in February 1944 to reinforce other units that were preparing for the D-Day landings. "When we got back to England," he says, "it became evident that the last thing the various units of the Third Division, who were fully trained, wanted was a bunch of strangers interfering with their well-developed team work, so most of us were sent to holding units in England."

Soon after, he was one of the three servicemen who were sent back to Canada for a Victory Bond tour which really meant a long and pleasant leave. After six weeks he was sent back to England as part of the reinforcement stream for the invasion of northwest Europe. On arrival, he met a group of officers, some from his own regiment, proceeding for flight training as part of an Army program to create aerial observation squadrons for use in the direction and control of artillery fire. There were 20 in the contingent, two of whom had failed the medical exam:

I jumped in. Within twenty-four hours I was given one of the vacancies of the unfit. I was sent to London to take the RAF medical. I passed it. The medical exam took place in a long hall with small offices on either side in which a doctor charged with a certain part of the examination presided. We formed along the hall from room to room in groups of three or four, where each doctor, after performing his part of the examination, made a note on the clipboard we all carried, and passed us on down the line. It was at the height of the Buzz Bomb attacks and while in one of the rooms, we heard one coming. As always, the sound grew louder and louder until we were all convinced that it was coming directly for us. We all crowded under a large table in the room — all on our knees, including the doctor, but he was fully clothed and we were not. As the sound grew louder one of the boys said "Hey Doc, is that part of the test?" It broke the tension. Everyone laughed and we never did know where the Buzz Bomb landed, but it was nowhere near us.

McIntyre was sent to Cambridge for flight instruction and later to Andover in Hampshire for operational training, but by the time he had learned to fly Austers the war was virtually over, and he never flew operationally.

In London, MacIntyre was able to indulge his lifelong interest in music, particularly the opera. There were regular performances at the new Sadler's Wells theatre and on occasion at the Sheppard's Bush Empire. The Carl Rosa Opera Company was also active during the war, and while these performances were produced on a modest scale and their choruses and orchestras were often small, they were no less captivating to McIntyre, whose love of music started early. "I was the third in the family," he said, "and my older brother and sister had already had music lessons. When it came to my turn, I told my father I wanted to play the horn. He got me a trumpet and a friend of his who was bandmaster in the Salvation Army Band agreed to give me lessons. The Salvation Army was certainly known for training their musicians thoroughly. Later, I got into the Canadian Legion Military Band.... I was able to become second or third cornet. I was able also to learn something about orchestration. I was in the band for about five years leaving it when I went to University at Saskatoon." His older brother Hugh remembers the sadness with which Bill returned his cornet and uniform to the band when he left.

While taking his flight training in Cambridge, McIntyre met his future wife, Hermione "Mimi" Reeves, at the English Speaking Union. Mimi was running the cafeteria, which served a buffet dinner every night. She also worked at the bar. Mimi's family on both her father's and her mother's side were trainers of thoroughbred racehorses. Her paternal grandfather had been the chief trainer for the Hungarian Rothschilds in Alag, just outside Budapest, where Mimi was born. Her father was an assistant trainer at the same establishment. Once, on a visit to the Mendel Art Gallery in Saskatoon with her own daughter Elizabeth, Mimi recognized a picture of a rural scene with horses as a depiction of her birthplace. She hadn't been back to see the village of Alag since 1919, but felt that sudden flash of recognition. She retained a sense of attachment for her native country throughout her life.

Mimi's grandfather was one of a number of English trainers who are said to have introduced the sport in its Anglicized form to Hungary in the latter part of the nineteenth century. Her mother was the daughter of Fred Webb, another English trainer who had gone to Hungary.

In 1914, both trainers and their families were interned in Hungary as enemy aliens for the duration of the war. Much later, in Victoria, Mimi still had some pewter and glassware that her family had buried before the internment so that it would not be confiscated by the state. One of her earliest memories, as a child of eight or so, was of a train trip from Budapest to Austria, taken when the horses, attendants, and their families were moved out of the path of a much-feared communist takeover at the war's end. The Rothschilds abandoned their racing interests in Hungary and Mimi's father became a trainer in Vienna. Her schooling was completed there except for one year in England to improve her English accent.

The Reeves family moved to France about 1930, living at Chantilly, where Mimi's father continued to train horses. Mimi herself left to live and work in England in the early 1930s. She held several jobs, including one as governess for the two young children of a major in the Royal Artillery. His military service took her to India for a year. Upon her return to England she worked for the well-known travel agency, Thomas Cook & Sons. In this capacity she lived in various Swiss hotels where Cook's tourists were sent on vacation, and acted as liaison officer and guide for English and American visitors. Her ability to speak German and French was, of course, a great asset in this work. She brought the last Cook's Tour home to England from Switzerland in September 1939, to escape the war in Europe.

Unlike her husband, Mimi had enjoyed a cosmopolitan upbringing. As a child, she spoke German, Hungarian, and English. She later learned French. She had worked as a governess in Kashmir and, in the same capacity, taught English to the two daughters of a Jewish lawyer in Bratislava. She also worked as a bookkeeper in London. By contrast, McIntyre was not even particularly interested in horse racing, although the couple's widely different interests and backgrounds never seemed to be a source of contention. Elizabeth says that her father always had the highest respect and appreciation for Mimi's intelligence, and she considers that it was her mother's influence that made her father, intellectually and socially, a much broader person than he would otherwise have been. Madam Justice Bertha Wilson attests to Mimi's charm, conversational gifts, and engaging manners. She added zest to social functions held by the Supreme Court, where she was the life of the party.

"We just got married," says McIntyre. "My older brother Hugh was a medical officer in the RCAF stationed in Yorkshire. I wrote home to inform the family that I was going to get married. Mimi's full name was Hermine (later modified to the Greek form of the name, Hermione) Elizabeth Reeves. The name Mimi resulted from a younger brother's inability to say Hermione, and the short form survived. Hugh came down to Cambridge and was best man at the wedding. He was delighted with her from the meeting — as were all others — and any fears that I might be bringing home a chorus girl were dispelled."

At the end of the war, McIntyre considered joining the diplomatic corps and wrote the External Affairs exam in London. He passed the written exam and was called before a panel of seasoned foreign service officers for the oral, but was not finally chose to fill one of the small number of existing vacancies. A premium was placed on linguistic skills for those aspiring to a career in the foreign service, and the unilingual McIntyre was outdistanced in this instance by candidates having a knowledge of French or German.

With millions of service personnel awaiting repatriation, there was a great shortage of shipping when it came time to return home, and Mimi, as a war bride, had a relatively low priority. McIntyre, accordingly, returned to Moose Jaw alone in the spring of 1946, being demobilized with the rank of captain. The Department of Veterans Affairs allowed him a year to complete his articles in Saskatchewan at a stipend of $90.00 a month. He took out his articles with Fred J. Gilmour, QC, of Moose Jaw in March 1946. Mimi arrived from England in August. When asked whether Mimi, who was now caring for their daughter Elizabeth, found the transition from the sophisticated capitals of Europe to Moose Jaw a difficult one, McIntyre simply says no. She was resourceful and adaptable and had the knack of making friends wherever she went and McIntyre was fortunate in his articling. "Fred Gilmour was a great man and great teacher. I wasn't used as cheap labour, but got a thorough grounding in practice fundamentals in Moose Jaw. Gilmour had no particular legal specialty but took up whatever cases 'walked in the door.'" In this respect, Moose Jaw was much like Victoria during McIntyre's practice, for in these smaller centres intensive specialization was still a thing of the future. Fred Gilmour also left Moose Jaw and practised for several years in Vancouver. That Gilmour had taken his responsibility for training law students seriously was reflected in the scope and the level of concentration that came to characterize McIntyre's career.

Elizabeth remembers that her father was never a strict disciplinarian. He reared his children by example rather than through chastisement or punishment. If a child did something stupid or unbecoming, he would typically say, "Why in the world would anyone want to do that?" He encouraged his children to make the maximum effort to achieve their desired goals, and thought that if you told a child he or she could not do something, the child would not make the attempt. He always encouraged people to do their best. Elizabeth considers the long conversations and arguments she had with her father and others in the family circle as key to learning about life. Any proposition advanced by a family member would be put to the test. Her father's greatest pleasure at the table was serious conversation. While some might think it curious that neither of McIntyre's children entered the legal profession, he never exerted any pressure on them in the choice of a career. Elizabeth became an archivist with a deep interest in legal history, and John became a history master at a private co-educational institution, St. Michael's University School in Victoria. Elizabeth reflects that had she been born ten years later she might have become a lawyer. "At a certain time, my father was fed up with the law," she adds, "and thought I should become an academic. He considered that the woman lawyers he knew before his appointment to the Bench didn't have a happy life. The hours demanded in the profession were long and there was little time left over for family or leisure activities. He wouldn't encourage anyone at that time to go into law, neither me nor my brother. In fact he was very supportive of our alternative career choices."

Madam Justice Wilson recalls that a number of judges of her acquaintance had tried to discourage their daughters from entering the legal profession. Mr. Justice John Arnup of the Ontario Court of Appeal discouraged his daughter, Jane, in such strong terms that she sought reassurance from members of the profession that there was a place for women in the practice of law. Her father had told her that women had no future in litigation, but that they could perform a role in legal research. (Jane Arnup did become a lawyer, serving as counsel in the Ontario Attorney General's Department.) Judge Wilson affirmed that a woman would not gain the immediate acceptance in a law firm that a man would. When a man was hired, she said, there was an assumption that he was capable of doing the job. In the case of a woman, the partners, who were predominantly male, had to be persuaded. There is a much stronger onus on a woman to prove herself.

The Saskatchewan that McIntyre returned to after the war did not seem an attractive place to begin a new career. After years of drought, grasshopper infestations, and economic depression, parts of the province were virtual desert. Postwar havoc and the restriction of markets made it difficult for farmers and others to clothe their children, let alone make a decent living. McIntyre was so impressed with Vancouver Island while he was receiving his military training at Gordon Head, that he resolved to settle in either Vancouver or Victoria to practise law. McIntyre went out to the coast with letters of introduction to Vancouver lawyer Tom Norris (later of the British Columbia Court of Appeal), from Fred Gilmour and former Saskatchewan Attorney General M.A. MacPherson. He met a young woman in Vancouver with whom he had been at law school. She told him with delight that she had been hired by Norris. He then had qualms about seeing Norris because he thought it might affect her job prospects. Finally, Mimi told him, "See Mr. Norris. Don't be rude." So McIntyre went to the Rogers Building to meet Norris, whom he described as a "bear with a hearty voice." Norris said, "I don't need you. See Mr. Whittaker in Victoria; he needs a man. I've already written to him." Norman Whittaker was impressed with McIntyre and offered him a job. He accepted gratefully and returned with Mimi to Saskatchewan to wind up his affairs.

In order to transfer from the Saskatchewan Bar, to which he had been admitted earlier in the year, he had to write examinations in British Columbia statutes and in practice and procedure. He spent a few evenings studying the B.C. Rules of Court, which were essentially the English rules, and mastering the intricacies of local statute law. He passed the required examinations and had to pay $1500 of an $1800 gratuity from the army as a transfer fee charged to barristers from outside the province. The fee was a very high one, amounting in some cases almost to a disincentive to transfer. He bade Mr. Gilmour goodbye and in a few weeks was back in Victoria in the offices of Norman Whittaker and John Raymond McIlree. The latter was one of Canada's most distinguished soldiers, and a competent solicitor, who suffered from partial deafness as the result of congenital trouble in one ear and a war injury in the other. McIntyre went with the firm in June, being admitted to the British Columbia Bar in July 1947. Then, with dramatic suddenness, Whittaker was elevated to a judgeship on the British Columbia Supreme Court in September. McIntyre became the only lawyer in the office other than McIlree.

On the threshold of his legal career, McIntyre looked back on his Saskatchewan boyhood, the depression, his time at university, and his wartime experiences, with complex feelings. He may have regarded his life so far as promising, but uneven. While his parents' ruling values of industry and integrity were personally inspiring, his academic career had been chequered and must have left him feeling dissatisfied. However, he left law school with a deep and abiding interest in legal history and theory, subjects on which he continued to read widely. In the future McIntyre would set high standards for himself and almost always achieve them. The dreariness of post-Depression Saskatchewan impelled him to leave Moose Jaw but on Vancouver Island, with his wife Mimi and their children Elizabeth and John, he prospered in his profession and earned a growing respect in his community. To all who fought, the war was a dreadful experience. Even now, McIntyre is reluctant to speak about that time. Yet the war undoubtedly tempered him. He returned to Canada with polish, authority, and a new singleness of purpose. Coming to Victoria with nothing but a firm resolution to succeed at the bar, he was determined to spare no effort to that end.

NOTES

1. There is an excellent profile of Dr. King by Professor Len Findlay, "Engaged Intellectual: The Case of Carlyle King," in *Vox* 15 (Saskatoon: University of Saskatchewan Faculty Assn.), April 1996.
2. For example, Elmer A. Driedger, *The Construction of Statutes*, 2nd edn. (Toronto: Butterworths, 1993).
3. P.B. Waite, *Lord of Point Grey: Larry MacKenzie of U.B.C.* (Vancouver: University of British Columbia Press, 1987), 154.
4. B.C. Legal History Collection Project (transcript of tape), interviewee, Dr. George F. Curtis; interviewer, F. Murray Fraser; February 1980, p. 22.
5. *Ibid.*
6. J.W. Pickersgill, *Seeing Canada Whole: A Memoir* (Markham, ON: Fitzhenry and Whiteside, 1994), 85.
7. E. Russell Hopkins, Confederation at the Crossroads (Toronto: McClelland & Stewart, 1968).

II

PRACTICE IN VICTORIA

WHEN MCINTYRE BEGAN PRACTISING LAW in Victoria in 1947 it was still a small city with a population of about 50,000[1] and fewer than 80 lawyers. As the provincial capital it was the main governmental and administrative centre, and then as now its salubrious climate and natural beauty attracted many tourists in the summer and fall. As a retirement home for its disproportionately large number of older people, many of whom were well-to-do, it presented opportunities for the legal profession to engage in wills, trusts, and estate work.

There were few changes in the size of law firms in Victoria in the 1940s and 1950s. Work for lawyers had declined substantially during the Great Depression and few new legal practitioners had arrived in Victoria since that time. During the war years, young people who might have entered the profession were in the armed forces. In effect, the Depression and World War II comprised a 16-year hiatus where the ranks of the legal profession came increasingly to be filled by older men, many of whom were veterans of World War I. Given the gap in age between the two generations of lawyers when McIntyre arrived in 1947, there was little overcrowding and competition for places among fledging barristers.

The British Columbia Attorney General's Department was much smaller than it is now, while most other government departments had their own legal counsel. The growth of administrative law consequent upon the proliferation of boards and regulatory bodies in Canada was a later phenomenon, and the greatest increase in constitutional litigation has occurred still more recently, after the adoption of the Canadian Charter of Rights and Freedoms in 1982.

The relatively small number of lawyers in the government service worked to the benefit of the new arrivals. Much of the government work now done by in-house counsel was still farmed out to general practitioners. Amongst the work the province assigned to firms were criminal prosecutions at the spring and fall assizes, and litigation involving the reassessment of the forest industry for taxation purposes. The fees paid for such work were not necessarily large, but if work was contracted out on a regular basis the proceeds were a valuable supplement to other professional income. In addition, and especially in the case of younger lawyers, useful publicity from newspapers and other media could be obtained when they were hired to do criminal prosecutions. As in any profession, name recognition was important.

As noted in Chapter 1, Norman Whittaker's elevation to the bench in September 1947 left John R. McIlree and McIntyre as the only remaining lawyers in their small Victoria firm. They agreed that McIntyre would receive $150 for the first month of employment as an associate with a $25 increase monthly over the next six months, when salary would be discussed again. However, Whittaker's sudden departure so affected the balance of work and the future of the firm that an earlier discussion of financial arrangements became expedient. McIlree said to McIntyre, "I've just settled up all my affairs with Norman. Everything here — all the books — are mine. How would you like to be my partner?" McIntyre responded that he would love such an arrangement but that he did not have any money. The older man replied, "That's O.K., I don't need money." Thinking aloud, McIlree said, "A two-thirds one-third split wouldn't be very fair ...". Thinking that a lesser share would be more than adequate, McIntyre assented. Then McIlree added, "I would think a 60-40 split would be about right." Even with McIntyre assuming liability for 40 percent of the losses, the arrangement was a generous one. McIlree was the more experienced senior partner of a firm that had acquired considerable goodwill in the community, and he was supplying the library and working quarters for the partnership. They then shook hands, sealing the only partnership agreement they would ever need in a business relationship founded entirely on trust and mutual respect. The only variation over time was that McIntyre's share of the profits grew larger. He was a hard worker and took on all of the counsel work of the firm. The only other condition that McIlree made was that his son, then attending law school, would have a place in the firm once he was admitted to the bar. To this McIntyre promptly agreed.

McIntyre had actually won his first case in Saskatchewan shortly before coming to Victoria. *Dobson v. Dobson*[2] concerned a farmer who had asked a real-estate agent to draw up his will leaving his personal property to his wife, and also to prepare a transfer of eight quarter-sections of land to his two sons, the respondents. When the transfer documents were completed, the agent was cautioned by the farmer to say nothing about them and not to register them until after his death. When the man died, McIntyre acted for the widow. The court held that the purported transfer could not take effect as an escrow, but was actually a testamentary document, as McIntyre had submitted, but because it was unwitnessed and therefore void, the widow as residuary legatee took the real property, which otherwise would have gone to her sons. In fact, she took the whole estate.

"The first year of my partnership," says McIntyre, "I got through three or four heavy pieces of counsel work. Later on I served as counsel for the Royal Trust Company in a number of their local cases. In fact we did much of their Victoria litigation. It was not an exclusive arrangement, but they relied on our firm to do much of their local work. This type of work led me into probate and chancery work generally, and I did a lot of work in that field, including wills and estates. I also acted as prosecutor for the municipality of Esquimalt and did their police court prosecutions."

McIntyre recalls a case where he was confronted by opposing counsel who sought to question a priest about what he had been told in the confessional. The priest had an absolute theological duty, of course, not to divulge anything. The only clear case of privileged communication then recognized in law, was that between solicitor and client. Before the priest could answer the presiding judge, the much-respected Chief Justice J.O. Wilson said, "I'm quite aware that there is no privilege here. If you put a question as to what happened in the confessional and the priest, as I think he will, refuses to answer it, he would be in contempt of court; but if you ask that question and it turns out to be anything but an absolutely vital question I will be very disappointed." After this gentle but firm admonition, counsel did not put the question.

McIntyre worked not infrequently as a Crown prosecutor during the assizes. When he was elevated to the Supreme Court of Canada in 1979, he found that he had more experience in criminal law and in other areas of practice than his colleagues, with the exception of Lamer, who later became Chief Justice. Not only was he experienced in criminal law, he read widely in the area, in Holdsworth, Maitland, and other legal historians; he immersed himself in the theory of the law. Because of the pressures of opinion-writing, he found much less time for such reading when he was on the bench. His criminal law practice never hardened McIntyre, however; his judicial colleague Madam

Justice Bertha Wilson later said, "He had a very benign and compassionate attitude to people, despite his work as a prosecutor."

In the early years of McIntyre's practice he and his family lived at 799 Linkleas Avenue, and in the smaller city of that time there were a number of vacant lots and some bush in the vicinity. His son John, a product of the postwar baby boom, says that "Victoria was a great place to grow up." The family moved to a larger house at 339 Foul Bay Road in the early fifties, when John was aged 7 and Elizabeth 10. A neighbour here was Graham Odgers, an Australian expatriate who became an astronomer at the local observatory. He was a frequent visitor to the McIntyres and a fascinating conversationalist. Another good friend was Edward Cantell, a lawyer, who became Superintendent of Insurance for British Columbia, and served later as a provincial deputy minister.

Elizabeth remembers being fascinated as a youngster by the conversation of her parents and their guests. Before bedtime she would often lodge herself unobtrusively in a corner of the room where she could listen to the animated give-and-take for as long as possible. Having retired to Victoria, Grandmother and Grandfather McIntyre also called frequently. John remembers going with his father to pick up his grandparents from church on Sunday, and going to Sunday school himself without, however, becoming deeply religious. "All of the children — aunts and uncles — were not particularly religious," he says, "but there had been such a strong ethical and moral influence in their parents' home when they were growing up that the moral dimension remained."

George MacMinn, QC, the Clerk of the British Columbia Legislative Assembly, frequently acted as a junior for McIntyre when they both practised in Victoria in the fifties and sixties. He contrasted Bill's meticulous preparation with the more spontaneous forensic style of his law partner Lloyd George McKenzie. The latter made brilliant addresses to the jury from a few assorted notes written on scraps of paper; he could extemporaneously develop scattered thoughts into a coherent and dramatic discourse. McIntyre's style was different but it was the one that MacMinn found himself emulating as time passed. McIntyre's research was thorough and his approach scholarly. He set out a detailed written record of his pleadings while remaining highly effective without such preparation when cross-examining witnesses. MacMinn considers that although both partners were versatile, McKenzie was the better jury pleader and McIntyre the superior appellate advocate.

In 1975 Harry Rankin, QC, a longtime Vancouver alderman and criminal defence counsel, acted for John Harvey Miller, accused of murder in a case where McIntyre held in his dissenting judgment that capital punishment was contrary to the Canadian Bill of Rights. Rankin appeared before McIntyre a number of times when the latter was a trial judge in Vancouver. He considered McIntyre to be a true adherent of the common law and essentially liberal-minded. Later it was Rankin's impression that McIntyre disliked the Charter, and on this issue he tended to agree with the judge. He thought McIntyre had a good mind and admired his crisp, intelligible judgments. Rankin recalls that Chief Justice Sloane of British Columbia once said that judges could rarely write more than a few pages without falling into error. The concision of McIntyre's work was thus all the more appealing.

McIlree, who was a solicitor at the law firm, did much of the general work, particularly involving estates, although in that age of generalists McIntyre also undertook such work. Relations between the partners were close, and there were never any serious disagreements. McIlree's father, John Henry McIlree, had been an original member of the North-West Mounted Police and worked his way up through the ranks to become assistant commissioner in 1892. He retired to Victoria, and died in 1925. The younger McIlree had wanted to join the force but was rejected because of defective hearing in one ear. However, he was considered fit enough to join the army in World War I. Commissioned in the field, and gassed at Ypres, McIlree won the Distinguished Service Order and returned to Canada as a major. He was a very close friend of all the McIntyres, and became John's godfather.

One aspect of law that McIntyre disliked was divorce work, because of the adverse impact of family break-up on children. Occasionally, however, he would handle divorce cases. Although in non-legal areas he would discuss anything frankly with Mimi, he respected client confidentiality and never discussed their cases or private communications at home. Once Mimi heard from a bus driver that someone she knew was getting divorced and told Bill. "Yes I know," he said, "I'm handling it." She was upset that he had not told her, but he never discussed professional business in the home.

McIntyre helped those in unfortunate circumstances, often for little or no fee. A Victoria barrister J.C. Scott-Harston, recalled a case where McIntyre helped a fellow barrister who had qualified as a solicitor in England and later transferred to the British Columbia bar only to be disbarred there. He went east and qualified for a semi-legal job, but he needed a sponsor to pass the required exam and get reinstated to the bar. McIntyre took on the task, and Scott-Harston observes that such altruism was typical:[3] many lawyers would simply say that their disbarred colleague had been the author of his own misfortune, and leave it at that. McIntyre was compassionate.

A major preoccupation of McIntyre's during his practice in Victoria was his *pro bono* work as legal adviser to the Salvation Army. The lawyer who had hired him as an associate, Norman Whittaker, had been chairman of the Army's advisory board. After Whittaker's judicial appointment a Salvation Army officer visited Bill to invite him to go on the board, and he accepted. Eventually, he too became chairman and came to know many of the Army's personnel and their concerns very well. He recalls that Stuart Keate of the *Victoria Colonist* and Monty Drake (now Mr. Justice Tyrwhitt-Drake) were also on the board. At one dinner held at the Salvation Army Citadel in honour of General Bramwell Booth, grandson of the founder, who was visiting Victoria in the course of a world tour, Monty declared to the assembled officers, "Yes, the name of Booth is famous for two things we got from England, the Salvation Army and gin." There were some chuckles, some shock. As a tribute to his work, McIntyre was awarded the Salvation Army's highest decoration, the Distinguished Service Order. He is one of the very few civilians who is not actually an Army member to possess this award.

Indicative of the catholicity of his interests was his friendship with and interest in the work of the distinguished American poet, Theodore Roethke. Winner of the Pulitzer and Bollingen prizes and the National Book Award, Roethke taught at several American universities before coming to berth at the University of Washington in Seattle, in 1947. He was a frequent visitor to Vancouver Island, where the McIntyres met him at a summer camp at Saratoga Beach. The son of a Saginaw, Michigan florist, Roethke was "a bear of a man with an ego to match." He wrote poetry concerned with "childhood, nature and the exposed psyche."[4] Several poems relate to scenes on Vancouver Island, and the McIntyre children recall some interesting exchanges between the poet and the lawyer, as well as Roethke's girlfriend and her frolicsome little cat. The poet was interested in law, and the lawyer so interested in poetry that he can still recite long passages from memory. Sadly, Roethke died suddenly of a heart attack in 1963, while only in his fifties.

McIntyre first met Lloyd McKenzie in Victoria in 1948, during an enquiry by the Benchers of the Law Society into the fitness of one Gordon Martin to be a member of the provincial bar. Martin was a self-professed communist and member of the Labour-Progressive Party. The case against Martin, as presented by the Law Society, was that his political ideology rendered suspect his sincerity in taking the oath of loyalty, and also (somewhat artificially), that while he was a man of good character he was not one of good repute. McKenzie was a classmate of Martin's and president of the inaugural 1948 law-school class at the University of British Columbia. (The Vancouver Law School had been staffed entirely by a part-time faculty of downtown practitioners for three decades, but in 1945 a permanent university law faculty was established.) McIntyre remembers coming out the front door of the old Vancouver courthouse on Langley Street where the Benchers had their quarters, to find McKenzie and a few other law students in animated conversation. McKenzie proclaimed that denying admission to Martin because of his political views was an outrageous infringement of his civil rights. As his classmate, McKenzie was ready to testify to Martin's good character. Another scheduled character witness was Vancouver lawyer John Stanton, whose political views ran as far to the left as Martin's.

McIntyre joined in, saying the Benchers were wrong. They had to accept the oath, which represented the only available means of ensuring that a person would speak the truth. The oath was administered to everyone, irrespective of their good reputation or lack of one. When a prospective lawyer promises to be loyal under oath that promise must be accepted, since there is no other way of empirically substantiating loyalty. If Martin was willing to take the oath he should be admitted to the Law Society. McKenzie agreed. The group adjourned to Cap Cameron's Coffee Shop for further disquisition. McIntyre and McKenzie, who would both become distinguished judges, soon became good friends.

An opposing view on the controversy came from Reginald Tupper, Treasurer of the Law Society. Tupper maintained that if you were a Communist, you were not bound by oaths. In effect, your first lie as a lawyer would be spoken as you took the oath. McKenzie obviously disagreed. Just before he was scheduled to give character evidence, the Vancouver *News Herald* ran a story that two well known communist sympathizers, Stanton and McKenzie, were to give testimony for Martin the following day. Of course the allegation was patently false in relation to McKenzie. On reading this report, William H.M. Haldane, KC, a Bencher from Victoria, was so indignant that he summoned Ken Drury, the *Herald's* editor, to the courthouse and demanded that he print an equally prominent retraction, which he did.

In due course McKenzie testified before the Benchers that as class president he had gotten to know Martin well, that he was an honest, decent person and a good husband and father. They differed in their political beliefs, McKenzie said, but he emphasized that he had no doubt of Martin's sincerity and veracity under oath, a matter of primary concern to the Benchers. He remembers being crisply cross-examined by J.W. de B. Farris, a former attorney general of the province, who was counsel for the Law Society, but he remained steadfast in his testimony.

The Benchers rejected the petition of Martin for admission to the bar because although "the evidence clearly indicates that the personal morals of Martin cannot be questioned [and] that he was a hard worker at the University and conscientious in his work,"[5] he also "subscribed to revolutionary doctrines involving the forcible overthrow of the state and was not, therefore, of good repute." They also ruled that, "the mere statement of willingness on the part of an avowed communist to take the oaths[6] — lip service to the letter of the law — is not sufficient to justify his acceptance as a person who, in truth, would carry out in its true meaning the requirements of the oath."[7] In so ruling the Benchers asserted an exceedingly broad discretion: "In the case of the Martin application the only requirement is that the Benchers exercise their discretion honestly in the public interest and on considerations of good sense. They are not otherwise fettered."[8] It appeared immaterial to them that in every respect Martin had complied with the statutory requirements for admission to the bar set out in the *Legal Profession Act*[9] and that his good character was unimpeachable. The presumptive insincerity of his oath, based solely on their reading of abstract Marxist doctrine, and the narrow distinction between "good character" (which he possessed), and "good repute" (which he apparently did not), precluded his admission to the bar. On appeal, the Benchers' decision was upheld by Coady, J., who held that, barring some error, the court should not substitute its opinion for that of the Benchers, and that the Benchers in arriving at their decision could take judicial notice of all matters reasonably relevant for consideration. In due course the decision was unanimously upheld by the Court of Appeal.[10]

McIntyre, who served as a Bencher from 1965 to 1967, said later that in such capacity he would have had no hesitation in voting for Martin's admission. Martin was in all respects qualified. The fact that one suspects that a person is not telling the truth when he takes the oath is not a factor. In the legal system we rely on the oath because it is not possible to remove suspicion. Adequate or not, putting someone under oath when they go into the witness box is the only step we can take, and there are serious penalties for perjury.

Long after the dispute, McKenzie wrote to Martin to invite him to the 25th anniversary reunion of the class of '48. He had never been admitted to the bar and was working as a timekeeper near Courtney. He expressed his appreciation for the invitation but politely declined, adding, "I'm afraid I'd be a spectre at the feast." McKenzie says that he knew other law students at the time who, while every bit as sympathetic as Martin to the communist cause, were not as argumentative in law school corridors, and were admitted to the bar without question.

The Martin case was the last of its kind in British Columbia. McIntyre observes that this local controversy cannot be separated from the pathological anti-communism sweeping the West and especially the United States at the time. The widespread fear of a "communist conspiracy" to overthrow Western democratic governments through subversion from within is actually mentioned by the Benchers in their ruling: "The history of the Communists in Canada, in Britain, and in the United States during the last 3 or 4 years has shown that the doctrines of Communists are dictated from abroad and involve traitorous conspiracies and attempts against these countries."[11] This climate of anti-communism had intensified in Canada just three years earlier when Igor Gouzenko, a cipher clerk at the Soviet embassy in Ottawa, defected with incriminating documents disclosing the names of Canadians allegedly spying for the USSR. About half of those named were eventually convicted of espionage, including Labour-Progressive M.P. Fred Rose. Gouzenko's revelations led to the Kellock-Taschereau Royal Commission on Espionage, which is also referred to in the Benchers' decision.[12]

A dispute took place when McIntyre was practising in Victoria that involved Craig Monroe, a friend and fellow law graduate of the University of Saskatchewan who practised law in New Westminster, and Mr. Justice Manson of the B.C. Supreme Court. In this case McIntyre's sympathies were entirely with Monroe. E. Davie Fulton, Diefenbaker's Minister of Justice, had secured a constitutional amendment from the U.K. providing for the compulsory retirement of superior court judges at the age of 75. Before the amendment was obtained senior judges could work indefinitely. The amendment, which was retroactive,[13] had the effect of compelling the retirement of Manson and a couple of other judges who were over the stipulated age limit. When Monroe was offered Manson's job the latter asserted that if he accepted it would be a nullity, since the amendment itself was clearly unconstitutional. The retired judge warned of dire consequences. Monroe could be sued by any party who lost before him on grounds that he lacked jurisdiction due to the irregularity of his appointment. Monroe accepted his appointment nonetheless, and none of the awful scenarios forecast by Manson transpired. McIntyre enjoyed discussing disputed points of law with Monroe, whom he found to be a judge of pre-eminent common sense.

After the retirement of McIntyre's senior partner, J.R. McIlree, in the mid-1960s, he and Lloyd McKenzie agreed to merge their firms. Both firms were flourishing but they felt that if they combined they could offer better service to the public and attract more clients. For McIntyre this involved a move from the Central Building to the Yarrow Building, at 645 Fort Street. In the small city of Victoria of that time, Harman & Company, as the new firm was called, with its complement of seven lawyers, came to rival Crease & Company, Victoria's largest firm, with a dozen barristers. The merger was augmented when Hugh Henderson joined it, and soon comprised twelve members. The lawyers from McIntyre's firm involved in the new arrangement were John N. McIlree (his partner's son) and Robert M. McKay, while Mr. McKenzie's associates were J. Howard Harman, Robert H.G. Harman, and Kenneth C. Murphy. Although lawyers in Victoria continued to engage in a general practice, the burden of litigation in the new firm fell largely on McIntyre, McKenzie, and Murphy. McKenzie had, in fact, been counsel for B.C. Hydro in a recent case that was the biggest in the province in its time. No fewer than three members of Harmon & Company — McIntyre, McKenzie, and Murphy — were later elevated to the Bench.

"Bill McIntyre always introduced me as his junior partner," recalls McKenzie with amusement. "Actually, when our firms merged there wasn't any seniority or juniority; we were all equals." Sometimes, when ordering a meal in a restaurant, McIntyre would gesture toward McKenzie and ask the waiter to see what "his father" wanted — the partners had been born five months apart. Although his manner in the courtroom or on the bench could be reserved, in private gatherings McIntyre had a wry humour. McKenzie says that McIntyre was painstaking, conscientious, and thorough in his practice. He had an excellent grasp of the law, and his clients evinced loyalty and gratitude to him long after their professional links had lapsed. McIntyre did many forestry taxation and assessment cases. Because of their convoluted statutory framework,[14] these were intensely disliked by judges. Another lucrative area was general estate practice. In addition, both partners were in demand for criminal prosecution or defence cases during the spring or fall assizes, prestigious work that could bring local renown and press recognition. McKenzie appeared for the defence in several highly publicized cases and, with respect to local profile, McIntyre became solicitor for the University of Victoria upon its formation in 1963. Its predecessor, Victoria College, had existed since 1903, and awarded its first bachelor's degrees in Arts and Science (through the University of British Columbia) in 1961. Two years later the university became independent. McIntyre also worked with other officials in acquiring land and facilitating construction of the new campus in the Oak Bay area.

McIntyre was a strong opponent of capital punishment, and before their firms merged, McKenzie had been involved in a cause célèbre on Vancouver Island that raised the issue dramatically. In the late fifties, McKenzie prosecuted a murder case that ended with the last legal execution in British Columbia.[15] Leo Anthony Mantha, a 31 year-old tugboat sailor, stabbed a young navy man to death at the naval barracks in Esquimalt. The two men had been lovers but the victim had recently left Mantha for a woman. George Gregory defended Mantha. The accused was found guilty and sentenced to hang. Gregory attended the execution at Mantha's request, and McKenzie thinks he never fully recovered from the spectacle. The sentence of death, which was mandatory, was pronounced by Mr. Justice Jack Ruttan, and the execution took place in April 1959. At a ceremony held by his colleagues to celebrate 25 years on the bench, Ruttan spoke of this case. He related that the minister of justice and cabinet had been regularly commuting death sentences to life imprisonment, and that he had written to the minister giving the circumstances of the case and describing it as a crime of passion. He strongly recommended that clemency be exercised, but received only a terse telegram from the minister saying that the sentence would be carried out. There were subsequent executions in Ontario's Don Jail in 1962, but all death sentences in Canada were thereafter commuted by cabinet until 1976, when the death penalty was finally abolished by the Trudeau government.

Throughout the McIntyre/McKenzie partnership there was never a disagreement over money or "division of the spoils," as McKenzie has put it. The partners held a monthly meeting to arrange such things and it was always amicable. Not much heed was paid to charging clients on a strict "time" basis, in contrast to the almost obsessive concern of many contemporary law firms with "billable hours." The partners would heft the case file and consider what the result in court might be. They were inclined to charge more for a successful result had been. A recurring nightmare of McKenzie's was having to go to a partners' meeting where he could not think of a cent he had made for the firm that month. He imagined McIntyre saying, "Do you mean you didn't make *anything at all?*" Each partner brought business from his former practice and there was little transferring of files. All the partners tended to do anything that came along: "Whatever came in the door," as one of them put it.

In one assizes case where McIntyre led for the prosecution, the accused was a convict with many prior convictions who appeared without counsel. McIntyre confirmed to the judge that the accused had refused legal aid but just before recessing, the judge asked him to have another word with the accused just to confirm that he still intended to represent himself. The accused told McIntyre that if he was provided with legal aid counsel he would probably end up with some wet-behind-the-ears kid: "I've been in court a lot and I know as much as anybody. I'll act for myself." When the judge returned McIntyre gave him a sanitized version of what the accused had said at which point the judge turned to the accused and said, "Since you don't have counsel I will intercede for you from time to time." McIntyre's junior, George MacMinn, leaned over and said to him, "I can see this is going to be one of those outrageously fair trials."

The proper demeanour of a trial judge is always a matter of some dispute. In this case Crown counsel were concerned that the judge, in seeking to be fair, would overcompensate on behalf of the accused, making their work the more onerous. However, if the accused went unrepresented by counsel and there were no interventions from the bench, he would be at a severe disadvantage, especially where technical points of law or procedure were involved. An overzealous judge who intervenes excessively, especially when attempting to anticipate future lines of argument, can make counsel's task extremely difficult. These considerations prompted McKenzie, perhaps ironically (since McIntyre ordinarily was a non-intervening judge), not to appear before his partner after the latter's elevation. "The reason was," he explains, "that he'd be striving so much to be fair that he'd lean over backwards and probably fall on top of me. He'd be giving me the hardest job of all. I'd have to be twice as precise as the other side. That's how I saw it. I never did appear before him."

McKenzie has also praised McIntyre's exceptionally retentive memory, in a profession where a complex case might entail mastering a wide range of relevant technical detail in order to represent one's client well. When McKenzie defended in a naval court-martial, for example, he had to learn all about radar. In cases involving collision at sea or the stranding of ships such knowledge was essential. The art of the advocate sometimes consists of being a jack of all trades. McIntyre agrees that a lawyer has to be sponge-like and soak up information in many different areas. This aptitude for osmosis is equally useful at the bar as on the bench. "You *hear* all the expert testimony, then you make an evaluation. You do this at the bar and you continue to do it as a judge on trial and appellate courts."

However, a lawyer's knack for describing, summarizing, and encapsulating a proposition can lead to intellectual dishonesty. McIntyre observes that an advocate can pose as a learned expert and yet not really "know which end is up." A lawyer must be very careful not to be overconfident of newly- acquired knowledge, and should be extremely careful when cross-examining expert witnesses. By virtue of extensive study, experience, and practice, an expert witness is bound to know much more than counsel, and such experts can confound a case if counsel is not careful.

Speaking from his own experience as counsel and judge, McIntyre has observed that the conduct of a case often depends on the courtroom manner of the judge. Some judges are virtually impossible for counsel to argue before because of their propensity to interrupt and interfere, conduct that can approach actual harassment. A judge must ask some questions, but a strong line should be drawn between necessary questioning and a disconcerting intrusiveness. Judges should remember Sir Francis Bacon's admonition that, "It ill suffers a judge to learn by inquiring what he would in due course learn by silence."

In his final two years of practice (1965-67), McIntyre was elected a Bencher of the Law Society, and took the weekend ferry from Victoria to Vancouver for monthly meetings. The government and discipline of the law profession had been delegated by the provincial legislature to the Law Society, and Benchers were mindful that if they did not discharge their duties conscientiously the delegation could be withdrawn. They were concerned with issues of legal ethics and the disbarment or discipline of delinquent members for dishonest or unethical practices. They were also concerned, as in the Martin case, with prescribing conditions under which students-at-law would be admitted as barristers and solicitors. In fact, they were concerned with almost every detail of the governance of their profession. One vexing and recurrent issue was whether it was consistent with the profession for lawyers or firms to advertise legal services and fees charged for particular kinds of work. Traditionally this had not been allowed, but in most jurisdictions limited advertising, subject to guidelines, is now permitted. An ongoing task McIntyre undertook as a Bencher was to consult with other lawyers on particular ethical dilemmas arising from practice. He found the work interesting and challenging but very time-consuming, and by the time his first term had elapsed he was appointed to the bench.

McIntyre has never played a leading role in politics, but he was active in supporting the candidacy of fellow-lawyer Allan Macfarlane, who ran as a Liberal in Oak Bay. For some time Macfarlane was one of the rare elected Liberal MLAs in the provincial legislature. Insofar as McIntyre had a political affiliation he was a Liberal, a disposition which, combined with his obvious qualifications, certainly did not impede his chances for elevation to the bench. In the summer of 1965 Chief Justice Jack Wilson asked him if he had ever thought of going on the bench. McIntyre admitted that he had considered the possibility, and the Chief Justice said, "You're not going to get the next appointment but you should get the one after that." This prediction was not entirely accurate, in that the next appointees were Nathan Nemetz and Peter Seaton. Some patience was called for under such circumstances. Later, when Mimi and Bill were at the Union Club, Chief Justice Bird came in and said, "I understand you're going to the bench." The next week Mr. Justice Jack Ruttan came over to their table and said, "Wilson's fixed it. You're going to join him." Jack Nicholson, the regional minister for B.C. in the federal cabinet then phoned, and asked whether McIntyre would accept if he were offered a superior court appointment. He said he would, and the appointment was made.

For McIntyre, the 20 years he had practised law in Victoria marked a period of personal and professional growth. He attained considerable stature in legal circles, and was seen as both a fine advocate and an excellent counselor. He also read voraciously, particularly legal history and criminal law but also in other areas, and his erudition impressed all who knew him. Perhaps the quiet ambience of Victoria was conducive to reading and reflection. He was as capable of analyzing the strategy of General Haig at the Battle of the Somme as the legal merits of an ongoing case, and his detailed knowledge of matters outside of his profession was a source of wonder to his friends. He was quiet and dignified, and while he had a rare sense of humour he seldom laughed aloud. He was not one to seek the limelight, and few of his legal cases attracted public attention. The title of Queen's Counsel, given to senior lawyers as a mark of distinction, was bestowed more sparingly in British Columbia than in other provinces, and he did not actually receive his QC until 1990, following his retirement from the Supreme Court of Canada. It is interesting, and perhaps reflective of a truly unique legal context, that two of the first three appointments to the nation's highest court from British Columbia were members of the small Victoria bar — the other was Lyman Poore Duff who was appointed in 1906, and from 1933 until 1944 was Chief Justice of Canada.

The McIntyre family was a close one, and it was one of life's great gifts that Bill's parents, Sidney and Pauline, lived to see him take the oath as a judge of the Supreme Court of British Columbia. Bill was equally proud of his own children, Elizabeth and John, and far from hoping that they would aspire to the law, quietly encouraged them to pursue careers of their own choosing.

NOTES

1. *The Canadian Almanac and Directory for 1963* (Toronto: Copp Clark, 1963), 439.
2. [1947] 1 W.W.R. 483 (Sask. K.B.).
3. Interview of Dr. Daniel Marshall Gordon, by J.C. Scott-Harston (transcript of tape), British Columbia Aural Legal History Project, 1978, 211.
4. Thomas J. Traviso, "Theodore Roethke," in *Benet's Readers Encyclopedia of American Literature,* George Perkins, Barbara Perkin, and Philip Leininger, eds. (New York: HarperCollins, 1991), 920-21.
5. *Re Martin* [1949] 1 D.L.R. 105 at 109 (Benchers of the Law Society of British Columbia).

6. The plural "oaths" indicates that there was one oath for barristers and another for solicitors.
7. *Re Martin* [1949] 1 D.L.R., 105, note 5 at 111.
8. *Ibid.*, 114.
9. R.S.B.C., 1936, c. 149, s. 39.
10. *In re Legal Professions Act* [1949] 1 W.W.R. 993 at 999-1000 (B.C.S.C.); and see the judgment of the British Columbia Court of Appeal in (1950) 8 *The Advocate*, 105-19.
11. *Re Martin* [1949] 1 D.L.R., note 5 at 111.
12. *Ibid.*
13. *An Act to Amend the British North America Act*, 9 Eliz. II, c. 2 (20th December, 1960). See section 2 of the Act, which reads: "A Judge of the Superior Court, whether appointed before or after the coming into force of this section, shall cease to hold office upon attaining the age of seventy-five years, or upon the coming into force of this section if at that time he has already attained that age."
14. See *The Logging Tax Act*, R.S.B.C., 1960, c. 225.
15. "Last Judge to Order Hanging in B.C. Dies at 83," *The Ottawa Citizen*, October 4, 1996, A3.

III

A JUDGE IN BRITISH COLUMBIA

MR. JUSTICE MCINTYRE served successively on the Supreme Court of British Columbia (1967-73) and on the provincial Court of Appeal (1973-78) before being appointed to the Supreme Court of Canada in 1979, where he served for a decade.

Although he enjoyed all his appointments, it was McIntyre's tenure on the Supreme Court of British Columbia that gave him the greatest satisfaction. He had always been a champion of common law and it was the Court of King's Bench, the English forebear of the court to which he was appointed, that had defined and developed common law jurisprudence for almost a thousand years. Quickness of mind and a mastery of substantive law and procedural rules and evidence were essential attributes for a judge in this court. In contrast to appellate court judges, who worked in a different environment and had more time to deliberate, judges in the Supreme Court sometimes had to make rulings within a few minutes of a challenge at trial, and an error could lead to the reversal of previous decisions. The major dispute-resolution function took place in trial courts, while their appellate cousins served in a more rarefied atmosphere as "correctors" or courts of revision.

In the Canadian legal hierarchy the provincial courts (whose predecessors were known as magistrate or police courts), have a more circumscribed jurisdiction than superior courts (such as the B.C. Supreme Court), but decide about 90 percent of the cases in Canada. Their powers are defined by statute. They decide small claims falling under a stipulated amount that varies from province to province, adjudicate on preliminary hearings to determine whether a *prima facie* case exists to send an accused to trial, and hear the majority of criminal cases (except for more serious crimes like murder). The attorney general of each province is responsible for the appointment and remuneration of provincial court judges. By contrast, provincial superior courts and courts of appeal are established under provincial law, but incumbent judges are appointed and paid by the federal government.

The Supreme Court of British Columbia is a superior court of general jurisdiction. Its competence includes deciding cases not typically delimited by statute, and it has inherent, historically-based powers to define its own jurisdiction.[1] Under a jurisdictional compromise made at Confederation, the power to establish and set the size of membership in Canadian superior courts rests with the provinces, but the power of appointment for superior court judges rests with the governor general under section 96 of the Constitution Act, 1867. While such courts have extensive original jurisdiction they also serve as appellate tribunals for provincial courts and for certain administrative boards and tribunals.

With McIntyre's appointment, the initial approach had been made by John R. Nicholson, the federal minister of labour, who was also regional minister for British Columbia. But the appointment itself was recommended to the federal cabinet by the then Justice Minister, Pierre Elliott Trudeau. After his swearing in, McIntyre moved with Mimi to Vancouver to take up his new duties. By this time the children, Elizabeth and John, were studying at university. There were only two other superior court judges residing in Victoria, Mr. Justice A.D. Macfarlane in the 1950s and later, Mr. Justice Wootton. Victoria barristers were sometimes unhappy with the fact that they always appeared before the same high court judge, while their confrères in Vancouver had a much wider legal forum.

Chief Justice J.O. Wilson, who admired McIntyre and was instrumental in elevating him, was described by Canadian journalist Bruce Hutchison, his friend of 70 years, as "the most popular judge British Columbia has ever known."[2] While both judges, of course, retained their independence in decision making, the Chief Justice became McIntyre's treasured friend and mentor and was always available to discuss common concerns. He served as Chief Justice for virtually the whole of McIntyre's tenure on the B.C. Supreme Court.

Wilson was himself the son of a lawyer. He had enlisted in the Canadian army in 1915, at age 16, and fought at the Somme and at Passchendaele, where he was wounded in April 1918. He achieved the rank of lance-corporal, and after returning from the front was admitted to the University of British Columbia in the fall of 1919. One of his good friends there was Howard Green, a future External Affairs minister in the Diefenbaker cabinet, but Wilson's strongest political ties were to the Liberal Party, with whom he worked while studying law in his father's law office in Prince George. After his admission to the bar

Wilson was engaged principally in litigation and criminal law work, but also became campaign manager for Gray Turgeon, who successfully ran in the 1935 general election. Turgeon later became a senator, and his brother Alphonse, after a distinguished diplomatic career, was appointed chief justice of Saskatchewan.

In March 1944 Wilson was appointed to the Supreme Court of British Columbia, which then had a complement of six judges. While interviewing Wilson in 1979, Bruce Hutchison suggested that Canada should have a Bill of Rights "embracing both federal and provincial jurisdictions and in which should be enshrined certain rights." There had been extensive debate within the Trudeau government concerning the entrenchment of a bill enumerating all the basic rights and freedoms possessed by Canadians. While conceding the objective, Wilson responded that such a bill would entangle the Supreme Court of Canada in political decisions. If the Supreme Court was already being criticized for bias in ordinary cases (the argument of Chief Justice Laskin, a proponent of entrenchment), Wilson considered that public criticism would only be increased and intensified by an entrenched bill. Enshrining rights would lead to a wave of litigation of a political nature, and if you have that kind of litigation and Parliament is not clearly supreme, Wilson stated, then the courts become a political rival. He raised the question, really, of whether the courts were the proper vehicle for developing social policy, and regarded this development with apprehension. Given that Wilson was the only head of the Supreme Court during McIntyre's tenure, and the latter's own deep reservations about the effect of entrenching fundamental rights, the degree of agreement between the two jurists is striking.

Wilson did not enjoy the administrative side of his office, but said that it was a trait in a good Chief Justice to know which judge to assign to a particular kind of case. He assigned McIntyre to circuit soon after his appointment in 1967, where he would acquire experience in litigation and criminal law. Wilson had a friendly disposition. When he asked one of his colleagues to do something, McIntyre recalls, he rarely couched it as an order, yet his fellow judges seemed to comply naturally with his wishes. Combine this personal forcefulness with the fact that Wilson considered that "the essential things" were already set out in the Diefenbaker Bill of Rights,[3] and the extent to which he influenced McIntyre's constitutional views starts to come into focus.

This is not to say that they always agreed on legal issues. For example, when a dispute arises between solicitor and client over fees, the client can apply to an official assessor to have the fees "taxed," or verified, to ensure they fall within professionally-prescribed norms. Regarding a proposal made by the B.C. bar to raise fees, Wilson thought that solicitor/client costs, such as the hourly rate charged for lawyer's services, was increasing too much and too quickly in relation to fees assessed for doing specific legal tasks. In Wilson's words, "It might be twenty, twenty-five years ago when I thought that the bar people wanted too much; my views did not prevail. I remember Bill McIntyre was on that committee and he was fresh on the bench and presented the bar view and his view prevailed but I think in general the disparity between taxed costs and solicitor and client costs has been increasing and I regret that."

Despite such incidental disagreements, Wilson and McIntyre respected and liked one another and relations between the two were very cordial. McIntyre was valuable to the chief justice because of his trial experience, and was made circuit judge for Quesnel, Cranbrook, Kelowna, and Nanaimo, especially to hear criminal cases. McIntyre appreciated this appointment; from his earliest days at law school he had wanted to be a judge. He was a welcomed presence both at the bar and among his judicial colleagues, but a difficult test lay before him.

The late David Ricardo Williams, QC, a lawyer from Duncan who wrote several acclaimed works on legal history and later became writer-in-residence at the University of Victoria, got to know McIntyre well. He has vivid memories of a criminal trial where he was a Crown prosecutor before McIntyre, and which fully reflected the latter's careful approach to judging. The *Tatauche* case was heard early in McIntyre's tenure in a court house in Nanaimo. It was a rape trial, and the victim was a Native girl who was only 12 or 13 years old. The alleged assailant was also Native. Evidence indicated that the victim had been very badly injured during the course of a brutal sexual assault. After she was taken to the police station, a matron had taken photographs of the wounds and bruises she had suffered during an obviously violent physical attack. All signs belied any suggestion that she had consented to intercourse. Williams wanted to put these photographs into evidence so that they could be shown to the jury. He was concerned about a rule of evidence, however, that enabled judges to prohibit the placing into evidence photographs of an "inflammatory" nature during a criminal trial. It was thought such photographs could be so disturbing that jurors would not be able to render an objective verdict based on the evidence as a whole, and that they would create a bias against the accused.

McIntyre refused to let the pictures go to the jury. Williams remembers, during the *voir dire*, having a really animated argument with the judge over his prohibition. He told him there were worse things on television than these pictures; there was all kinds of blood and gore in the media. "Well I'm not going to admit them," McIntyre said. In the end, the accused was acquitted. "I was really very angry about that," Williams recalls. "He wasn't able to break out of that mould and say jurors could put up with this sort of stuff! In thirty years we've become so inured to violence that nobody thinks of it anymore, but photographs of a little girl that had been raped weren't deemed admissible then. There was lots of other evidence — the jury was just perverse."

Of course, if McIntyre had admitted the sensational photographs, his decision could have been reversible error if a conviction were secured and the defence were to appeal. To McIntyre, fair process was always of prime importance. However desired a particular result might be, it should only be arrived at after a fair trial with appropriate safeguards for the accused. Despite his disappointment in this case, Williams was McIntyre's staunch friend and admirer throughout his career. Williams recalls McIntyre in the role of adversary counsel as an affable, eminently fair, and easygoing colleague, but also as a resolute and determined courtroom opponent. He was equally formidable as a judge. Williams appeared before McIntyre several times when he was on the Supreme Court of British Columbia and later the Court of Appeal. He had a quality of inscrutability. "It was very hard to read him when he was on the Court of Appeal," said Williams.

He didn't say very much. He was a cerebral type both on the bench and off it. He didn't interrupt you and you seldom heard any jokes or quips from him. He was the best-read judge on the bench of his time, I would say, not only in the law, but in subjects outside the law. He could converse on any topic in literature and would always have an informed view. It made him a bit on an oddity in a way. Outside the courtroom he was a very agreeable companion. He enjoyed good food and good wine. He was humorous. He had a dry wit about him, an ironic wit. He was excellent company, but you didn't see that in court. He drew a line between his private and his public appearances.

Although Chief Justice John Farris once declared that any lawyer going to the bench would be making a financial sacrifice, McIntyre's promotion did not entail a major loss of income. In 1967 the difference between what he made as a judge and what he had pulled in as a lawyer was about $14,000, but he concedes that the disparity would have increased in the following years. Financial security remains an important aspect in attracting and keeping capable persons on the bench. McIntyre has mixed feelings about the assessment of judicial pensions:

> There should be an adequate pension and a residual pension to your wife if she survives you. At first judicial pensions were non-contributory, but those appointed after 1974 do contribute; those appointed before don't have to. To qualify you must be 65 and have served for 15 years. That will have to be changed. It's difficult to recruit younger judges. If you're appointed at 49 it's all right since your necessary 15 years of service will be up at age 65. If you're appointed at age 30, however, and have served 20 years on the bench by the year 2000, you'd still have to wait to 2015 for a pension. A judge should know precisely what the rules for pension eligibility are. You shouldn't have to hang on tenaciously when you're physically ill to get a pension. I think the present pension is extremely generous — the quantum is O.K.

The craft of judging was much as McIntyre had expected it to be. He was a natural "preparer," and he studied in advance for each case. Some judges do not prepare until they come to a case: they take the view that they might acquire a bias. McIntyre reasons that bias can be avoided while reading the pleadings and checking the cited authorities. McIntyre alerted himself to possible evidentiary problems arising out of statements, admissions, and confessions. However, judges never read "discoveries," of course, a practice forbidden on the grounds that to read them is potentially prejudicial. In the appellate process there is less danger of prejudice, because the record is complete. McIntyre explains, "At some time you are going to have to resist prejudice before you hear counsel. At some stage you will hear all the evidence. A judge, actually, is in a good position. A judge is secure and independent; nobody can fire him. He listens to a dispute between people he will never see again. He is not interested in the outcome other than to produce a fair result. You should always listen to both sides with an open mind: when you hear the plaintiff's side it frequently seems unassailable until you hear the defendant's response."

Judges can either give a judgment from the bench at the termination of proceedings or reserve, and give a written judgment later. One of the proverbial faults of courts since Lord Eldon's time, as parodied by

Dickens in *Bleak House*, has been procrastination. McIntyre was never a delayer.

We didn't give judgment from the bench as much as they do now, but there were never long gaps. I was always a bit nervous about judgments from the bench. I may have been too cautious. There were occasions when I could have given judgments from the bench, but I wrote. On appeal, I'm against frequent judgments from the bench. You need more care, because the judgments are more likely to be recorded and thereby influence the development of the law. You need time for reading and reflection. Even on the Supreme Court of Canada there were occasions when we gave judgments from the bench. The court would announce that reasons would follow after the oral judgment.

McIntyre cites the Supreme Court of Canada case of *Tremblay v. Daigle*,[4] where an oral judgment was necessarily expeditious. It was the case of a young plaintiff who was asserting "father's rights" in order to prevent his pregnant girlfriend from having an abortion. The Court held that the fetus was not a rights-bearing human being, and that there was no legal basis for affirming "father's rights." Even before the oral judgment was delivered, however, the young woman obtained an abortion in the United States. McIntyre considers there was no real justification for an appeal to the Supreme Court in this case, but by the time the judgment was delivered he had just retired and did not participate in it.

McIntyre was always conscious that the accused, arraigned in the dock and facing the whole panoply of state authority, was likely to feel overawed by the trial court. He tried to let the people at trial know that as a judge he was genuinely sensitive to their concerns. He tried to be polite, saying "Thank you witness," after their testimony, and he did not let counsel abuse or browbeat witnesses. He remained cognizant of how opposite parties might react in difficult circumstances, and strove to create an atmosphere that would relieve tensions. One example demonstrates this even-handedness. In a drug conspiracy case where he presided, one of the four or five defendants was the father of a small baby. His wife had come to the trial and the baby started to whimper. As the baby continued to fret the woman got up and headed toward the courtroom door. "Madam, you don't need to take that baby out," McIntyre said. "It doesn't bother me; it doesn't both the jury; if it bothers anyone else they can leave." His cardinal rule was to be polite to witnesses, the accused, and to his or her family. In this case, the woman's husband was convicted and received a ten-year sentence.

In a personal injuries case over which he presided in the early 1970s, a young Japanese woman of about 20 years of age had been hit by a vehicle on a crosswalk in Vancouver, and her hip was seriously fractured. It was impossible to do a hip replacement because there were so many fragments. At issue was whether she had crossed the street at the proper intersection, but she succeeded at trial and the amount of damages had to be decided. This was a difficult case because damages can turn on cultural distinctions. In Japanese culture any damage to the body rendered the victim "not completely whole," with adverse social consequences. The victim's mother had testified, in fact, that in the Japanese community a crippled woman has very little status. "I considered that," McIntyre says, "in my award of damages. I mentioned the cultural issue to Craig Monroe one day and he said, 'What place is there in *our* society for a crippled woman?'" In terms of compensation the social effect of incapacitating physical injury was considered, as well as the fact that men had a wider range of employment opportunities than women.

As a superior court judge McIntyre sat on a large variety of cases, both those involving the broad original jurisdiction of the court and those involving appeals, often from the provincial court. An example of the latter was *R. v. Bagnall*, where a provincial court judge had acquitted the respondent of driving drunk, a condition defined under section 236 of the Criminal Code.[5] When the driver was apprehended and detained in custody overnight, he asked the police to give him a blood test, which he hoped to use in his defence. No test was made, and he was not advised that the police had no facilities to make such a test. While McIntyre had some sympathy with the accused, he noted that the police are under no legal obligation to furnish facilities for blood tests. Nor had the man requested legal advice on the matter, or called for an independent test from his own physician. Accordingly, the appeal by the Crown was allowed, and the case was remitted back to the trial judge for disposition.

The question whether a Vancouver city bylaw validly delegated powers to the supervisor of the motor inspection station to inspect vehicles arose in an appeal of the case *R. v. Horback*. A police magistrate, Levey, had dismissed a charge against the respondent for failing to return a vehicle for reinspection within a stated time. The respondent admitted all the facts but contended that the inspector did not possess valid powers to charge as delegated by the city; these were discretionary or judicial powers which were beyond the city's capacity to grant. His determination, therefore, was a nullity. Relying on the principle *potestas delegata non est delegari* (a delegated power must not be redelegated), McIntyre found that the city could not grant the inspector more than administrative power, but had in effect granted him an unsupervised discretion to set safety standards. This amounted to an abdication of power; safety standards should be set, according to the delegation to it, by city council itself. The appeal was dismissed.

In a divorce action, *Pybus v. Pybus*,[6] the issue was whether the wife, who had petitioned for divorce, could satisfy the court that she was living "separate and apart"[7] from her husband when they were in fact continuing to live under the same roof. The husband had moved into a basement bedroom and there had been no sexual relations between the parties but the wife had continued to do the cooking, shopping, laundry, and other necessary household duties. On this evidence McIntyre considered it impossible to find that the parties had been living "separate and apart" for the then mandatory three-year period required for divorce on the grounds of marriage breakdown. In *Rushton v. Rushton*,[8] however, where the estranged spouses continued to live in the same suite because they were joint caretakers of an apartment building, McIntyre decided on the facts that they were essentially leading separate lives and could satisfy the requirement of "living separate and apart." They lived in separate rooms, had no sexual relations, and there was almost no contact between them. The wife performed no domestic services for the husband and shopped and cooked only for herself.

In *Brooke Enterprises Ltd. v. Wilding and Jones*,[9] the case concerned exactly when a cause of action for negligent design of a motel arose; if the cause had arisen more than six years earlier it was barred by the Statute of Limitations.[10] There were no contractual relations between the plaintiffs and the defendant, although the latter was alleged to be liable for negligence in design. If the cause of action arose when the defendants made the defective design, the action would be statute-barred because the alleged negligence had occurred more than six years earlier. However, if the action arose when the plaintiff became aware of past defects by observing existing faults in the building, it could be maintained. It was held that the latter standard was the correct one and that the suit was maintainable.

A petition by a son for a larger share in his father's estate under the Testator's Family Maintenance Act was the issue in *Re Stubbe Estate*.[11] In that case the deceased left an estate valued at $54,000 in equal shares to his son, the petitioner, to the daughter of his first wife by a former marriage, and to the four daughters of a second wife by a former marriage. During the first marriage, the domestic situation of the testator's family had been unhappy. The testator had not provided adequately for his wife and son and they lived in penury while the petitioner was growing up. The son had not enjoyed a proper home environment, nor had he received an adequate education, and advancement in life had been prejudiced thereby. Since the son was the only blood relative of the deceased, McIntyre decided the latter had failed in his moral duty to provide adequately for his child. His testamentary disposition was varied so that his son would receive a one-third interest in the estate, with the remainder divided in equal shares between the other five children, who were not blood relatives.

The foregoing very selective list of McIntyre's B.C. Supreme Court cases affords a glimpse of the remarkable range and variety of subject matter tried in that forum. While the cases do not always involve large sums of money (indeed, they could potentially involve *any* amount), they are all of great importance to the contesting parties. The very rationale of the historic English Court of King's Bench was to administer justice to the subjects of the realm, no matter what the cause, and the British Columbia Supreme Court is furthering the heritage of its English predecessor to the same purpose.

In 1973 McIntyre received a telephone call from the Honourable Otto Lang, minister of justice in the Trudeau cabinet, enquiring whether he would accept an appointment to the British Columbia Court of Appeal. At first McIntyre thought the offer was a practical joke. He had had no prior notice of the appointment. As their conversation progressed he realized that it was really the minister speaking, and indicated he would accept gladly. When he told Chief Justice Wilson of the offer, the latter just smiled and waved "Bye-bye." Relations between Wilson and McIntyre were more than cordial; through their close association on the court the two judges had developed a deep mutual respect and become firm friends. McIntyre remembers that the chief justice was truly "revered" by colleagues, and for both personal and professional reasons McIntyre himself left the trial court with a certain sadness.

In both of his British Columbia judicial appointments McIntyre served under one chief justice. This was Chief Justice J.O. Wilson in the British Columbia Supreme Court, and on the Court of Appeal, Chief Justice John Lauchlan Farris, the son of one of Canada's great advocates, J.W. de B. Farris. While Wilson had many years of judicial experience, Farris was a rare example (Chief Justice Sherwood Lett was another) of a chief justice elevated to the highest position on his court without first serving as a puisne judge. Farris became chief justice in 1973, the year McIntyre joined the court. After Farris's call to the bar in 1935, he had rapidly become known as an effective counsel, often appearing with another outstanding advocate, Claude McAlpine. Before the abolition of Privy Council appeals in 1949, he appeared several times in that august forum. He was sought out by labour unions, and handled cases involving such varied fields as civil and mechanical engineering, geology, and marine architecture. Like McIntyre, he was known as someone who prepared cases assiduously and was unfailingly courteous to other counsel during trial.

McIntyre's two most significant decisions on the British Columbia Court of Appeal were *R. v. Miller and Cockriell*,[12] in which he made a forceful dissent against imposing capital punishment, and *R. v. Rourke*,[13] in which he held for a unanimous Court of Appeal that, in a clear case, a trial court judge at any level had jurisdiction to direct a stay of proceedings to prevent an abusive process. The remedy, however, was not available in the *Rourke* case. Neither of McIntyre's decisions commended themselves to the Supreme Court of Canada. His liberal dissent in *Miller* was not decisive, since the court unanimously affirmed the majority decision upholding capital punishment,[14] and his decision in *Rourke* was also reversed.[15] Although these opinions were not ultimately decisive, their very liberality must be recognized by those who consider McIntyre to be a conservative jurist overly concerned with the preservation of public order.

In his opinion on capital punishment, the facts as stated in the majority decision by Robertson, JA, were as follows: that the accused, Miller and Cockriell, had been drinking beer in a Fort Langley beer parlour, and on returning to Miller's house had consumed more beer. According to the evidence presented in court, something was said about the death of Miller's brother during a police chase, and the two were said to have discussed shooting a policeman. They decided to go for a drive. Miller took with him a .30/30 Winchester rifle loaded with one shell in the chamber. They drove the short distance to Cloverdale, where the courthouse and the police station are situated side by side. Miller drove around the block and Cockriell threw a beer bottle through the window of the courthouse. Later, in another part of town, something attracted the attention of Constable Roger Pierlet, who pursued the men in a marked police car. At a certain point he stopped their car. Miller had the cocked rifle resting on his arms with the muzzle pointing toward the open window. The constable asked Miller for his driver's licence, but he did not have one. When he asked Miller to get out of the car, Cockriell pulled the trigger, and the bullet struck the policeman in the chest. The constable managed to get to his car and radio for help. He was found collapsed beside his car by the officer who arrived to cover him, but died almost immediately. In due course, the two men were tried before a jury, found guilty of murder as charged, and sentenced to death.

Josiah Wood, who was counsel for Cockriell and later appointed to the Court of Appeal, argued eloquently against capital punishment in the subsequent appeal, contending that it had been rendered inoperative because the provisions of the Criminal Code relating to murder (sections 214 and 218) infringed section 2(b) of the Canadian Bill of Rights,[16] which directed judges to construe the law so as not to "impose or authorize the imposition of cruel and unusual treatment or punishment." All the judges who participated in the Court of Appeal decision agreed that this was the governing standard, but there was a disagreement between McIntyre and the majority over whether capital punishment did, in fact, constitute "cruel and unusual treatment or punishment." The issue on appeal was not, of course, whether the appellants should go unpunished, as everyone agreed that they had been properly convicted of murder, but whether, because of section 2(b), the death sentence should be reduced to life imprisonment. Harry Rankin, who was Miller's counsel, adopted Wood's argument on capital punishment in its entirety.[17]

While there were other grounds of appeal, the one of most interest here concerns the constitutional validity of capital punishment. Speaking for the four-judge majority,[18] Mr. Justice Robertson contended that section 2(b) of the unentrenched Bill of Rights "is nothing more than a canon of construction," which Parliament could repeal or exclude from applying under the notwithstanding clause: "The Bill of Rights is no more sacrosanct than any other statute and the usual canons of construction apply to and in respect of it as much as to and in respect of any other Act. Such a repeal or exclusion does not need to be expressed; it can be implied."[19]

What Robertson meant here was that to the extent of inconsistency, the 1973 amendments on capital punishment, which were central to the whole case, took precedence over the Bill of Rights, and not the converse, as McIntyre was arguing. He cited *Daniels v. The Queen*,[20] which had adopted statements in Halsbury's *Laws of England* discountenancing "repeal by implication," or "the repeal of a general enactment by a particular one."[21] Punishment by death for murder, moreover, might be "cruel" but it was not "unusual."[22] When Parliament last enacted the provisions on capital punishment in 1973, it was fully cognizant of the Bill of Rights, and "there was no need to use the magic words 'shall operate notwithstanding the *Canadian Bill of Rights*,'" because the punishment of death for murder was not "unusual";[23] consequently, it did not offend the Bill.

McIntyre agreed with all of Robertson's conclusions on the other grounds of appeal, but disagreed with his disposition of the capital punishment issue. He agreed that the accused were rightly convicted of killing a police officer. Unlike the majority, however, he did not see the legislative intent of Parliament in passing sections 214 and 218 as overriding by implication section 2(b) of the Canadian Bill of Rights; nor did he see, as Robertson, JA, argued, that section 2(b) had no impact on the provisions because capital punishment was not "unusual." As the majority had declared, the Bill of Rights was indeed a statute but it was a statute that, according to its plain words, had consequences, and in this case section 2(b) of the Bill was not concerned with parliamentary intention but with the consequences of the Criminal Code provisions on murder, which Parliament had enacted: "It has not forbidden the passing of laws but it has directed the Courts in the exercise of their historic function of construing the laws to refrain from construing any Act of Parliament not excepted from the operation of the Bill of Rights so as to 'impose or authorize the imposition of cruel and unusual treatment or punishment.'"[24] This distinction was the key consideration for McIntyre. In enacting sections 214 and 218 in 1973, Parliament had not excepted them pursuant to section 2 from the operation of the Bill of Rights. It was the duty of courts to construe these sections, therefore, in order to ensure that their consequential effects did not result in "cruel and unusual treatment and punishment," and this duty had been imposed by Parliament.

McIntyre read the terms "cruel" and "unusual" in section 2(b) disjunctively, "so that cruel punishments however usual in the ordinary sense of the term might come within the proscription." He then goes on to say, "I am of the opinion it would be cruel and unusual if it is not in accord with public standards of decency and propriety, if it is unnecessary because of adequate alternatives, if it cannot be applied on a rational basis in accordance with ascertained or ascertainable standards, and if it is excessive and out of proportion to the crimes it seeks to restrain."[25] According to all of these criteria, McIntyre finds capital punishment to be "cruel and unusual," and so to be proscribed by section 2(b). Public standards of decency and propriety are not static but evolve: "Over the centuries the popular mind has turned away from the worst forms of punishment and the number of offences for which drastic physical punishment could be imposed has been greatly reduced."[26] Human sensibilities have developed to the point where the propriety of the death penalty is doubted by increasing numbers of people.

Canadian statistics on the death penalty for the century between 1867 and 1965 indicate that, while the ratio between those actually executed and those sentenced to death varied from decade to decade, from the inception of the statistics a substantial number under capital sentence had had their sentences commuted to life imprisonment or had otherwise escaped the death penalty; in McIntyre's words, "for a century Canadians have applied the death penalty with some reluctance." There was a marked decrease in the 1960s because of the increasing disposition of the federal cabinet to commute such sentences to life imprisonment. As far as adequate alternatives are concerned, McIntyre considered a term of life imprisonment, more rigorously enforced than before so as to ensure that the sentence is served, to be suitable.[27] Was the death penalty arbitrary as applied in Canada? Referring to the statistics, McIntyre concludes that it is: "A punishment which is visited upon only a few of those who qualify for it is likely to be found to have been arbitrarily applied and arbitrarily withheld. Only a relatively small percentage of those convicted of capital crimes in Canada, prior to the *de facto* suspension of the death penalty in 1962 suffered execution." Among factors he found compounding the arbitrariness were the capricious use of the commutation process and the discrepantly numerous executions of men as compared to women. And mistakes do occur: innocent persons have been executed. The awfulness of the death penalty resides in the fact that if the wrong person is hanged the mistake is irremediable. "In my view," concludes McIntyre, "the sentence of death is in all circumstances excessive punishment. It far exceeds the need that can justify it and renders any errors in its application, and errors will occur, impossible of correction."[28]

By way of penalty in *R. v. Miller and Cockriell,* McIntyre would have allowed the appeal to the extent that he would have directed the entry of a conviction for both appellants of murder punishable by life imprisonment. The words providing for the death penalty in ss. 214

and 218 having been found inoperative, there is nothing left in the legislation to distinguish murder punishable by death and murder generally, and the conviction merits the lesser penalty.[29]

On appeal McIntyre's dissent was not followed by the Supreme Court of Canada, which unanimously upheld the Court of Appeal's majority judgment.[30] In the meantime the Supreme Court had been overtaken by Parliament, which in 1976 repealed the death penalty for murder.[31] Accordingly, by the time the Court rendered its decision the question was moot. In the corridors of Parliament if not in the courts, McIntyre and those who agreed with him had prevailed. A political solution superseded the judicial one. In 1987, under Mulroney, there was further debate in Parliament and throughout the nation about the possible reimposition of the death penalty, and once again the abolitionists prevailed.

Several years after the Court of Appeal's judgment in *Miller*, during an interview between Mr. Justice A.B. Robertson, the author of the majority decision, and a concurring member of the panel, Chief Justice John L. Farris, the following colloquy took place:

Mr. Farris: "I always thought about that judgment of Bill McIntyre's that he felt very strongly on the impropriety or immorality of hanging, of capital punishment, and that dissent of his wasn't really a judgment, it was a diatribe against the concept of capital punishment."

Mr. Robertson: "It was emotional."

Mr. Farris: "It was a purely emotional matter."

Mr. Robertson: "Yes."

Mr. Farris: "That doesn't mean that Bill McIntyre isn't a fine judge; he is a fine judge."

Mr. Robertson: "Oh yes."[32]

If one grants the premise of his fellow judges that McIntyre did harbour strong sentiments against the death penalty, would that in any way affect the validity or cogency of his judgment? Oliver Wendell Holmes once said that a judge could put any conclusion in logical form, so the main consideration in a legal judgment must be whether the supporting reasons, whatever their emotional wellspring, substantiate the conclusion. On an issue like capital punishment it would be odd if mature members of the legal system did not entertain strong feelings, acquired over years of practice as prosecutors or defence counsel or in some other capacity. McIntyre's judgment is controlled and closely reasoned. His interpretation of section 2(b) of the Canadian Bill of Rights is reasonable, and his consideration and dismissal in turn of each of the arguments favouring capital punishment is thorough. Whether one agrees with him or not, there is no indication of imbalance.

In *R. v. Rourke* an indictment was preferred against the respondent containing one count of kidnapping and one of robbery in relation to an incident that had occurred on October 5, 1971. The indictment was preferred on November 21, 1973. The following day the trial judge, acceding to a motion by the respondent, stayed proceedings "as an abuse of the Court's process which would deprive the respondent of his right to a fair trial in accordance with the principles of natural justice."[33] Originally, police had intended to apprehend the respondent on October 29, 1971, when he was scheduled to appear on a traffic charge at the police court in Vancouver, but he did not appear. The authority for his apprehension was a pick-up order, a notification to police officers that he was being sought and that if they encountered him "they may but not must arrest him."[34]

The respondent was living in Creston, British Columbia, and made no effort to conceal himself:

The respondent said he knew nothing of the matter until April 1973. He says he had lived openly at Creston for the previous two years. During that period he was employed at Creston, had a motor vehicle registered in his name, knew several RCMP officers with whom he played softball and was known to the parole authorities in Creston. If, he says, the Vancouver police had made any diligent inquiry they would have found him within a few days of 5th October, 1971 when these offences were said to have been committed. Because of the delay he has been seriously prejudiced in his defence.[35]

Rourke alleged that his defence had been prejudiced because in the time between the date of the offences in October 1971 and his actual apprehension at Creston in April 1973, and the further time that elapsed to his trial date in the following November, several witnesses who could have established alibis or provided other material evidence had either died or had disappeared. He argued that he had never been a fugitive, had played softball with police officers, and could easily have been found if the authorities had made an effort to find him. The fact that they had not sought him out earlier had gravely prejudiced his defence.

While denying the remedy Rourke sought in this case, McIntyre made a strong affirmation, in a clear case, of the right of a court at any level to stay proceedings in order to protect the process of the court from oppressive conduct on the part of the prosecution.[36] What constitutes a "clear case" giving rise to this remedy is difficult to define in abstract terms, both because of variability in different situations and the judge's discretion whether or not to grant the remedy in individual cases. Two illustrations drawn from actual cases are mentioned by Chief Justice Laskin. If the accused is removed for trial to a place remote from where the offence occurred and cannot procure essential witnesses because of prohibitive costs, or in a case where the accused committed an alleged offence at the instigation and with the encouragement of a police officer, this remedy could probably be successfully invoked. The minority agreed with McIntyre that the court had power to provide a remedy for abusive process, but considered that the facts in Rourke did not warrant such a remedy. Laskin's practical considerations were as follows:

> The time lapse between the commission of an offence and the laying of a charge following apprehension of an accused cannot be monitored by courts by fitting investigations into a standard mould or moulds. Witnesses and evidence may disappear in the short run as well as in the long, and the accused too may have to be sought for a long or short period of time. Subject to such controls as are prescribed in the Criminal Code prosecutions initiated a lengthy period after the alleged commission of an offence must be left to take their course and to be dealt with by the Court on the evidence, which judges are entitled to weigh for cogency as well as credibility. The Court can call for an explanation of any untoward delay in prosecution and may be in a position, accordingly, to assess the weight of some of the evidence.[37]

Laskin, speaking for four judges,[38] agreed with McIntyre that in a clear case the court had a right to stay proceedings to prevent abuse of prosecutorial discretion, but a bare five-judge majority[39] held against the Court of Appeal on this point.[40] The main argument of the Court majority, speaking through Justice Pigeon, was that the Criminal Code had preserved common law defences, but that such defences did not embrace a discretionary stay of proceedings.[41] There being no legal basis for such a stay in the codified Criminal Code, a slim 5-4 majority found the postulated inherent power not to exist.

Some years later, in a bookstore in Portland, Oregon, McIntyre was browsing through an edition of Justice William O. Douglas's U.S. Supreme Court decisions, where he found cited some early-nineteenth century English cases that were directly on point. The Court majority had doubted the very existence of relevant case authority. By this time McIntyre was a member of the Supreme Court of Canada, and when he showed the citations to Mr. Justice Pigeon the latter was silent for a moment. Looking up, finally, he said with a grin, "But you didn't find them either Bill." The key passage as cited by Mr. Justice Douglas in *U.S. v. Marion*, 404 U.S. 307 (1971) is as follows:

Lord Mansfield held in *Rex v. Robinson*, 96 Eng. Rep. 313 (K.B. 1765), that the issuance of an information was subject to time limitation: "If delayed, the delay must be reasonably accounted for." In *Regina v. Hext*, 4 Jurists 339 (Q.B. 1840), an information was refused where a whole term of court had passed since the alleged assault took place. Accord: *Rex v. Marshall*, 104 Eng. Rep. 394 (K.B. 1811).

Baron Alderson said in *Regina v. Robins*, 1 Cox's C.C. 114 (Somerset Winter Assizes 1844), where there was a two-year delay in making a charge of bestiality:

It is monstrous to put a man on trial after such a lapse of time. How can he account for his conduct so far back? If you accuse a man of a crime the next day, he may be enabled to bring forward his servants and family to say where he was and what he was about at the time; but if the charge be not preferred for a year or more, how can he clear himself? No man's life would be safe if such a prosecution were permitted. It would be very unjust to put him on his trial.[42]

One wonders whether the result would have been different if the above authorities had been before the court in *Rourke*.

In the era of the Canadian Charter of Rights and Freedoms, as the authors of a recent text declare, "a prosecution may be so tainted by the Charter breach that a stay of proceedings is appropriate."[43] The common law stay has been adapted as a Charter remedy, but is used only sparingly, in cases of severity. As the Supreme Court of Canada has said, the remedy of a stay should be granted only "'in the clearest of cases,' where the prejudice to the accused's right to make full answer and defence cannot be remedied or where irreparable prejudice would be caused to the integrity of the judicial system if the prosecution were continued."[44]

In *Harry v. Kreutziger*[45] McIntyre had an opportunity to consider the equitable doctrine of contractual relief on the basis of unconscionability. The appellant was an Indian living in Powell River who suffered from a congenital hearing defect, but was not deaf. He had a Grade Five education and was described as a "mild, inarticulate, retiring person" who was inexperienced in business matters. Pressure was exerted on him by the defendant to sell his fishing boat, the *Glenda Marion*, for a price substantially below its fair market value. The defendant was an experienced business man. Evidence was adduced that Harry had attempted to refuse the offer but that Kreutziger had exerted considerable pressure. When the plaintiff sought relief from performance of the contract as an unconscionable transaction the motion was denied,[46] from which denial the present appeal was taken. Concurring judgments granting the relief sought by the plaintiff were delivered by McIntyre and Lambert, JJ.A Craig, JA, concurred with both judgments. McIntyre held that an improvident transaction would be set aside as unconscionable where it was induced by an inequality in the position of the parties due to the ignorance, need, or distress of the weaker: "In my opinion, it is clear from the evidence that the respondent, a man of greater business experience, greater education and with a full knowledge of the value attributable in the autumn of 1973 to a commercial fishing licence, took advantage of his general superiority and prevailed upon the appellant to enter into this bargain against his best interests."[47] In his concurring opinion, Lambert asked whether "the transaction, seen as a whole, is sufficiently divergent from community standards of commercial morality that it should be rescinded."[48] In answering this question in the affirmative he gave more weight to Canadian cases than those from elsewhere, where different standards of commercial morality might apply.

An interesting constitutional point arising under the division of powers between Canada and the provinces was decided in favour of federal jurisdiction by McIntyre in *Jebsens v. Lambert*.[49] The plaintiff was a shipowner who sent a ship into the harbour in Vancouver with a cargo of some 15,000 tons of raw sugar. The recipient of the sugar, B.C. Sugar Refinery, had locked its employees out, and was being picketed by the union representing its employees. As a result of the picketing, the crews of longshoremen ceased unloading the plaintiff's ship. The picketing here had caused damage, and was aimed solely at an innocent third party. McIntyre found that the union lacked power to picket a federal "undertaking" authorized under section 92(10) of the British North America Act, 1867. The Labour Code of British Columbia,[50] which would have made the picketing lawful, simply did not apply in this case. Consequently, he allowed the appeal, in an oral judgment, and directed "the injunction prayed for in the notice of motion go in the terms sought."

Having served on both judicial forums, McIntyre is well qualified to compare the work of an appellate and a trial judge. His first impression of the Court of Appeal was of a certain unreality. As a trial judge he had been engaged, along with counsel, in endeavouring to establish, according to legal rules, what had actually happened in given cases. In the Court of Appeal this process had been accomplished, and argument centred not on the parties at law but on the conduct and rulings of trial judges. "In the trial process," McIntyre observes,

you see the whole picture emerge piece by piece. That created picture then goes to the Court of Appeal. You should not fiddle around with findings of fact by the trial court during an appeal. The whole focus changes. The question is not "what happened?" but "is what happened right or wrong?" When the transition from a trial court to an appeal court is made by a newly-appointed judge, it calls for a very significant mental adjustment. In the trial court a judge sits alone; in the court of appeal a judge rarely functions without associates.

"It's great to have the others there," McIntyre reflects, "to assist in what is really a common enterprise. But you can't, during an appeal, reach over behind the trial judge and seize on what somebody said in the trial court. You are bound by the record or 'case,' and by the trial judgment."

McIntyre considers it a mistake to have all Court of Appeal judges drawn from the trial bench, but it would be equally mistaken not to have any trial judges. The biggest danger facing the trial judge on an appeal court is the temptation to defend the trial judge from whom the appeal is taken. The function of an appellate tribunal is to serve as a court of error — to correct and rectify any errors that were made at trial. McIntyre remembers that when James McDonald was elevated to the Court of Appeal he was asked whether he found it hard to overrule his former colleagues. With a characteristic sly grin he replied, "No, after a couple of times you get to enjoy it."

For those who have not been trial judges it is a different experience. The work is more academic, and some judges and lawyers would find it sterile. In form it is a higher court because it can reverse trial court judgments, but McIntyre says that such well-qualified trial judges as Jack Ruttan or Lloyd McKenzie have turned down appointments to the Court of Appeal. They did so not out of false modesty but because the trial court was the more ancient common law forum; there, real-life struggles took place, adversarial parties actively engaged, and law emerged in the process. There was no monetary incentive to go from one court to the other as the salaries were the same. Some judges simply preferred the trial to the appellate court. In many ways McIntyre himself preferred the trial court to the other forums on which he sat.

Looking back on his years on the bench, McIntyre considers that his happiest ones were spent on the trial court in British Columbia: "You're the real judge," he observes. "The appellate process merely reviews what you've done. The judge of first instance (and often of last instance) is the one who presides over a serious criminal trial with a jury. You experience in that setting the great heritage of the common law that has been passed down to us." Chief Justice Wilson apparently felt the same way. When it was suggested to him that a prospective appointee might not wish to come to the B.C. Supreme Court, he replied, "Nobody has to apologize for sitting on the British Columbia Supreme Court, which is a direct lineal descendant of the historic Court of King's Bench of Henry II. All the majesty of the law is there. It was the height of my career." He recalled a rather evocative metaphor for the distinction between trial and appellate courts made by Judge Montague Tyrwhitt-Drake, who compared the two tribunals to a physician and a pathologist: the trial court deals with the living and the appeal court with the dead.[51] The trial judge, says McIntyre,

will get 20 seconds to make decisions on points of law that the House of Lords will take six months to disagree about; or to agree. The trial judge is the real judge: the only judge possessing inherent jurisdiction pertaining to the office of the appointment. A High Court judge has all the jurisdiction; it can only be ousted if it can be shown that it's been taken from him. The courts of appeal or the Supreme Court of Canada only have that jurisdiction that is given to them by statute. Original jurisdiction in all issues is that of the Supreme Court of British Columbia. Appellate courts are statutory tribunals charged with limited powers of review. The only judges who can issue prerogative writs are superior court judges.

There are different qualities to look for in different benches. What the Court of Appeal needs are competent second-guessers; it looks at the finished product. If Napoleon had gone there instead of here would he have won the battle?

In the Court of Appeal it's harder to sit and listen to legal argument for two hours than to preside at trial. The greatest difficulty is in keeping awake. You don't have breaks and interruptions. Time on the trial bench goes much more quickly.

Appeal court work may be more attractive academically, but McIntyre considers that it is only rarely that one can find it truly satisfying. The workload is heavy and there is too little time for reflection. The first thing that Chief Justice Bora Laskin said when he arrived at the country's highest court was, "There's only one problem with this court: we don't have time to think." A revised opinion-writing schedule has lately provided more time for academic consideration.

McIntyre found sitting with other judges on the Court of Appeal legally stimulating. That court sits in threes for the most part. "The chemistry is different, depending on who the other judges are," he said. "It's only rare that you have to act on your own. There's also nothing wrong with dissenting. You know your judgment even if wrong isn't going to be decisive. A dissenting judge can write with a free hand. I used to think you should never dissent unless the point of principle was very grave. I decided with the onset of the Charter that that wasn't the rule anymore. In its formative stages varying views should be expressed about the Charter with reasons for the dissent. In the old days such dissents wouldn't have been written."

McIntyre recalls the strong contention between the British Columbia Supreme Court and the Court of Appeal when the latter court was established in 1907 over who should be styled "Chief Justice of British Columbia." There were those who argued that because the existing Chief Justice of British Columbia presided over the province's historic superior court of general jurisdiction he should continue to bear that designation. On the other hand, in terms of hierarchy, the newly-established Court of Appeal could reverse superior court decisions. (Before the innovation, three judges of the Supreme Court of British Columbia would sit *en banc* during an appeal on a colleague's decision, there being an appeal from a single judge to the full court.) There were partisans for both points of view. The compromise arrived at was to leave the title "Chief Justice of British Columbia" with the incumbent for the time being, with the head of the newly-created forum being called "Chief Justice of the Court of Appeal"; when the present Chief Justice of British Columbia ceased to hold office, however, the statute provided that the title was to devolve upon the Chief Justice of the Court of Appeal and his successors,[52] with the head of the trial division then to be styled Chief Justice of the Supreme Court.

Later, when McIntyre was appointed to the Supreme Court of Canada, his prior judicial experience compared favourably with that of any of his colleagues. His circuit court experience in criminal and other trials was invaluable when he came to deliberate on issues of criminal law and procedure in the nation's highest court, matters on which he and Justice Antonio Lamer (as he then was) were the court's acknowledged experts. As a judge he was fair-minded, painstaking, and lucid in writing his opinions. He always prepared thoroughly, and believed in brevity and clarity of expression: those who read an opinion are entitled to understand what the law is. His view of the judicial function was that judges should exercise self-restraint and not intrude into areas of policy making appropriate for resolution by cabinet or legislature. He was insistent in his appellate work that the facts on which an appeal was based should be those admitted into evidence by the trial court, without additions, deletions, or embellishments. On rare occasions this could lead to controversial results, as when he prepared an opinion in 1991 for Justice Minister Kim Campbell on the regularity of David Milgaard's conviction in 1970 for the murder of Gail Miller. After receiving an opinion based on the evidence then submitted, the justice minister said: "There has been a thorough and diligent review of every piece of evidence.... I have concluded that there is no reason to believe that a miscarriage of justice is likely to have occurred in this case."[53] Later, of course, DNA evidence was examined that fully exonerated Mr. Milgaard.

NOTES

1. *Crevier v. A.-G. Que.* [1981] 2 S.C.R. 220.
2. *British Columbia Aural Legal History Project* [transcript of tape]. Interviewee, Hon. J.O. Wilson (C.J.S.C., B.C., Trial Division, 1963-73); interviewer, Bruce Hutchison, July 1979, 1, 13, 60, [second transcript], 4, 7, 18.
3. *Ibid.*, 20.
4. [1989] 2 S.C.R. 530.

5. R.S.C. 1970, C.C.-34. [1973] 5 W.W.R. 665 (B.C.S.C.).
6. (1968) 65 W.W.R. 129 (B.C.S.C.).
7. (1970) 72 W.W.R. 315 (B.C.S.C.) Section 4(1) of the Divorce Act, 1967-68, c. 24.
8. *Rushton v. Rushton* [1969] 2 D.L.R. (3d), 25 (B.C.S.C.).
9. [1973] 5 W.W.R. 660 (B.C.S.C.); R.S.B.C. 1960, c. 370.
10. R.S.B.C., 1960, c. 378.
11. [1973] 1 W.W.R. 354 (B.C.S.C.).
12. [1976] 63 D.L.R. (3d), 193 (B.C.C.A.).
13. *R. v. Rourke* [1975] 6 W.W.R. 591 (B.C.C.A.).
14. *Miller v. The Queen* [1977] 2 S.C.R. 680.
15. *Rourke v. The Queen* [1978] 1 S.C.R. 1021.
16. R.S.C. 1985, Appendix III.
17. [1976] 63 D.L.R. (3d), 193 (B.C.C.A.), at 205-06.
18. Farris, C.J.B.C., Maclean, Robertson, and Carrothers, JJ.A.
19. [1976] 63 D.L.R. (3d), 193 (B.C.C.A.), at 246.
20. [1968] S.C.R. 517.
21. 36 Hals., 3rd ed., 465, 468.
22. [1976] 63 D.L.R. (3d), 193 (B.C.C.A.), at 245-46.
23. *Ibid.*, 246.
24. *Ibid.*, 255.
25. *Ibid.*, 260.
26. *Ibid.*, 262.
27. *Ibid.*, 265-66.
28. *Ibid.*, 270-72.
29. *Ibid.*, 273.
30. *Miller et al. v. The Queen* [1977] 2 S.C.R. 680.
31. S.C. 1974-75-76, c. 105, ss. 4-5.
32. *British Columbia Aural Legal History Project* [transcript of tape]. Interviewee, Hon. A.B. Robertson; interviewer, Hon. John L. Farris, March 1980, 100.
33. *R. v. Rourke* [1975] 6 W.W.R. 591 (B.C.C.A.), at 592.
34. *Ibid.*, 592.
35. *Ibid.*, 593.
36. *Ibid.*, 593-94, 599-600.
37. *Rourke v. The Queen* [1978] 1 S.C.R. 1021, at 1040-41.
38. Laskin C.J.C., Judson, Spence, and Dickson, JJ.
39. Pigeon, Martland, Ritchie, Beetz, and de Grandpre, JJ.
40. *Rourke v. The Queen* [1978] 1 S.C.R. 1021, at 1045.
41. *Ibid.*, 1044.

42. Vern Countryman, ed., *The Douglas Opinions* (New York: Berkley, 1978), 382-83.
43. Robert J. Sharpe and Katherine E. Swinton, *The Charter of Rights and Freedoms* [Essentials of Canadian Law Series] (Toronto: Irwin Law, 1998), 177.
44. See *ibid.*, 177, where the above passage by L'Heureux-Dubé, J. in *R. v. O'Connor*, (1995), 103 C.C.C. (3d) 1 at 43, is quoted.
45. (1979), 95 D.L.R. (3d) 231 (B.C.C.A.).
46. 3 B.C.L.R., 348.
47. (1979), 95 D.L.R. (3rd) 231 (B.C.C.A.), at 239.
48. *Ibid.*, 241.
49. (1976), 64 D.L.R. (3d), 574 (B.C.C.A.).
50. 1973 (B.C. (2d. sess.), c. 122.
51. *British Columbia Aural Legal Project* [transcript of tape]. Interviewee, the Hon. J.O. Wilson, interviewer, Bruce Hutchison [second transcript], 114.
52. See The Court of Appeal Act, 1907, S.B.C., 1907, c. 10, and sections 2(1) and 2(2).
53. Carl Karp and Cecil Rosner, *When Justice Fails: The David Milgaard Story* (Toronto: McClelland & Stewart, 1991; rp. 1998), 151-52.

IV

THE SUPREME COURT OF CANADA

MR. JUSTICE MCINTYRE spent exactly a decade (1979-89) on the Supreme Court of Canada, serving first under Chief Justice Bora Laskin from 1979 to 1984, and then under Chief Justice Brian Dickson. He decided when he was appointed to stay on the court for precisely ten years because he felt strongly that institutions such as the Supreme Court benefitted from the infusion of new ideas and that it was appropriate and desirable for older judges to make room for new appointees. Short terms of office help combine continuity with constructive innovation. Also, Mimi was not in good health and longed to return to British Columbia.

Former Justice Minister Marc Lalonde, who recommended McIntyre's appointment to the Trudeau cabinet in 1979, had known McIntyre personally before his elevation to the country's highest court. He held a very favourable opinion of McIntyre both personally and as a judge, an impression reinforced in a personal interview with him in Vancouver just prior to selection. McIntyre had the right personality for the Supreme Court; he was impartial and independent, but he also possessed a sympathetic disposition. While he was attached to his home province, he was not a narrow regionalist; McIntyre had the breadth of vision to realize through his judicial work the needs of all Canadians. He had expertise in law generally, Lalonde thought, not just in one or two areas, and was obviously thoughtful and widely-read. The minister was impressed with McIntyre's extensive judicial experience on both the superior and appeal courts of his province, and convinced by a broad canvass of the provincial bench and bar that yielded positive comments on McIntyre's judicial abilities, experience, and personality. McIntyre was a superlative candidate for the appointment.

Three years after he was summoned to the nation's highest court, a dramatic constitutional change took place. On April 17, 1982, in Ottawa, the Queen signed the document proclaiming the Canadian Charter of Rights and Freedoms, along with an amending process, into law. Thus the venerable British North America Act of 1867, as amended, was patriated, along with an acknowledgment by the U.K. that, in future, the renamed Constitution Act, 1867, could be amended only in Canada. Prime Minister Pierre Trudeau had finally achieved a measure of political autonomy that Canadian prime ministers and premiers had been seeking since 1927. Yet, because of the federal government's resolute determination to push constitutional changes through in the face of stormy opposition by a majority of provinces, the process had not been an easy one. On the legal front, a majority of the Supreme Court had ruled, over strong dissent by Chief Justice Laskin and Justices McIntyre and Estey, that substantial provincial consent was necessary for patriation of the Act. Their decision entailed further negotiations with the provinces, and these negotiations resulted in a breakthrough in November 1981.

Unlike most of his colleagues, McIntyre did not see the substantial changes introduced in April 1982 as a revolutionary break with the past. Some observers thought that the Canadian Constitution was bound to become more "Americanized" by these changes, with a widening rift between the court on the one hand and the legislature and executive branches on the other as judges used their new Constitutional powers to declare federal and provincial laws unconstitutional. This gap could result in a politicization of the Supreme Court and rising tension between the judicial and the more traditionally "political" branches of government. At first McIntyre was hopeful that such a development might not occur. As a strong proponent of gradualism, and conscious as he was of the organic continuity of the common law as it prevailed in Canadian decision-making to that time, he saw the Charter operating essentially as a supplement and occasional corrective, not as a rival to the common law. There was no doubt, however, that the Charter (along with other laws having constitutional force) was now the "supreme law" of Canada and that laws in conflict with it were of no force or effect. With an instrument defined in such a way at their disposal, it would be very tempting for judges to use their new powers expansively. If they succumbed to temptation, they would, however, strain the flexible perimeter dividing the judicial from the legislative branch of government. In its worst expression, this tendency could give rise to the court's becoming a "super-legislature," second-guessing the social policy of Parliament and the provincial legislatures. McIntyre, with his great sensitivity to the essential separation of powers, resisted this temptation. It is doubtful, however, that most of his colleagues did so, or even wanted to do so. His first impression, that a constructive relationship was possible between traditional common law concepts and the Charter, gave way to increasing pessimism as the Court invoked new constitutional norms. It began, in effect, to substitute its own social policy for that of the legislative branches throughout the country.

THE SUPREME COURT AS AN INSTITUTION

According to statute, three places on the nine-member Supreme Court of Canada bench are reserved for judges from Quebec,[1] trained in the civil law system; there is no statutory requirement for representation from other provinces or regions of the country. Because the court is a federal institution, however, and its judgments need to have national legitimacy, it is customary to select judges from the main geographic regions of the country.

In addition to the three judges on the Supreme Court from Quebec, there have traditionally been three from Ontario, because of its dense population and political and economic centrality. The custom has arisen to appoint one judge from the Atlantic provinces, at least one from the three prairie provinces, and one from British Columbia. Except in the case of Quebec, the foregoing distribution is not always strictly adhered to. When Justice McIntyre was appointed, for example, there were only two judges from Ontario (Chief Justice Bora Laskin and Justice W.Z. Estey), with two from the prairie provinces (Justice Ronald Martland from Alberta and Justice Brian Dickson from Manitoba), but none from British Columbia. Justice Roland Ritchie, a Nova Scotian, was the appointee from the Atlantic region. In 1984, when Martland retired, his vacancy went not to Alberta, but to Ontario, with the appointment of Bertha Wilson, the first female judge on the Supreme Court. The record indicates that the appointing authority attempts to make an equitable distribution of judgeships from across the whole country, thus reflecting the federal structure of Canada, but that sometimes there are minor adjustments in the relative numbers allotted on the court to the various regions. In 1949, for example, when the St. Laurent administration abolished overseas appeals to the British Privy Council, judgeships on the Supreme Court increased from seven to nine. While McIntyre had never shared the strong antipathy of some Canadian nationalists to the fact that a transoceanic body served as the country's highest court, he did consider it both appropriate and timely to have the newly enlarged Supreme Court serve as the ultimate legal authority in Canada. It was another necessary step on the road to true nationhood.

There is no law or convention determining that the most senior puisne judge will succeed to a vacant chief justiceship, nor is it required that the office alternate between French-speaking and English-speaking incumbents. When Chief Justice Gerald Fauteux retired in 1973, Ronald Martland of Alberta was the senior puisne judge, but Prime Minister Trudeau selected a relatively junior member of the Court, Bora Laskin, to succeed Fauteux. There was some suggestion at the time that Trudeau, a strong centralist, preferred the more centralist Laskin to the westerner Martland, who had been a Diefenbaker appointee — an evaluation that is plausible but difficult to verify. When Dickson succeeded Laskin in 1984, Justices Beetz and Ritchie were more senior and may have been considered too old for the post. Ritchie, born in 1910, would have had an incumbency of less than one year if he had been chosen because of the rule that Justices must retire at age 75.

Mr. Justice Louis-Philippe Pigeon studied the record of rotation between French- and English-speaking incumbents in the Chief Justiceship and found no historical evidence for it. While there is some history of alternation, the succession of Anglin by Duff in 1933 and of Laskin by Dickson in 1984 can be cited against it. McIntyre discussed the historical evidence with Pigeon and agreed with his conclusion: the appointment of the chief justice is entirely the prerogative of the prime minister and he may choose any qualified person regardless of language. According to McIntyre, Dickson was a popular choice among his colleagues on the Court, the various bar associations and members of the profession, and with the public at large. His appointment as chief justice in 1984 coincided with the inception of the adjudication of Charter claims, an exciting time in Canadian law. The legal and general public seemed to regard him as both the ablest and most sympathetic "helmsman" for inaugurating this new legal era, with all its challenges and problems. Chief Justice Dickson certainly saw his central task as that of developing a coherent and well-integrated system of Charter norms to guide future lawyers and tribunals.

When the federal government appoints Chief Justices or other judges to the Supreme Court, a question is sometimes raised as to whether it should consult with the attorney general of the judge's home province. While the prime minister or minister of justice may advise the attorney general of the appointment beforehand, there is no strict requirement to do so. As matters stand, the constitutional prerogative rests entirely with the federal authorities. Before McIntyre was approached by Justice Minister Marc Lalonde in 1978, for example, there was no indication that the latter had consulted the Social Credit government in British Columbia, nor was there a constitutional reason to do so. There had been only two British Columbians before McIntyre to sit on the Supreme Court of Canada: Sir Lyman Duff, who was appointed in 1906 and was Chief Justice from 1933 to 1944, and Charles H. Locke, who served from 1947 to 1962.

In view of British Columbia's growing size and economic importance in the Canadian federation, its politicians had argued for decades that the province should be considered one of five geographic regions in Canada. In September 1978, in a B.C. White Paper on "Reform of the Supreme Court of Canada," the main implication of this position was clearly stated: "British Columbia recommends that the Supreme Court be composed of eleven members consisting of *at least one person* from each of Canada's five regions."[2] Although this recommendation was not adopted by the federal government, they did acknowledge a provincial grievance. Marc Lalonde's predecessor as justice minister, Otto Lang, stated in August 1978 that under the current informal appointing system, British Columbia could not expect another judge until Justice Ronald Martland of Alberta retired in 1982 (at age 75), or until Justice Dickson of Manitoba retired almost a decade later. "Consequently," Lang admitted, "it can be argued that the present constitution of the court does not adequately reflect the importance of the West or parts thereof."[3]

On McIntyre's appointment his very liberal dissenting position on capital punishment was emphasized by Geoffrey Stevens in *The Globe and Mail*. "[McIntyre] concluded not only that the death penalty was cruel and unusual [under Diefenbaker's Canadian Bill of Rights] but there is no evidence it has a special deterrent effect and it is not necessary for the safety of the community." He also quoted McIntyre's friend from St. Andrew's College days: "As J.A. Davidson says ... 'Bill McIntyre was never a radical, but he was on the radical side of the centre in the postwar days. He had a great feeling for the underdog.'"[4]

Under a constitution where the federal division of powers and entrenched rights are central features and where judges have the power to strike down "inconsistent" provincial or federal laws, it is necessary to have politically neutral judges to decide whether an impugned statute is valid or not. It is a basic requirement of a federation, in fact, that there be a written constitution allocating defined powers to the centre and the regions, and that this document not be unilaterally alterable by any unit within the federation. When differences arise concerning the ambit of a particular government's jurisdiction, a neutral supreme court is needed to act as an impartial arbiter. It must decide which of the contending powers has jurisdiction. If the federal units, including the central government, were able to reallocate powers or adjudicate the scope and validity of their own powers, the federal system would break down. If they were capable of deciding in their own interest whenever disputes arose, the coherence between the division of powers and the vitality of the constitution as a dispute-resolving mechanism would disappear. Ideally, there should be a shared perception among members in a federal system that appointees to their highest court, acting as "constitutional umpires," are completely independent of the disputing parties. Without perceived and actual independence, the court's decisions would lack legitimacy and be difficult to implement completely or at all.

Insofar as appointments to the Supreme Court of Canada may be politically motivated, McIntyre had only tenuous ties to the Liberal administration. An inactive member of the party, he had done little more than support his local MLA in provincial elections. His appointment was not perceived as political and was acclaimed accordingly by the bench, the bar, and the general public. Scholars who have examined the question closely have found little evidence of politically motivated judicial appointments at the highest level. While there have been allegations of patronage or political favouritism regarding appointments at the superior court level, few, if any, recent appointees to the Supreme Court have been politically active, in the sense of running for provincial or federal office, prior to their appointments. Many, indeed most, appointees have had careers in law practice, sometimes combined with teaching, and culminating in service on provincial superior courts or courts of appeal. "Two of the main differences between the Canadian and American Supreme Courts," said Madam Justice Bertha Wilson,

> were that appointments to the Canadian Supreme Court were not made on a political basis, and the Canadian tribunal did not resort to a "framers' intent" approach in interpreting constitutional provisions,[5] which left more scope in Canada for the development and evolution of law in a changing society. There is a constant need to adapt legal principles to new conditions.

Not only liberal members but conservative members of the court emphasized that we had no time for a "frozen rights" approach in Canada. That's no part of our tradition; it's a U.S. tradition. The room for rights to evolve in tune with a changing society: it's fundamentally very basic.

Although it is difficult to prove that the 1981 *Patriation* case is an example of political bias, the context of the case was clearly political. There had been a lengthy and bitter controversy in Parliament between the government and the official opposition over whether Trudeau's constitutional package was potentially subversive of provincial legislative powers, and if so, whether it could be entrenched by Parliament in the U.K. without some measure of provincial consent. Members were split on the issue that provincial consent was a conventional prerequisite for passage. McIntyre did not consider constitutional convention to be less important than law, but he and a minority of his colleagues nonetheless held that there was insufficient evidence to demonstrate the existence of a convention and that facts contradicted the majority's conclusion. Had the necessary threshold of evidence been met, McIntyre would have agreed that it barred the federal request. However, a majority of the Court argued that both the legal norms and convention were part of the Constitution of Canada, and that if the prime minister sought patriation and entrenchment without the consent of an unspecified majority of the provinces, he would be acting unconstitutionally. There was a clear conflict between the majority and the minority on the existence of the convention.

On the other hand, looking at the Supreme Court panel that decided the *Patriation* case, it is difficult to argue otherwise than that their decision reflected a highly charged political climate. Indeed, the strongest anti-government position on the court was taken by the two Diefenbaker appointees, Ronald Martland and Roland Ritchie, who voted both against the legal right to patriate and for conventional constraints preventing the government from taking action without consulting the provinces. The strongest pro-government stance was taken by the three Trudeau appointees, Bora Laskin, William McIntyre, and W.Z. Estey, who voted for the legal right to patriate and considered the supposed constitutional convention not to have been established. These two camps may have reflected an admixture of political propensities and rival visions of federalism, and when such viewpoints converge it is difficult to assess their relative weight in the decision-making process. Between the most polarized positions, Julien Chouinard, a 1979 appointee of Prime Minister Joe Clark, and the Trudeau appointees, Brian Dickson, Jean Beetz, and Antonio Lamer, endorsed the government's legal power to present any amendment it chose to Westminster, but demurred on the convention issue, insisting on provincial consultation because the package derogated from provincial powers. There were judges appointed by both Conservative and Liberal administrations on both sides of the issue, and few of them had been actively involved in politics before ascending to the bench. At the highest level appointments have tended to be non-partisan, and the judges in this, one of the most "political" cases ever to be decided by the Court, did not make their rulings based on politics. It is interesting that McIntyre, who has manifested a growing uneasiness with the adjudication of the Charter by the Court, and Dickson and Lamer (two future chief justices), who would have limited government action by imposing a "conventional" constraint but who went on to become ardent devotees of the Charter, all voted in 1981 against their later biases with respect to its passage into law.

Chief Justice Lamer recalls that through the unusually hot summer of 1981, the entire Court had been working assiduously on the concept of constitutional convention. Lamer, who strongly disagreed with the pro-government stance taken by Laskin, McIntyre, and Estey, is unequivocal in his assessment of the result of the *Patriation* case: "I think we saved the ruddy country."[6] Former Chief Justice Dickson takes a similar view in retrospect. As a result of the Court's requiring "substantial provincial consent" prior to entrenchment of the Charter, Dickson maintains, "[Trudeau] got nine out of ten provinces. That was substantial support, whereas two out of ten would be anything but that. If the prime minister had gone to England with just two provinces, and eight either strongly against it or cool to it, the whole situation would have been quite different."[7] There are indications that Prime Minister Margaret Thatcher was very unhappy about the Canadian government's request that the British Parliament enact the Trudeau package against the determined opposition of eight provinces. While Trudeau put on a bold face and maintained to the Canadian public that Britain would comply in due course, Thatcher sent an experienced Conservative parliamentarian, Sir Francis Pym, to warn Trudeau late in 1980 that his package would not pass unless his "Charter of Rights" proposal were dropped.[8] It is interesting to speculate what would have happened had Trudeau proceeded to seek entrenchment without "substantial provincial consent," and the British prime minister had refused to act on his behalf. A refusal, in the opinion of some, might have triggered a constitutional crisis in Canada and precipitated the abolition of the monarchy.

In one of the first thorough examinations of constitutional convention, the Supreme Court came to a rather startling conclusion. On one level it did not alter the classic Diceyan formulation — conventions were still political in character and not enforceable by courts — but in constitutional cases it seemed that this was a distinction without being a difference. By subsuming both law and convention under the rubric of the Canadian Constitution, the Court indirectly gave convention the force of law by positing that political action that violated convention, as defined by a majority of the court, would be "unconstitutional." Because no government wants to be perceived as acting unconstitutionally, the formulation of the convention rule by the Court majority on that subject essentially precluded the government from proceeding without further negotiations with the provinces.

The two future chief justices who concurred in the result on convention consider that the effect of Mr. Trudeau's going to Westminster with only two provinces supporting his initiative would have been catastrophic. Inferentially, it was an act of statesmanship for the Court to give a partial victory to both sides, thereby compelling the disputants to return to the negotiating table in order to secure substantial provincial consent before the package was presented to the Queen. The alternative was increasing dissension in Canada and, with only two provinces supporting the federal government, possible blockage of the Canada Bill by foes of the measure in the British Parliament, and particularly in the House of Lords. Canadians who opposed unilateral action had already travelled to London to register their strong opposition to a unilateral process, and their allies in the British Parliament could justify obstruction on the basis that the Bill did not have the consent of Canada as a "structured federal whole," and was therefore not entitled to passage.

There was a large measure of political calculation in what a majority of the Court had done. The bifurcation of the constitutional question into separate issues of "law" and "convention" was contrived to produce a political result — to force reluctant parties to negotiate further. Today Justice McIntyre is still unsure of whether the court's decision in this case was productive of Canadian unity. Is the political situation in Canada at this time better — is the country more united

— than it would have been if the majority had squarely confronted the fact that conventions were political and let the chips fall where they may? This alternative, of course, was the preference of the three dissenters (including McIntyre) on convention. In attempting to answer this question one must be aware both of the *Patriation* decision and the political negotiations that followed it.

With the Court requiring support by a substantial majority of the provinces for the entrenchment of the Charter, a virtual veto over *Patriation* had been ceded to this group. In view of the new conventional requirement, it was now necessary for Trudeau to attract more provincial allies before entrenchment. In ensuing negotiations through November 1981, Trudeau managed to secure the consent of the nine anglophone provinces, but not Quebec, by offering certain jurisdictional concessions. Quebec was isolated in this process, and separatist politicians would in future interpret her isolation as a "betrayal," with dire consequences for Canadian unity. In a dramatic rejection of the "compact theory" of Confederation, both the Quebec Court of Appeal[9] and the Supreme Court of Canada[10] affirmed in a later constitutional case that, given the support of a substantial provincial majority, Quebec's consent to the *Patriation* package was not necessary. Accordingly, when Justice McIntyre asks whether the federation is better off today than in 1982, the question cannot be divorced from the isolation of Quebec indirectly caused by the court majority on convention. Securing the constitutional package by weighing English Canada against Quebec's protest has been a continuing irritant to the government and people of that province. It is significant that in retrospect former Chief Justice Dickson and ex-Premier Lougheed of Alberta have expressed doubt about the wisdom of achieving patriation over Quebec's opposition in 1982. They now regard that policy as a mistake having incalculable consequences for the future of the federation.

In an effort to overcome the divisive political consequences of Quebec's rejection of the 1982 amendments, the Mulroney administration put forward the 1987 Meech Lake and 1992 Charlottetown Accords which featured the "distinct society" and other provisions, but the rejection, in turn, of both of these proposals has made the situation worse. The refrain of Quebec nationalists is that their "minimal" demands have been twice rejected by English Canada since 1982 (although the electorate of Quebec joined with a majority of provinces in voting against the Charlottetown Accord in October 1992). The sequence of events since the *Patriation* decision has enabled nationalist leaders to argue that Canadian federalism is a failure. The 1995 referendum registered a much closer vote in favour of Quebec sovereignty than in 1980, with federal forces prevailing by a mere one percent. Perhaps the whole political dynamic is moving in the direction of eventual separation. Separatism would have continued to exist no matter what the Supreme Court decided in September 1981, but McIntyre is sure that the decision on convention led to results unforeseen by its authors. Politically, it has probably made the break-up of Canada more likely.

Prime Minister Trudeau has praised publicly the judgment formulated by Laskin, McIntyre, and Estey in the *Patriation* case, and criticized in the strongest terms the decision of the Court majority (led by Dickson). This criticism was made in his dedicatory address at the inauguration of the new Laskin law library in Toronto, with Chief Justice Dickson present in the audience. Trudeau began by praising Chief Justice Laskin's outstanding human qualities, "his great intelligence, combined with a concern for human beings and an apparent desire to live in a society which permitted self-fulfilment to all."[11] These qualities, he continued, "contributed mightily to the wisdom of the dissent he formulated along with Justices Estey and McIntyre in the *Patriation Reference*."[12] "That dissent," he argued, "was not only the better law, but the better common sense, and consequently it was also wiser politically. Had it prevailed over the majority view, I believe that Canada's future would have been more assured."[13] On the other hand, "the majority judgment on the existence of convention fatally tilted the doctrine of Canadian sovereignty away from the people and towards the several governments, that is to say, towards one form or other of the compact theory of confederation."[14] Finally, he added, "because conventions are enforceable through the political process, the courts should not even have engaged in declaring their existence. In choosing to answer the question there is little doubt the Supreme Court allowed itself — in P.W. Hogg's words — 'to be manipulated into a purely political role,' going beyond the lawmaking functions that modern jurisprudence agrees the Court must necessarily exercise."[15] Rarely has a head of government criticized his chief justice's decision in such corrosive terms.

Dickson was mortified by Trudeau's comments, particularly because he considered that if the prime minister had gone to England with only two out of ten provinces supporting him, his request would have lacked the "substantial support" that the Court held was constitutionally required. In Dickson's estimation the decision on convention had facilitated the breakthrough without which the very enactment of the Canada Bill at Westminster would have been problematic. If one agrees with this position, Trudeau's remarks sound churlish. One of the prime minister's strongest objections to the Court's decision was that the judges had ruled that a "substantial majority" of provinces was needed but had refused to specify the number — was it six, or seven, or eight? Dickson's answer to this criticism is straightforward. The Court could determine the existence of a convention in this case, he replied, but only the political actors could define its content. The sequel to the 1981 decision makes this clear. Nine provinces eventually agreed to *Patriation*, and when Quebec sought a ruling that this number was insufficient without Quebec's concurrence, the courts disagreed. In this case any nine provinces would probably have satisfied the conventional requirement. This division is not necessarily definitive in all cases where a "substantial majority" threshold is required. It is possible that in other cases the concurrence of seven or eight provinces would suffice.

Trudeau would obviously have preferred the Court to declare that the federal government possessed the legal power to present any amendment to Westminster and leave it at that. To superadd a requirement that a "substantial majority of provinces" was necessary was, in his view, gratuitous and insupportable. This, too, was the position of Laskin, McIntyre, and Estey. Trudeau considered the majority's decision on convention to be political, and it distressed him that a political constraint should become a constitutional barrier to patriation when the court had already declared that there was no legal impediment to the process.

In the United States, the Supreme Court was established as a coequal branch of government in the Constitution of 1789. It can confront the president and the legislative branch on equal terms in constitutional controversies and in the present century, especially, has done so on more than one occasion. In the British and Canadian systems, courts have not traditionally enjoyed a comparable constitutional status, although with entrenchment in 1982 the Canadian Supreme Court is evolving in that direction. There have not been many confrontations in Canada between heads of government and chief justices. The contretemps between Trudeau and Dickson stands out as a result. In the United States, there have been numerous historic clashes: between President Grant and Chief Justice Chase on "legal tender,"[16] between President Roosevelt and Chief Justice Hughes on the New Deal statutes,[17] between President Truman and Chief Justice Vinson on the President's seizure of the steel mills when a strike was pending during the Korean War,[18] and between President Nixon and the Burger Court on executive privilege.[19] With the Supreme Court of Canada's accession to much enhanced powers after 1982, a question arises as to whether the frequent disputes between executive and court in the republic to the south will now occur here. Signs of potential conflict may be seen in the Court's growing tendency to invoke Charter provisions to invalidate laws passed by either the federal government or the provinces. In Canada the courts have traditionally had a more deferential attitude to governments than their U.S. counterparts, but with the adoption of the Charter most of the factors conducive to confrontation in the U.S. are now present here. It may only be a matter of time until jurisdictional disputes become a more prominent feature on the political landscape. Another difference between the Canadian system and the American, perhaps, can be seen in the civility shown by members of the Canadian Court to each other, despite sometimes substantial policy disagreements. "In the States, they pan each other's judgments right in the judgments," Justice Wilson said. "That's considered a 'no-no' here. If you have something to say, you say it in legal terms — that's the civilized way of going about it."

Madam Justice Wilson agreed with Chief Justice Mifflin of Newfoundland that in the formative year after the Charter was entrenched, when the Supreme Court was most intent on developing Charter norms, there was little scrutiny of private law matters such as contracts, torts, and property, where no Charter provisions applied.[20] Indeed, in the first few years of Charter jurisprudence the Supreme Court had to devote so much of its time and resources to defining and applying Charter norms that private law actually suffered. Mifflin is sure that in some areas, because of the Supreme Court's concentration on public law, provincial courts of appeal were becoming *de facto* the ultimate authority over private law. McIntyre does not fully agree. He points out that, in an average year in Canada, up to one million legal decisions might be rendered. Of this number it is possible to subject only a minuscule fraction of cases to judicial review. The greatest need is not to crowd the docket, but instead to carefully select those cases that are of public importance for adjudication; in the years immediately following enactment many of these were bound to be Charter cases.

Madam Justice Wilson reflected that this was a general problem for the Supreme Court:

> If the Court didn't grant leave to appeal it bestowed a finality on the lower court decisions. What should be considered in granting leave to appeal was a highly controversial issue on the Supreme Court. At times the Court was uncomfortable that three judges made the decision. Frequently one or two would say, "Well, look, there's a split here and perhaps we should take the matter for final decision to the full court. We should get input from others." I never thought that we achieved a satisfactory *modus operandi* for leave-granting right until the time I retired. In my time there were too many leaves granted on family matters. The selection depended on interests of members of the court rather than on specific issues of property or contract which may have great importance but interest judges less. It's an unsatisfactory process. I don't have any magical answers. There is, generally, insufficient attention given to the tremendous importance of granting or withholding leave to appeal.

"When I was appointed to the Court," Wilson continued, "Bill McIntyre was great. He was very supportive and we became very good friends. The fact that we thought differently about the Charter and other issues didn't seem to affect us. Bill and Gerry La Forest were my two closest friends on the court, but they were most conservative jurists. Jean Beetz, Bill, and Gerry were viewed generally as three of the most conservative judges." Madam Justice Wilson considered that the more recent split decisions of the Court, along with the multiplicity of judgments being written by individual judges, made the problem of legal interpretation very difficult. "How on earth can the courts below or the lawyers know what the law is?" she reflected. "We are not confronted with an occasional multiple judgment, but it is happening constantly. What use would a 5-4 split on Quebec's secession be?"

JUDICIAL LEADERSHIP

One of Justice McIntyre's complaints about the present Court is that the length and prolixity of judgments make it occasionally very difficult to determine what the law is. Both Dickson and Lamer think that a measure of judicial leadership by the Chief Justice is therefore appropriate so as to lend decisions greater weight and to make the process of determining what the law actually is less troublesome for counsel and lower courts. Dickson has observed that 5-to-4 decisions tend to produce weak law. The more cases for which there is a unanimous result, the stronger the ensuing jurisprudence will be. He adds, "Quite often I, and other members of the Court, would make modifications — maybe not major ones — in a draft judgment in order to get somebody else's concurrence, and to get as few dissents as possible. The authority of the judgment is not very formidable where the Court divides three or four ways."

While Chief Justice Lamer says that he never "campaigned" to achieve a certain result, it was not unhealthy to attempt to exert influence over one's colleagues through persuasion and argument.

If I feel that a case can be decided on one issue rather than two issues, and one of the issues is irking one or two judges, I prefer to have a 9 to 0 decision than a 7 to 2 decision, or a 9 to 0 with concurring reasons. I'll horse-trade. I'll leave the other one to another day. If I see we're going to get a dog's breakfast, however, then I'll call a meeting. Before holding the meeting, I'll have a very, very thorough analysis, sort of a working paper, prepared by my clerk and circulated a week in advance of the meeting to see if we can't pull together with the view of coming out with two sets of reasons instead of four sets of reasons. In most cases, this was successful. The cases where it wasn't successful coincided with the arrival of new judges; new judges tend to dig in their heels. They want to get their names in the books and I understand that. Dickson and I used to co-sign judgments; I wrote "Bill 101." Instead of concurring, it's better to co-sign; it gives the opinion more strength.

The achievement of consensus, collegiality, and unanimity if possible, has been a common aim of chief justices on both the Canadian and American Supreme Courts.[21] Just after the inception of the U.S. Supreme Court, Chief Justice John Marshall was able, through a combination of historical circumstance and sheer moral and intellectual tenacity, to lay down operational principles that had a powerful and lasting influence both on constitutional law and procedure. In Canada, before 1949, when appeals to the Judicial Committee were abolished, the Supreme Court always functioned in the shadow of the former body, making the two North American courts very different in terms of their milieu and constitutional role. There were strong chief justices in Canada: Anglin, Duff, and Rinfret before 1949, and Laskin, Dickson, and Lamer afterward, but in the parliamentary system, at least until the advent of the Charter, they tended to be more deferential to the legislature than their American counterparts. It was not until recently that Canadians began referring to the Supreme Court as the third branch of government.[22] With the establishment of the Supreme Court as a final Court of Appeal for Canada in 1949, and the entrenchment of the Charter in 1982, the conditions for its accession to a much greater role in the public life of Canada, for better or worse, were created.

When McIntyre arrived on the Court in 1979 he resolved, whenever possible, to help form a consensus. He knew that the authority and precision of the law is enhanced when unanimity or a strong consensus is secured. Never one to seek the limelight (at least not in the beginning), he worked in a truly collegial spirit to develop a well-defined and intelligible corpus of public and private law. In line with his attachment to the common law and his view of its complementarity to the Charter, which he thought should be invoked more sparingly than most of his colleagues did, he began increasingly to differ from his colleagues on the ambit of Charter provisions. Dickson, Lamer, and Wilson saw these instruments in more radical terms. They were seeking to use the Charter to make a sweeping overhaul of Canadian law, while McIntyre's vision of its purpose and the judges' functions was far more modest. At times he considered the Court to be encroaching on legislative functions and prerogatives. Consequently, as time passed, and against his initial inclination to act as part of a team, McIntyre felt more compelled to dissent, particularly on criminal law issues in Charter cases.

McIntyre discerns a trend in recent years toward overtly political decision making by the Supreme Court. This trend has been accentuated by the duty imposed on judges since 1982 to interpret the broad, expandable terms of the Charter, a reach which at its widest can involve the Court in making legislative policy. Even before 1982, however, the temptation had been present. The Court could indulge occasionally in policy making at the invitation of the government, particularly when reference questions were put to it by the Governor-in-Council pursuant to the reference procedure. According to that procedure, the Court must answer *any* question of fact or law submitted to it by Cabinet.[23] In 1935 the Court was asked by the Liberals for a reference opinion on whether their predecessors' "New Deal" social program was constitutionally valid.[24] Later they were consulted about whether Canadian citizens of Japanese origin could be deported to Japan after the Second World War,[25] and later still, on the validity of Trudeau's Wage and Price Control legislation of 1975 (a topic hotly-contested in the general election the year before).[26] Most recently the Supreme Court asked about the conditions under which Quebec could separate from the Canadian federation.[27] In effect, judges are really being asked to address questions of a largely political nature. In such instances they are constrained to answer circumspectly so as not to arouse suspicions of improper motivation. Although the duty to answer reference questions is statute-based and appears to be unavoidable, McIntyre would regard the reference on Quebec separation to be one bearing so centrally on federal policy that in answering it the Court is assuming the mantle of the executive. When such highly charged political questions are sent to the Court by the government, the issue of the politicization of the Court naturally arises because parties are not acting at the appropriate arm's length required by the doctrine of the separation of powers.

When the provinces challenged the constitutional propriety of the federal Cabinet's presenting questions concerning the validity of *provincial* laws to the Court by using references in 1912, Lord Chancellor Loreburn said, "No one who has experience of judicial duties can doubt that, if an Act of this kind were abused, manifold evils might follow, including undeserved suspicion of the course of justice and much embarrassment and anxiety to the judges themselves."[28] The reference questions Loreburn is speaking of do not arise, initially at any rate, in an adversarial context, as do private lawsuits, but are questions put by the Crown to the Court. Later the provinces may intervene, especially when questions of federal constitutional law are involved, at which time the process becomes more adversarial in form. However, the judgment given by the Court is still advisory, and not binding, although it is invariably followed, and now perhaps has obligatory force by virtue of convention. Lord Loreburn goes on to say that since members of the Judicial Committee were all privy councillors and bound to advise the British Crown in that capacity when required, it did not seem inconvenient or improper for the Court to assume a similar role in Canada,[29] nor should such a role be "stigmatized as subversive of the judicial function." His Lordship may have overlooked the fact that in the more flexible British Constitution, powers tend to overlap more than they do in Canada. For example, Canada does not have Law Lords who sit in Parliament and are called upon to give advice to the sovereign or government ministers. When Law Lords advise the Crown on reference-like matters they may be acting in an executive capacity, in which case Loreburn's own example could be cited against him. In any event, his example related to the Constitution of a unitary state and should not be applied to a federation having a constitutional division of powers. The crux of the province's 1912 objection to the reference procedure related more to the latter context.

Other federations have been sensitive about the relationship between executive and judiciary and do not possess an exact parallel to the Canadian reference device. When George Washington formally requested the U.S. Supreme Court's views on a treaty in 1793, he was told by the Court that there were "considerations which afford strong arguments against the propriety of our extra-judicially deciding such questions."[30] While this pronouncement can be cited against the practice of rendering advisory opinions, in this century "all Chief Justices served as presidential consultants."[31] Taft actually helped to formulate the 1924 Republican Party platform while he was Chief Justice.[32] In the 1911 case of *Muskrat v. U.S.*,[33] the Court emphasized that it would not explore the validity of an Act of Congress in a vacuum, but would consider executive requests where a case or controversy already existed.

In Australia, Commonwealth legislation providing for references to the High Court was held to be *ultra vires* in the Judiciary and Navigation Acts.[34] Here the High Court declared: "We can find nothing in Chapter 111 of the Constitution to lend colour to the view that Parliament can confer power or jurisdiction upon the High Court to determine abstract questions of law without the right or duty of any body or person being involved."[35] Very liberal treatment of the declaratory judgment procedure in public law litigation has, however, permitted the High Court to deal with issues similar to those raised in Canadian reference cases.[36]

Formally or informally, in the United States and Australia, judges do, from time to time, at the request of the executive, explore abstract questions where there are no adversary parties. In Canada, however, a formalized statutory procedure for presenting such questions to the Court has existed from the time of its establishment in 1875. The unrestrained use of such a power, as in the Quebec reference example, makes McIntyre apprehensive in that when it answers questions the Court may be acting in a political rather than a judicial manner. He has serious concerns as to whether such questions should be referred to the Court at all.

In an article on the contemporary Supreme Court in 1988, *Maclean's* magazine stated that, "defining and enforcing Canada's Charter of Rights makes the judges perhaps the most powerful people in the nation."[37] As the laws enacted by Parliament must conform to the Charter and other parts of the Constitution of Canada, as interpreted by the Court, this observation has some force. Since the proclamation of the Charter on April 17, 1982, the judges of Canada's highest court have acquired significant new powers. Now, more than ever, the characters and backgrounds of the judges themselves have assumed great importance. Who are the persons who discharge this vital interpretive function?

McINTYRE'S CONTEMPORARIES ON THE COURT

When McIntyre was appointed to the Court on January 1, 1979, Bora Laskin had been Chief Justice for six years. It was he who told McIntyre that in view of the volume of work, there was simply not enough time to study and reflect on the law. Born at Fort William, Ontario, in 1912, Laskin obtained his B.A., M.A., and LL.B. at the University of Toronto before proceeding to Harvard for his Master of Laws degree. He read law with W.C. Davidson, QC, and was called to the Ontario bar in 1937. He taught law at the University of Toronto and Osgoode Hall in the 1940s, and from 1949 to 1965, when he was appointed to the Ontario Court of Appeal, he taught law at the University of Toronto. His special interests were constitutional and labour law, and his proficiency in the latter resulted in his appointment as arbitrator in many labour disputes. He was an advocate of the final disposition of appeals in Canada, an authority defined in 1949 by the St. Laurent government when overseas appeals were abolished and the number of judges on the Supreme Court was increased from seven to nine. He was a strong centralist in disputes between the provinces and the federal government on the constitutional division of powers, and was with the Court majority in finding that the Supreme Court could overrule not only its own past decisions but also those of the Judicial Committee.[38] As the ultimate Court of Appeal for Canada, this enlarged and reconstituted domestic forum achieved the same level of authority as the Judicial Committee. When Laskin died of leukemia in 1984, he was succeeded as chief justice by Brian Dickson.

A lover of horses and country life, Dickson lived in retirement at "Marchmont," his estate in Dunrobin, Ontario. Born in Yorkton, Saskatchewan, he graduated with the gold medal and his LL.B. from the Manitoba Law School in 1938. He lost most of his right leg while serving in the artillery at the Battle of the Falaise Gap of August 24, 1944. In the 1980s, no fewer than six of the nine Supreme Court judges, Dickson, McIntyre, Lamer, Ritchie, Le Dain, and Chouinard, had served as artillery officers in the Canadian army. Could it be that an analytical, problem-solving capacity is essential to both gunnery and law, and that the same aptitudes that led these men to study law also fitted them, when they joined the army, for service as artillerymen? An expert in company law with his practice in Manitoba, Dickson also served as chancellor of the Anglican diocese of Rupertsland, and became chief justice in 1984. It was his task to lead the court in its formative years of Charter interpretation. Although his legal and church associations in Manitoba were conservative, in this work he was to become known as one of the most liberal members of the Court.

The chief justice who succeeded Dickson in 1990, the Right Honourable Antonio Lamer, was born in Montreal in July 1933 and received his law degree from the University of Montreal in 1956. The descendant of a French mariner who served the governor of New France from 1688 to 1700, Lamer grew up in the tough east end of Montreal where, he recalls, everyone on his block except himself and another boy, who became a dentist, went to the penitentiary.[39] His clients' experience of the forceful methods of the Montreal police may have prompted him to invoke the Charter as often as he did, so as to refashion constitutional remedies for the accused in criminal appeals. In addition to his legal practice with the Montreal firm of Cutler, Lamer, Bellemare and Associates, he lectured in law for many years at the University of Montreal. He was a founder of the Defence Attorneys' Association of Quebec and national chairman of the criminal justice section of the Canadian Bar Association. He also served as vice-chairman and chairman of the National Law Reform Commission. He served as a Justice of the Superior Court of Quebec from 1969 to 1978 and as a Justice of the Quebec Court of Appeal from 1978 to 1980, and was appointed to the Supreme Court in 1980. Politically, he was a low-profile Liberal, having served as past president (1960) of the Montreal district Young Liberals. Although they often disagreed on Charter cases, Lamer and McIntyre were close friends. They sometimes walked together to the Supreme Court building from their respective Ottawa homes.

The two Diefenbaker appointees, Ronald Martland and Roland A. Ritchie, brother of the distinguished diplomat and diarist Charles Ritchie, came from the provinces of Alberta and Nova Scotia respectively. Both were Rhodes Scholars, Martland at Hertford College, and Ritchie at Pembroke. Martland practised law in Edmonton from 1932 to 1958, when he was appointed to the Supreme Court, while Ritchie practised in Halifax from 1934 to 1959, the year of his appointment. Both were Anglicans and members of the prestigious Rideau Club in Ottawa. In contrast to most of their Supreme Court colleagues, neither had prior judicial experience when they were appointed. McIntyre had especially cordial relations, on the Court and socially, with Martland, whom he often visited in Ottawa after they had both retired.

An especially close friend of McIntyre's on the Court, Jean Beetz, was born in Montreal in 1927. He graduated from the University of Montreal in 1950 before taking his B.A. and M.A. at Pembroke College, Oxford. From 1953, he taught at the University of Montreal, serving as dean of the Civil Law Faculty from 1968 to 1970, while acting concurrently as special constitutional advisor to his former teaching associate, Prime Minister Pierre Trudeau. He served as assistant secretary of the Cabinet and assistant clerk of the Privy Council during the early days of the Trudeau administration, and was appointed to the Court in 1974. Beetz, unlike Laskin, tended to support the provinces in disputes with Ottawa on the division of powers, as in his well-crafted dissent in the Anti-Inflation reference.[40] Along with Beetz and La Forest, McIntyre was sometimes classed as a legal conservative, but this assessment depends upon one's definition of conservatism. While he was an admirer of the common law, public order, and an evolutionary rather than a revolutionary approach to legal questions, on closer examination McIntyre was the author of a significant number of liberal judgments, and it is difficult to encapsulate his legal philosophy using such labels. Beetz and McIntyre often discussed legal problems and enjoyed each other's company. Beetz suffered from a painful illness in his later years and retired in 1988, one year before McIntyre.

McIntyre's University of Saskatchewan law school colleague Willard Zebedee Estey served as chief justice of Ontario for about a year prior to his appointment to the Supreme Court of Canada in 1977. He had sat on the Ontario Court of Appeal from 1973 to 1975, and was chief justice of the High Court from 1975 to 1976. Like Beetz, he retired in 1988, one year before McIntyre. Estey's middle name, Zebedee, reflects the Baptist pedigree of his family, who came to

Saskatchewan from New Brunswick early in the century. (The Galilean fisherman of that name was the father of Jesus's disciples, James and John.) Estey was, however, universally known as "Bud" in legal circles. His father, J.W. Estey, became a member of an earlier Supreme Court bench after having served in Liberal cabinets in Saskatchewan in the 1930s and 1940s as attorney general and minister of education. Both Esteys studied at Harvard; the father earned his undergraduate law degree there and the son his LL.M., after serving in the army and the RCAF during World War II.

A much cited concurring judgment by the older Estey in the *Saumur* case upheld the right to proselytize in the case of a Jehovah's Witness who was being prosecuted by the Quebec government in Premier Duplessis' time for distributing religious tracts without a permit from the chief of police: "The right of the free exercise and enjoyment of religious profession and worship, is a personal, sacred right for which, history records, men have striven and fought. Whenever attained, they have resisted restrictions and limitations thereon in every possible manner."[41] The vigorous strain of libertarianism reflected in his judgment certainly stems in part from his family's nonconformist heritage.

The younger Estey was on the Law Faculty at the University of Saskatchewan in 1946-47, after his return from war service. Because he was starting his law practice in Toronto, he lectured concurrently, from 1947 to 1951, at Osgoode Hall. He was an accomplished woodworker and, like his father, an ardent sports fan. Both were enthusiasts for the Red Sox from their Harvard days. The younger Estey was a much sought-after member of government commissions of inquiry, both during his period on the bench and afterward. In the mid-1970s he conducted a public inquiry in Montreal into financial dealings involving Air Canada, and later into the mysterious crash at Gander, Newfoundland of a U.S. military aircraft carrying servicemen back to the United States on leave. The exact cause of this crash was never determined.

Appointed a few months after McIntyre in 1979 by Prime Minister Joe Clark, the Honourable Julien Chouinard, a graduate of Laval and Oxford, was called to the Quebec bar in 1953. He served on the Court for eight years until his premature death on February 6, 1987. His background was in the provincial public service rather than the judiciary. He was general secretary of the Quebec cabinet and provincial deputy minister of justice, taught corporation law at Laval, and was commanding officer of the Sixth Field Regiment, RCA, with the rank of lieutenant-colonel. In 1970 he advised the Bourassa government on the constitutional implications of the Victoria Charter, a precursor to the Charter of Rights and Freedoms which failed when the Quebec premier withdrew his province's provisional support for the measure. In the early 1980s Chouinard, along with Ritchie and Martland, was one of three Conservative appointees sitting on the Court. The other members had Liberal connections, although none of these Supreme Court judges had a highly partisan political background.

Some see it as an irony that the two members of the Court with the most polarized views on the Charter — McIntyre and Madam Justice Wilson — were also perhaps the closest friends. While McIntyre thought the Charter should be used less often, Wilson used it frequently, especially in the criminal law to mitigate or eliminate penal sanctions. Wilson, who was appointed in 1982 and was the first woman to serve on the Court, is generous in her tribute to Bill McIntyre for making her feel at ease within that male-dominated institution. Wilson was the only judge to be born outside of Canada, in Kircaldy, Scotland (the birthplace of the economist Adam Smith) in 1923. After receiving her M.A. from the University of Aberdeen in 1944, she accompanied her husband to Canada and graduated in law from Dalhousie in 1957. She was called to the Nova Scotia bar the same year, then the Ontario bar in 1959, and practised with the Toronto firm of Osler, Hoskin and Harcourt until 1975, when she was appointed to the Ontario Court of Appeal. During her incumbency on the Supreme Court she was a strong advocate for the appointment of more women judges, contending that many of her brethren, however professionally capable, were insensitive to or biased against women's perspectives in legal disputes. She retired on January 4, 1991. Recently, she has expressed satisfaction at the increased number of female appointments to the bench. She was a member of the Royal Commission on Aboriginal Rights, which reported in 1996.

The next woman to be appointed to the Supreme Court was the Honourable Claire L'Heureux-Dubé, who was elevated from the Quebec Court of Appeal in April 1987. While working as a secretary in a law firm, she found she was smarter than her boss, which motivated her to enroll in law school at Laval University. Educated by the Ursulines at Rimouski and in law at Laval, she was called to the bar in Quebec in 1952. She served on the Court of Appeal from 1979 to 1987. A devoted skier and swimmer, she heads for the nearby Laurentians when conditions permit. She was a senior member of L'Heureux, Philippon, Garneau, Tourigny and Associates from 1969 until 1973, when she was appointed to the Superior Court of Quebec. She lectured in family law in the Cours de Formation Professionelle du Barreau de Québec. Her professional interests were to a large extent centred in the family law area, as reflected in her presidency of the family law committee and family court committee of the Quebec Civil Code Revision Office from 1972 to 1976, her vice-presidency of the Vanier Institute of the Family from 1972 to 1973, and the fact that she was awarded the medal of the International Year of the Family in 1994. She was also a member of the board of directors of the International Society on Family Law, and president of the International Commission of Jurists (Canadian section) from 1981 to 1983. She became an associate member of the International Academy of Comparative Law in 1992, and received the Quebec Bar Medal in 1987. In 1998 she received the prestigious Margaret Brent Woman of Achievement Award at the annual convention of the American Bar Association in Toronto.

Renowned for her probing interrogation of counsel from the Supreme Court bench, she has been an able envoy of the tribunal to the country at large. A hard worker, she often toils on cases until 2:00 a.m. She dissents often, which she regards as healthy — she says she doesn't see things the same as her male colleagues. While judges should avoid giving their own opinions in their judgments, they are shaped by their own experience. There is, moreover, an inescapable element of public policy in the law: judges have to consider what is good for the country in the long run.

Mr. Justice Gerald Le Dain, a distinguished legal educator proficient in both the civil and common law, served on the Court for the relatively short span of just over four years, from May 1984 to November 1988. Born in Montreal in 1924, he served in the army in World War II, and graduated in law from McGill in 1949. He proceeded to graduate studies at l'Université de Lyon, where he received the Docteur de l'Université degree. After a stint in the McGill law faculty in 1953-59, he worked as a corporation lawyer and as a partner in the Montreal firm of Riel, Le Dain, Bissonette, Vermette and Ryan before returning to academia as Dean of Osgoode Hall Law School from 1967 to 1972. He had been called to the bar of Ontario in 1968, and also served as special counsel on the Constitution to Prime Minister Trudeau. He also chaired the inquiry into the non-medical use of drugs from 1969 to 1973, and was appointed to the federal Court of Appeal in 1975. Like L'Heureux-Dubé, McIntyre, and most of his colleagues, Le Dain found the Supreme Court's workload hugely demanding, and sometimes the onus of making Charter decisions in areas where there were few precedents bore heavily upon him. In his youth he aspired to be a major league baseball shortstop, and later enjoyed tennis. He also shared McIntyre's predilection for military memoirs.

Another outstanding legal educator is the Honourable Gerard V. La Forest, appointed to the court in 1985. A fluently bilingual New Brunswick Acadian, he graduated in law from the University of New Brunswick in 1949, and attended St. John's College, Oxford (Lester Pearson's College), as a Rhodes Scholar from 1949 to 1951. After practising law in Grand Falls and serving as advisory counsel to the Department of Justice, he taught law at the University of New Brunswick from 1956 to 1963 before proceeding to Yale, where he received a doctorate in law in 1968. From 1968 to 1970 he was dean of law at the University of Alberta, serving concurrently as counsel on the Constitution to Trudeau. He became assistant deputy attorney general of Canada (research and planning) in 1970, and moved to the Law Reform Commission of Canada in 1974. He was a prolific author of legal works, including treatises on constitutional reservation and disallowance, extradition, natural resources, the allocation of the taxing power, water law in Canada, and the territory of Quebec. When he was elevated from the New Brunswick Court of Appeal to the Supreme Court in 1985, Chief Justice Stratton of the former tribunal expressed sadness that he would no longer have La Forest's guidance, especially on constitutional matters. He retired from the Supreme Court in 1997.

If one examines the career backgrounds of McIntyre's associates during his decade on the Supreme Court, certain factors stand out. For one thing, a large number of his colleagues had academic backgrounds or mixed backgrounds in teaching and practice. Le Dain, La Forest, and Beetz, for example, served as Deans of Law at Osgoode Hall, Alberta, and Montreal, respectively, and Laskin was for decades a distinguished professor of law and a constitutional authority at Osgoode Hall and the University of Toronto. Ritchie, Estey, Lamer, and Chouinard, had lectured in law on a part-time basis while engaged in practice or public service. A former president of the Canadian Bar Association who appeared frequently on appeals in the Supreme Court, and thought there were too many academics on the Court, once lamented that Madam Justice Wilson could also be described as an "academic," because she practised essentially as a solicitor at Osler, Hoskin, and Harcourt. Martland, Ritchie, La Forest, Chouinard, and Beetz had all pursued legal studies at Oxford as Rhodes Scholars, but only La Forest and Beetz taught law professionally. To varying degrees, and with some specialization, Dickson, Lamer, McIntyre, Ritchie, Martland, Estey, Chouinard, Wilson, and L'Heureux-Dubé were practitioners, as opposed to academics. McIntyre and Lamer had the most extensive criminal law backgrounds if one considers both their trial and appellate experience. Dickson, Ritchie, Martland, and Estey were more at home in corporate boardrooms, practising commercial and corporate law, and Chouinard had a more substantial background in government service.

There are strong arguments in favour of appointing academics to appeal courts because they are forums engaging in research and reflection on the law. The trend seems to have begun in the early 1970s, with Trudeau's appointment of Laskin and Beetz. The later appointments of La Forest, McLachlin, and Iacobucci were Mulroney's. Another avenue of appointment to the Supreme Court in Trudeau's time was the office of constitutional counsel to the prime minister, which Beetz, La Forest, and Le Dain each held. What is increasingly needed now is a court whose members have backgrounds both in practice and in teaching.

Some commentators think that the complement of law teachers on the Court was too great in the 1980s, that there were too many "philosopher kings." Although McIntyre was never an academic, he did immerse himself in the theory of the law through constant reading and reflection. In 1997, Justice La Forest said, "Bill was a model of conscientiousness and courtesy. I particularly enjoyed his historical approach to law. Like so many Saskatchewanians of his vintage, his legal training was considerably better than was available elsewhere in Canada. He was superb in criminal law and deeply sensitive to human rights."[42] McIntyre also possessed a boundless curiosity concerning the origins and evolution of legal rules and principles, and the historical rationales for certain legal practices. He had no difficulty relating to the more abstruse arguments of the academics on the Court. His love of legal theory had been nurtured at the College of Law in Saskatoon by his esteemed mentor, Dean Cronkite. McIntyre's considerable practical legal experience, a dimension some of his academic colleagues lacked, was of great assistance to the Court. In any important development of the law, theory and practice must complement each other. At the same time, he undoubtedly benefited from the specialized academic advice of associates who had been law teachers.

The late 1980s was not an easy time on the Supreme Court of Canada, with five judges departing within the space of two years. Problems of continuity and "corporate memory" can arise when a vacuum occurs. In February 1987, Chouinard died suddenly, and in 1988, Estey, Le Dain, and Beetz retired, followed by McIntyre in 1989. After Madam Justice Wilson's retirement on January 4, 1991, Antonio Lamer was the only remaining judge who had been appointed by Trudeau.

McIntyre's years on the Court straddled the epochal dividing line marked by the proclamation of the Charter of Rights and Freedoms in 1982. Since Charter cases did not begin to arrive on the Supreme Court docket from the lower courts until about 1984, his decade on the Court involved five years of more traditional adjudication, and five years during which the Court struggled to define the content and limits of the new provisions. McIntyre played a major role in this pathbreaking interpretative function, particularly with his definition of "equality rights" in *Andrews* and by identifying the boundary line between disputes where the Charter did apply and those where it did not in *Dolphin Delivery*. In criminal law matters he sometimes dissented from Dickson, Lamer, and Wilson, with whom, nonetheless, he remained close friends. Ideologically, McIntyre was closer to Beetz, La Forest, and Martland, the last judge to leave the Court before the Charter became operational. He remains convinced that the Court's judgments are too long, and that their sanctioning of headnotes will land them in difficulties if a case arises where a headnote contradicts the body of a judgment. His reservations will now be examined in detail.

McIntyre's Criticisms:
Caseload, Headnotes, Length of Judgments

Justice McIntyre considered that the Supreme Court took on too many cases annually for proper adjudication. Of the countless thousands of cases appealed in lower courts, only a fraction of one percent can be heard by the country's ultimate tribunal. The Court accepts realistically that many important cases will have to be decided at the lower Court level, and seeks to hear only those of critical significance for the development of the law. The Supreme Court of the United States, with the same number of judges and a similar mandate, has a comparable caseload in a country with ten times the population. Although more time has been made available now for judgment writing, the workload is still too heavy, leaving judges insufficient time for research and reflection. McIntyre's opinion on these matters is shared by his former colleague, Justice Claire L'Heureux-Dubé, who told a meeting of judges in Montreal in 1988 that judges no longer have time to reflect, remain informed of legal developments, or maintain even a semblance of a normal life.

The decision taken by the Court to scrutinize and officially endorse headnotes, although done in the interest of clearer communication, is also fraught with difficulty. This decision was made by the Court after McIntyre's departure. Obviously it is only a matter of time until a discrepancy arises between a headnote and the body of the judgment, both having been officially approved. In such a case, which prevails? Does the practice adopted by the Court conduce to the clarity and intelligibility of the law? McIntyre thinks not. Traditionally, headnotes were simply a guide highlighting some of the more important phases of the judgment, enabling practitioners and others to refresh their memories. It was never a substitute or microcosm of the judgment itself, and weary law professors used to admonish their students not to rely on headnotes for examination purposes. When asked to discuss a specific case in class, the professor, after hearing the student's version, would sometimes say, "You've given me the headnote, now how about the case proper?" Because of the need for brevity, any headnote must abbreviate, condense, select, and emphasize; some facets of the case are stressed and others are omitted, and it is inevitable that compression will sometimes be misleading. In a complex relation of law to facts, one or other, or both, may be inadequately dealt with. The overall effect of officially sanctioning headnotes is mischievous.

Another problem is that in more recent years the judgments of the Court have generally become too long and convoluted. They are frequently phrased in such terms that it is difficult for practising lawyers and judges on other courts to extract the *rationes decidendi* (the governing reasons of the decision) and apply them as precedents. The problem is compounded where there are in the same case a number of concurring judgments that come to the same conclusion, but for different reasons. When counsel cite such a decision in court, or in a legal opinion, it is often impossible to ascertain what the grounds are for the decision as a whole; it can only be cited in an unprincipled way for its actual result.

McIntyre's judgments, conversely, were models of precision, clarity, and succinctness. With an economy of words, in a style that was lucid rather than elegant, they were written with the express purpose of assisting lawyers and judges to comprehend and apply the legal principles enunciated. The usefulness of McIntyre's judgments for the instruction of juries during trial was favourably commented upon by Mr. Justice William Grant of the Supreme Court of Nova Scotia:

As a judge I (and most trial judges) spent a lot of time on our jury instructions; they had to be judicially correct and yet be understandable by laypeople (jurors). We always looked for guidance in judgments of the Supreme Court of Canada. We had the feeling that Justice McIntyre's decisions were legally correct and were sensible and practical guidelines for us. With some of the others, they were legally correct but hard to reduce to phrases suitable for jurors. We knew he knew the criminal law and having been a practitioner, we had confidence that he could reduce the theoretical to the practical.[43]

These sentiments were shared by many trial judges.

CHIEF JUSTICE LAMER ON McINTYRE'S CRITICISMS

Responding to McIntyre's criticism that the length of judgments made it more difficult to say what the law is, Chief Justice Lamer remembers that judgments were short when he arrived on the Court in 1980. The Charter of Rights did not yet exist but three centuries of legal history and common law were a forceful legacy, and for decision making, courts relied on precedent. Judges would search for controlling precedents in the law reports, and for prior cases where factual elements were similar to those before the court. Typically, a judge would state in his reasons that the pertinent facts here were such-and-such, the legal issues to be decided were so-and-so, and that x number of cases in the law reports dealt with the matters at hand. Then, after reviewing the precedents in relation to the current case, he applied the law to the facts and came up with the decision. The judging process was more straightforward than it is now.

However, Lamer recalls that even in pre-Charter times, Dickson began to change the way decisions were shaped. He started the process in order to present a more complete picture, summarizing in some detail the law set forth by the lower courts. For example, labour law cases can be very complex; they merit detailed examination and explication. Dickson analyzed the issues in light of case law found in the judgments and, contrary to McIntyre, took the view that doctrine and academic writing were very important within the body of the judgment. He was actually much more French than English in this sense, because in the civil law system used in Quebec there is no system of precedents. Moreover, Lamer maintains that professors are far more important in the civil law system than individual judges.

Even before the Charter, Lamer points out that Dickson wrote different judgments than Martland and the rest of the court. With the advent of the Charter there was no history of jurisprudence on which to rely for interpretation. All that existed was the American experience with the Bill of Rights. The court was asked questions that "black letter" lawyers were not trained to answer: questions with a political dimension. Could the court deal with these concepts and applications in the succinct manner that McIntyre recommended? He maintains that it simply could not. The rights to "life, liberty and security of the person" are broad concepts. They have to be defined and given content by courts. "We're stuck with, 'What *kind* of animal is this?'" Lamer says. "With all due respect to my friend Bill, it is impossible to deal with them in the manner that was formerly done."

Chief Justice Lamer also disagrees with his former colleague with respect to headnotes. McIntyre thinks there is a risk that the text of a case may contradict the Court's officially sanctioned headnote. However, Lamer says: "The Court decided as a matter of policy — Bill was no longer there — that there was very poor press coverage of Supreme Court cases in the era of the Charter. We examine the headnotes now. Bill McIntyre says there's sometimes a contradiction between the judgment and the headnote. The problem is we have too many judgments in Canada now and the lawyers can't keep up with the rules. And with greater attention to the headnotes, there's more accurate press coverage of our cases."

In terms of selecting cases for a hearing where there was no vested right of appeal, Lamer considers that the system of rotating panels of three judges to grant leave-to-appeal in applications for hearing by the Supreme Court generally works well. If there are disagreements, two of the three judges may decide to grant leave, or the matter might occasionally be referred to all nine judges for a decision. Lamer does not believe that too much time is devoted to specific areas such as family law, although he feels this may have been the case in Madam Justice Wilson's time.

One of Lamer's procedural improvements that has worked well was limiting the time for oral argument to one hour for each side, with extensions being allowed by leave of the Court. When this alteration was first broached, some lawyers said it was contrary to the English tradition. "One fall, I interviewed every lawyer presenting cases," Lamer recalls, "and asked them, 'What do you think about one hour for each side?' The average time then taken was actually one hour and fifteen minutes. 'What if we had a rule of one hour, being flexible on the extension of time?' When this rule was introduced, the lawyers liked it. I now hear no complaints. When I arrived on the Court, there was a backlog, a two and a half year wait before a case could be heard. Now, you're inscribed on the roll and you're on." McIntyre argues that Lamer's citing the "average time" formerly taken is misleading. In some cases arguments took up less than an hour and many arguments by counsel exceeded two hours. Eminent counsel from British Columbia, such as Brian Smith, initially opposed the more stringent limit, but the bar's reaction now is generally positive. McIntyre also wonders whether the time limit for argument is offset, in some cases, by the too-liberal granting of "intervenor" status to interested groups who are not parties to the action.

FAREWELL TO THE COURT

When Justice McIntyre's departure from Canada's highest court was announced in 1989, opinion was divided on the merits of his restrained approach to the judicial function in the Charter era. Most critics saw the Charter as a revolutionary vehicle for improving existing statute and common law, as a means of introducing greater fairness, equality, and "fundamental justice" into Canadian law, and of bringing the law into closer conformity with new social and political ideals. While he never opposed the Charter, McIntyre believed it should be applied more sparingly and selectively than did most of his colleagues. In his opinion, overusing the Charter could undermine existing common law, which he thought contained or embodied most of the ideals enshrined in the Charter. McIntyre took an evolutionary approach to the law and feared that an overzealous bench would, in effect, usurp the government's legislative role, thereby weakening the institutional credibility of the Supreme Court. In its worst expression, an activist court wielding the Charter too aggressively blurred the separation of powers between judges and legislators. Commenting on McIntyre's approach to judging, Professor Peter Russell said: "He'll be remembered as the most articulate spokesman for judicial self-restraint in regard to the Charter of Rights and Freedoms. I get some test of that when I mention him to law professors who love the Charter — they roll their eyes at the mention of his name."[44]

McIntyre's critics saw his restrained approach as obstructive of much needed legal reform, while supporters saw it as protective of inherited common law norms and as preserving the law-making powers of legislatures. In his judicial work he remained detached from public controversy: "Public pressures really don't push the courts.... They push the legislatures and Parliament and that is what is should do. The court's function is to do the best it can with the law."[45] However, three of McIntyre's Supreme Court judgments received considerable media attention: his holding in *Dolphin Delivery* that a "governmental" element had to be present in a case before the Charter would be engaged;[46] his influential definition of equality rights in the *Andrews* case;[47] and his dissenting judgment in *Morgentaler*, which upheld the therapeutic abortion provision in section 251 of the Criminal Code.[48]

The *Calgary Herald* described McIntyre as a conservative judge who did not want to strike down too many laws,[49] and he was quoted in the *Winnipeg Free Press*[50] as saying, "the Charter is not an empty vessel to be filled with whatever we might wish." McIntyre feels that the extent of its impact on the law is still largely unforseen and uncertain, and it might take another half-century before a definitive evaluation of this young legal instrument can properly be made.

NOTES

1. Section 6 of the *Supreme Court Act* R.S.C., 1985, c. S-26 provides: "At least three of the judges shall be appointed from among the judges of the Court of Appeal or the Superior Court of the Province of Quebec or from among the advocates of that province."
2. Province of British Columbia, *British Columbia's Constitutional Proposals: Reform of the Supreme Court of Canada*, paper no. 4 (Victoria: Queen's Printer, September 1978), 15; emphasis in original.

3. Canadian Press, "B.C. Judge Appointed to Top Court," *The Gazette* [Montreal] December 22, 1978, 2.
4. Geoffrey Stevens, "A Feeling for the Underdog," *The Globe and Mail* [Toronto] December 29, 1978, 6.
5. See, e.g., Leonard Levy, *Original Intent and the Framers' Constitution* (New York: Macmillan, 1988); also, Antonin Scalia, *A Matter of Interpretation: Federal Courts and the Law* (Princeton: Princeton University Press, 1997); and Jack N. Rakove, *Original Meanings: Politics and Ideas in the Making of the Constitution* (New York: Knopf, 1997).
6. Interview with Chief Justice Antonio Lamer by the writer, October 2, 1996.
7. Interview with former Chief Justice Brian Dickson by the writer, October 9, 1996.
8. S. Clarkson, and C. McCall, *Trudeau and Our Times, Volume 1: The Magnificent Obsession* (Toronto: McClelland & Stewart, 1991), 322-23.
9. Re A.G. Quebec and A.G. Canada (1982) 134 D.L.R. (3d) T19 (Que. C.A).
10. Re A.G. Quebec and A.G. Canada (1982) 140 D.L.R. (3d) 385 (S.C.C.).
11. "Patriation and the Supreme Court," in Pierre Elliott Trudeau, *Against the Current* (Toronto: McClelland & Stewart, 1996), 246-47.
12. *Ibid.*, 247.
13. *Ibid.*
14. *Ibid.*, 251.
15. *Ibid.*, 252.
16. *Knox v. Lee*, 79 U.S. 457 (1871).
17. See, e.g., C. Herman Pritchett, *The Roosevelt Court* (New York: Macmillan, 1947).
18. *Youngstown Sheet & Tube Co. v. Sawyer*, 343 U.S. 579 (1952).
19. *U.S. v. Nixon*, 418 U.S. 683 (1974).
20. Interview with Madame Justice Bertha Wilson by the writer, September 30, 1996.
21. David M. O'Brien, *Storm Center: The Supreme Court in American Politics*, 2d ed. (New York: W.W. Norton, 1990), 142.
22. Peter H. Russell, *The Judiciary in Canada: The Third Branch of Government* (Toronto: McGraw-Hill Ryerson, 1987).

23. See, e.g., section 53(2) of the Supreme Court Act, R.S.C., 1985, c. S-26, which sets out, "The Governor in Council may refer to the Court for hearing and consideration important questions of law or fact concerning any matter." The Acts of 1875, 1891, and 1906 contained similar provisions authorizing the Governor-in-Council to submit to the Court questions of law or fact.
24. W.H. McConnell, "The Judicial Review of Prime Minister Bennett's 'New Deal'" (1968) 6 *Osgoode Hall L.J.*, 39.
25. *Co-operative Committee on Japanese Canadians v. A.-G. Can.* [1947] A.C. 87, affirming the appeal decision of the Supreme Court of Canada on a reference by the Governor-in-Council ([1946] S.C.R. 248).
26. *Reference Re: Anti-Inflation Act* (1976) 68 D.L.R. (3d), 452 (S.C.C.).
27. Susan Delacourt, "Pox on Both Ottawa, PQ, Bertrand Tells Top Court," *The Globe and Mail* [Toronto], April 14, 1997, A-l. See, Reference re: Secession of Quebec (1998) 161 D.L.R. 385 (S.C.C.).
28. *A-G. Ont. v. A-G. Can.* [1912] A.C. 571 at 583 (J.C.P.C.).
29. *Ibid.*, 585.
30. Letter of August 8, 1793, reprinted in H.P. Johnson, ed., *The Correspondence and Public Papers of John Jay* (New York: Putnam's, 1890), 488-89, quoted in O'Brien, *Storm Center*, 119-20.
31. *Ibid.*, 120.
32. *Ibid.*
33. 219 U.S. 346 (1911).
34. (1921) 29 C.L.R. 257.
35. *Ibid.*, 267.
36. Zelman Cowen, *Federal Jurisdiction in Australia* (Oxford: Oxford University Press, 1959), 18.
37. Rae Corelli, "Here Come the Judges," *Maclean's*, January 11, 1988, 32-37. I have drawn on this useful article for several of the profiles of Canadian Supreme Court judges that follow.
38. *Re Agricultural Products Marketing Act* [1978] 2 S.C.R. 1198 at 1256-57.
39. Corelli, "Judges," 37.
40. *Reference re the Anti-Inflation Act* [1976] 2 S.C.R. 373 at 440.
41. *Saumur v. Quebec City* [1953] 2 S.C.R. 299 at 359.

42. The Honourable G.V. La Forest, to the writer, September 13, 1997.
43. The Honourable William Grant, a retired judge of the Supreme Court of Nova Scotia who presided over many trials, to the writer, October 10, 1996.
44. Quoted in David Vienneau, "Conservative Judge Quits Supreme Court," *The Toronto Star*, February 11, 1989, A-1.
45. David Vienneau, "Retiring Judge Paid No Heed to Public Opinion," *The Toronto Star*, February 17, 1989, A-9.
46. *Ibid.*, and the Canadian Press report "McIntyre Resignation Opens Supreme Court Seat," *Winnipeg Free Press*, February 11, 1989, 9.
47. "This was a major decision on equality rights and it will shape court decisions for many years to come," said Ottawa lawyer Les Vandor, judicial affairs adviser to then Justice Minister John Crosbie. Quoted in Vienneau, "Conservative Judge."
48. Peter O'Neil, "Charter Impact Called Unknown," *The Vancouver Sun*, February 13, 1989, A-6; there were similar references to the 1988 *Morgentaler* dissent in virtually all of the newspaper reports.
49. *The Calgary Herald*, February 11, 1989, A-3.
50. Canadian Press, "McIntyre Resignation."

V

McINTYRE'S CONSTITUTIONAL AND QUASI-CONSTITUTIONAL DECISIONS

CONSTITUTIONAL

- The *Patriation* Case
- The Controversy over the House of the Federation
- The Newfoundland-Quebec Power Controversy
- Dr. Morgentaler and the Abortion Controversy
- The *Andrews* Case: Equality Rights
- *R. v. Vaillancourt*: Constructive Murder
- *Dolphin Delivery*: The Scope of the Charter
- The Rule of Law and Labour Strife in the B.C. Courts
- Consumer Protection and Freedom of Speech

QUASI-CONSTITUTIONAL

Military Justice and the Jurisdiction of the Civil Courts
Mandatory Retirement and Provincial Human Rights
Adverse Effect Discrimination and Minority Rights
Freedom of Religion in the Workplace

METHODOLOGY

IF ONE WERE TO ASK which judge on the Supreme Court of Canada best combined an economy of words with incisiveness of meaning, the answer would undoubtedly be William R. McIntyre. There have been more polished stylists on the Supreme Court — one thinks of Laskin and Dickson — but for the sheer ability to communicate lucidly and precisely, McIntyre has few if any equals within the Canadian judiciary. The elegant phrase can beguile but it can also obfuscate. What did the great American jurist Felix Frankfurter mean when he said in one of his judgments that the public schools should be desegregated "with all deliberate speed"? He clearly meant that the present pace of desegregation was too slow, but how does one define in practical terms "deliberate speed" as a yardstick of progress? It can mean pretty much what school administrators want it to mean, and for decades after the U.S. Supreme Court's 1954 school desegregation decision, the advance toward the desired goal, even in northern cities such as Boston or Detroit, was painfully slow.

For McIntyre, the courts have never been the primary agency for the creation of social policy. As in his dissents in *Morgentaler* on abortion or in *Vaillancourt* on constructive murder, he would acknowledge generally the primacy of the legislature and the executive arm in that area. He was never an "empire-building" judge, in the sense of grasping at the expansible norms in the Canadian Charter of Rights and Freedoms to develop social policy and enhance the authority of the court against the legislature. In terms of the interpretative techniques of the Constitution, he was more inclined to "read down" broad statutory provisions to preserve their constitutional validity than to "read in" new terms from the bench that were deemed to have been omitted by legislative draftsmen. He tended to regard the latter technique as a usurpation by judges of the legislative function and an indirect assault on the separation of powers.

In his constitutional decisions, the careful definition of the parameters of legislative powers was a constant preoccupation. In the "Patriation" case, for example, he drew back from according full "constitutional" status to unwritten conventions because he did not consider the status of such conventions to be a question of "law." Once the legality of the use of the Joint Address procedure by the federal government had been determined, that was all that was required to dispose of the reference. Indeed, to accord constitutional status to conventions was mischievous, since in the terms that the majority on that issue defined it, it propelled the parties back to the negotiating table with unforeseeable results. His approach to the Constitution was careful and reasonable and he rarely, if ever, overreached his judicial mandate.

McINTYRE'S CONSTITUTIONAL DECISIONS

THE *PATRIATION* CASE

When the four original provinces entered Confederation in 1867, there was a significant omission in the British North America Act, 1867:[1] there was no provision to enable the central government and the provinces to amend the Canadian Constitution, of which the foregoing statute had become the central core. In the absence of a formal constitutionalized amending power, Canada resorted to the Joint Address procedure when amendments were from time to time required. This involved a resolution passed by the House of Commons and the Senate requesting the Queen to place before Parliament at Westminster, the body having exclusive power to amend the B.N.A. Act (a British statute), their proposal for amendment. Once enacted by the House of Commons and House of Lords and signed by the Queen, the amendment became a formal part to the Canadian Constitution. There are several features in the Constitution, such as the lack of a power to make treaties, that emphasize its original colonial character.

Canada's growth as a nation, her full participation in the First World War, and her increasing autonomy and influence in relations with the U.K., led to the enactment by the British Parliament of the Statute of Westminster, 1931, acknowledging that Canada (together with her sister Dominions) was an independent and co-ordinate member of the Commonwealth, fully the equal of the United Kingdom. Political leaders in the Canadian provinces were concerned that unless some mention were made in the Statute of the preservation and protection of provincial powers, authorities in Ottawa might attempt unilaterally to amend the Canadian Constitution to their detriment. They wanted it emphasized that the statutory enshrinement of Canadian sovereignty and independence did not carry with it the power to make amendments in provincial areas of jurisdiction without the consent of the provinces. This particularly concerned adherents of the compact theory of the constitution, who argued, on the analogy of a contract, that no amendments affecting the rights, privileges and powers of the provinces could be made without the consent of any, or all, of the provinces affected. This theory was especially popular in

Quebec, where it had general support, especially from such prominent politicians as Henri Bourassa, L.A. Taschereau, and Maurice Duplessis. Separatist Quebec Premier René Lévesque argued that the contemporary Canadian nation-state was too centralized and advocated a return to the compact theory, or a "true confederation," in the form of sovereignty for Quebec combined with a treaty-based form of association with the rest of Canada commonly referred to as "sovereignty association."[2]

However, it was an English-speaking advocate of the compact theory, Ontario Premier G. Howard Ferguson, who in 1930 had argued most strongly for the inclusion of section 7 in the Statute of Westminster. He thought the effect of that provision, (not everyone agreed with him), was that Parliament's legislative powers, arising from Canada's newly-proclaimed sovereign status, did not enable it to alter the B.N.A. Act without provincial consent.[3]

When Premier Lévesque held a provincial referendum in May 1980 asking the electorate to give him a mandate to negotiate sovereignty-association with Ottawa, Prime Minister Trudeau and Minister of Justice Jean Chrétien, along with Quebec opposition leader Claude Ryan, interfered forcefully in the debate in their native province, urging voters to oppose Lévesque's request. Trudeau promised Quebecers "constitutional renewal" in return for a "no" vote. When the Quebec electorate rejected Lévesque's proposal by a differential of 60-40 percent, Trudeau had to make good on his constitutional promise. His difficulty was that it had proven almost impossible in the past to secure provincial consent on a domestic amending formula or on the entrenchment of rights and freedoms in the Constitution. Throughout the summer of 1980 a federal-provincial constitutional committee led by Justice Minister Chrétien and Saskatchewan Attorney General Roy Romanow attempted unsuccessfully to thrash out a compromise proposal, but the sides were too far apart. At a federal-provincial constitutional conference in September, Trudeau decided that he would proceed unilaterally with a Joint Resolution, requesting the British Parliament to entrench a domestic amending formula and a Charter of Rights and Freedoms, on which only two of ten provinces, Ontario and New Brunswick, were agreed. Trudeau and Chrétien's position was that the contemporary Canadian Constitution was a colonial anachronism and that the historical record demonstrated that British authorities would not undermine a resolution emanating from the two Houses of Parliament in order to determine whether prior provincial consent had been obtained. The only party with standing to approach the Sovereign or the British Parliament in relation to amendments was the federal government and the two Canadian Houses of Parliament.

For their part, the eight dissenting provinces did not agree that Ottawa could unilaterally amend the Constitution in such a manner, especially when provincial rights, privileges, and powers might be adversely affected by the proposed amendment. A British constitutional authority, Profession H.W.R. Wade, Master of Gonville and Caius College, Cambridge, and an adviser to the Quebec government in the developing controversy, had this to say about section 7 of the Statute of Westminster:

The inescapable conclusion is that [section] 7 of the *Statute of Westminster 1931* had left the U.K. Parliament with not only legal but also political responsibility for upholding the federal constitution of Canada and acting as a guardian of the rights of the provinces. Anachronistic and unwelcome as this responsibility may be, it was deliberately preserved in 1931 and nothing has since happened to alter it. The U.K. Parliament therefore has the duty, when requested to amend the *British North America Acts*, to ask itself two questions: first, does the amendment adversely affect Provincial legislative powers; and, secondly, if so, have the provinces affected signified their consent.

Wade would answer the first question "yes" and the second one "no." His advice to the British authorities was forthright: "The simplest course would be for it [the U.K. Parliament] to enact a short statute empowering the Government of Canada to amend the British North America Acts in any manner provided that the consent of all the provinces was obtained."[4] The constitutional positions of Ottawa and the dissenting provinces were polarized; indeed, they could scarcely be further apart, although there were nuances and gradations in the opposition of some provinces compared with others.

Confronted by the determination of Trudeau, his government, and his two provincial allies to forge ahead without unanimous or even substantial provincial consent, Manitoba, Quebec, and Newfoundland initiated constitutional references in their courts of appeal challenging the constitutional validity of proceeding with Trudeau's "package." Saskatchewan and Nova Scotia hovered on the sidelines,[5] hoping to help break the impasse. Months later they joined the six other provinces to comprise what became known as the "gang of eight."

The dissenting provinces were in a procedural quagmire. They had no direct access to the Supreme Court of Canada. They wanted to demonstrate that the federal government's constitutional position was untenable but in order to create favourable public opinion for their own position they needed supportive judgments at the highest provincial court level. Although time was flying and there was a strong intimation that the federal government might present its Joint Address to Westminster at any moment, they initiated references in the three provinces where the respective courts of appeal would be most receptive to their arguments. If rulings were favourable, Ottawa would be forced to compromise, and even if they were unfavourable they could finally be appealed to the Supreme Court. The reference questions as drafted by the provinces typically asked: first, whether, if the proposed amendments were enacted, provincial powers would be affected; second, whether a constitutional convention precluded a proposed amendment from going forward without provincial consent if it affected provincial powers; and third, whether the prior agreement of the provinces was required where an amendment would alter provincial rights, privileges, or powers, or would affect federal-provincial relationships.

The initial Manitoba reference result was a 3-2 division in favour of the federal government,[6] followed by a strong 3-0 Newfoundland decision in favour of the provinces,[7] with the Quebec Court of Appeal finally deciding 4-1 in favour of Ottawa.[8] Although the federalist side could take comfort from the Manitoba and Quebec victories, when Newfoundland ruled unanimously against Ottawa in the intermediate decision on March 31, 1981 (coincidentally, the 32nd anniversary of that province's entry into Confederation), Trudeau, who had favoured immediately presenting the Joint Address to the Queen, retreated one step. He decided to clear the air by joining with all the provinces in an ultimate reference to the Supreme Court of Canada. Counting the judges in all three courts, the federal side had prevailed by a narrow 7-6 division. Practically speaking, this narrow victory tended to throw into doubt the validity of Trudeau's position that there was no constitutional problem about sending the whole package to Westminster immediately.

In the Supreme Court of Canada's decision, which was announced on Monday, September 28, 1981,[9] McIntyre, Chief Justice Laskin, and Mr. Justice Estey were strong proponents of the federal legal power to send the Joint Address to Westminster, if necessary without provincial consent. They agreed with the majority[10] on the legal issue that the federal government could present whatever amendment proposal to the British Parliament it desired. However, the Court severed the important third reference question into two parts.[11] By a 6-3[12] majority they ruled that as a matter of constitutional convention it was essential to obtain prior provincial consent (not quantified) before requesting constitutional amendments affecting federal-provincial relations or the rights, privileges, and powers of the provinces.

The strongest centralist position was enunciated by Justice McIntyre and his two colleagues. At the other pole were Justices Martland and Ritchie, the two Diefenbaker appointees, who held that the federal government had no basis to proceed in this instance either on a legal or on a constitutional basis. Between these factions the remaining judges adopted a compromise position. They affirmed that the federal government had a legal right to proceed, but added that as a matter of constitutional convention, where provincial powers or federal-provincial relations would be affected it was necessary to obtain the prior consent of the provinces before submitting the Joint Address to Westminster. Since both law and convention were defined as integral parts of the Constitution, the combined majority decisions signified that while the prime minister had a *legal* right to present his Joint Address to Westminster, if he did not, in the conventional sense, obtain the consent of the provinces before doing so, he would be acting unconstitutionally. Since he continued to enjoy the consistent support of only two provinces, the practical effect of this legal decision was to induce the parties to resume negotiations so as to arrive at a compromise position enabling the federal government to meet the requirement mandated by constitutional convention.

Mr. Justice D.M.M. Goldie, who argued the case as counsel for British Columbia, said that the *Senate* reference[13] had given a certain amount of confidence to counsel speaking for the dissident provinces. In that reference, the court had said the federal government could not do indirectly what it could not do directly, and here it was plain that Parliament could not enact those parts of the amendment that derogated from provincial powers. The effect of Ottawa's securing the amendment would be that provincial powers would still be diminished by the federal government's employing alternative means. He also said that overlapping legal teams had argued in Manitoba, Newfoundland, and Quebec, one notable exception being John J. Robinette, who argued for the federal Crown in Winnipeg. Mr. Justice Goldie recalled saying, "See you in Newfoundland," after the Manitoba hearing, and Robinette had replied, "No; it wouldn't do my client's cause any good for a Toronto lawyer to appear in St. John's." Goldie found the Newfoundland court an especially interesting one to argue before. Each of the three Newfoundland judges had started to practice before Newfoundland had joined Confederation and were very sensitive to the implications of these issues. Because of its momentous importance, the Chief Justice's final decision was to be broadcast live on television before a national audience. Few observers of the patriation controversy over the last year and more were neutral: they supported either the provincial or the federal position. Unfortunately, the CBC television broadcast foundered when the wrong switch was thrown and Chief Justice Laskin's reading of the decision could not be heard. As a final anticlimax Canadians had to rely on condensed news reports over the next few days.

Justice McIntyre joined the seven-member majority opinion on the legal right of the federal government to present any constitutional amendment it desired to Westminster for enactment, but he dissented, with Laskin and Estey, concerning the constitutional convention (as found by the six remaining judges) requiring the federal government to obtain provincial consent before proceeding.

It is instructive that none of the majority or dissenting judgments in the *Patriation* case had a single author. The Court acted in full consultation and Chief Justice Lamer recalls that they laboured intensively on these convoluted questions through the summer of 1981. The judgments were all joint works, with Justice McIntyre making a major contribution to both the majority opinion on law and the dissent on constitutional convention.

The Address that was passed by both Houses of the Canadian Parliament in 1980 was not a statute (since it had not received royal assent), but a request to the Queen to put before British Parliament a proposal for the enactment of a Canadian constitutional amendment. There was no disagreement in Canada that only Parliament was legally able to present such an Address to the Queen, the issue being rather what procedure was to be followed when a putative amendment affected or altered provincial powers or prerogatives. The majority (including McIntyre) decided that on grounds both of precedent and principle the amendment proposal could still go forward. In the words of the majority:

What is central here is the untrammeled authority at law of the two federal Houses to proceed as they wish in the management of their own procedures and hence to adopt the Resolution which is intended for submission to Her Majesty for action thereon by the United Kingdom Parliament. The *British North America Act* does not either in terms or by implication, control this authority or require that it be subordinated to provincial assent. Nor does the *Statute of Westminster, 1931*, interpose any requirement of such assent. If anything, it leaves the position as it was before its enactment. Developments subsequent thereto do not affect the legal position.[14]

Accordingly, even when a potential amendment affected provincial powers it could still be presented to the British Parliament for enactment without any need for prior provincial consent.

In dissenting from the above majority opinion on law, Martland and Ritchie emphasized the uniqueness of the present issue: in the 114 years since Confederation there had never been an attempt to obtain an amendment like the current one without provincial consent.[15] After an extensive review of legal authorities, they added, "In no instance has an amendment to the *B.N.A. Act* been enacted which directly affected federal-provincial relationships in the sense of changing provincial legislative powers, in the absence of federal consultation with and the consent of the provinces."[16] The attorney general of Canada, they said, had presented "a deceptively simple argument" to uphold the legality of the resolution involved in the present appeal: because what was involved was a resolution and not a law, it was not a proper subject for judicial consideration and the two Houses could pass any resolution they desired.[17] Regarded from a substantive rather than a formalistic perspective, however, where it was considered that an amendment could only be enacted pursuant to such a resolution, what was really being argued was that the two federal Houses could initiate any amendment, "even though that amendment subtracts, without provincial consent, from the legislative powers of the provinces."[18] The corollary was clear, at least to Martland and Ritchie: "The Attorney-General of Canada in substance is asserting the existence of a power in the two Houses of Parliament to obtain amendments to the *B.N.A. Act* which could disturb and even destroy the federal system of constitutional government in Canada. We are not aware of the possible legal source for such a power."[19] The federal position was that what Parliament could not achieve directly by way of legislation, it could cause to be done indirectly through a Joint Resolution;[20] such a procedure struck at the basis of the federal system.[21]

The six-judge majority on constitutional convention held that it would be contrary to the unwritten rules of the Constitution for the federal government to obtain an amendment affecting provincial powers without provincial consent. They were mindful that the conventional rules of the constitution were not laws and were not enforceable in the courts.[22] The violation of a convention could not result in a legal sanction but might result in a political one, such as defeat in the next election. Conventions also were unwritten rules arising often from the interaction of officials or political authorities. Their actions might be central to the convention not merely as mechanically repetitive motions, practices, or usages, but as actions these politicians carried out with the sense that they were bound or obligated to do so. The Queen or her Canadian representatives could refuse to give assent to a Bill presented to them after its passage by the legislature — they have the legal power to do so. But if they refused, they would be violating the comparatively modern convention of acting in compliance with responsible Canadian ministers by signing any bill presented to them. "We have here," the Court majority on convention observes, "a conflict between a legal rule which creates a complete discretion and a conventional rule which completely neutralizes it."[23] Nevertheless, if this convention were violated, the courts would uphold the law, not the convention. Conventions, moreover, can be of fundamental importance, such as the convention underlying responsible government, which prescribes that if the opposition obtains a majority at the polls, the government must resign.[24]

The Court underlines the great importance of convention: "It should be borne in mind however that, while they are not laws, some conventions may be more important than some laws. Their importance depends on that of the value or principle that they are meant to safeguard."[25] And in a statement of the greatest significance in the present reference, the Court adds, "The foregoing may perhaps be summarized in an equation: constitutional conventions plus constitutional law equal the total constitution of the country."[26] It followed from this mathematical analogy that if the government violated convention by failing to obtain the requisite provincial assent before sending the Address to Westminster it would be acting unconstitutionally.

Referring to a summary of procedure followed in the past to secure amendments, as set out in the Government White Paper (after surveying in detail the relevant precedents), the Court observes,

In our view, the fourth general principle[27] equally and unmistakably states and recognizes as a rule of the Canadian constitution the convention referred to in the second question of the Manitoba and Newfoundland References as well as in Question B of the Quebec Reference, namely that *there is a requirement for provincial agreement to amendments which change provincial legislative powers*.

The statement is not a casual utterance. It is contained in a carefully drafted document which had been circulated to all the provinces prior to its publication and had been found satisfactory to all of them (see Commons Debates, 1965, at p. 11574 and Background Paper published by the Government of Canada, *The Role of the United Kingdom in the Amendment of the Canadian Constitution* [March, 1981] at p. 30). It was published in a white paper, that is as an official statement of government policy, under the authority of the federal Minister of Justice as a member of a government responsible to Parliament, neither House of which, so far as we know, has taken issue with it. This statement is a recognition by all the actors in the precedents that the requirement of provincial agreement is a constitutional rule.[28]

In conclusion, the Court affirmed that the agreement of the provinces of Canada, without stipulating the number of provinces required, was constitutionally necessary to pass a Joint Address, "and that the passing of this Resolution without such agreement would be unconstitutional in the conventional sense."[29]

Chief Justice Laskin, Estey, and McIntyre begin their dissent on constitutional convention by observing that the majority opinion on law, in which they joined, should normally conclude the issue in the present appeals. The Supreme Court is a legal forum, and "no legal question is raised in the questions under consideration in these reasons and, ordinarily, the Court would not undertake to answer them, for it is not the function of the Court to go beyond legal determinations."[30]

Had the case been determined solely on the legal issue, of course, it would have been an unalloyed victory for the federal government. There is considerable force behind the position of the three dissenters on the law versus convention issue, since the definition of constitutional convention arises from the interaction of political actors in specific empirical contexts and not from the decisions of courts. The two realms are ordinarily seen as separate categories. However, this was an unusual case and the Court majority on the convention issue had decided, rightly or wrongly, that both law and convention had to be addressed. In fact, with eight provinces strongly arguing that convention was a decisive factor against the federal government, the issue was virtually unavoidable and joined in such a way that the Court had to respond to it. Moreover, the majority decision on convention was couched in such terms that had the federal government proceeded on the basis of the legal decision alone (and there appears to be an innuendo in the dissent that this was permissible), it could have been described as acting unconstitutionally by violating convention.

A complicating factor was that this was one of the most politically charged constitutional references ever argued in Canada. The eight dissenting provinces were aware that the ultimate deciding action would be taken by Parliament in the U.K.; otherwise Trudeau's whole constitutional package would remain a dead letter. Since conventions were an outgrowth of English constitutional history, there was a disposition on the part of non-concurring provincial counsel to separate the issues of law and convention and to put the conventional case against the federal government as strongly as possible. If the eight provinces prevailed on the conventional issue, unilateral action by Ottawa would be extremely difficult. If the federal government forged ahead nevertheless — and there were some early indications that it might do so — Justice Goldie, counsel for British Columbia, considered that the British Parliament, particularly the House of Lords, would be receptive to the argument that the federal action was unconstitutional. In fact, Prime Minister Margaret Thatcher sent Sir Francis Pym to Ottawa to warn Trudeau that there could be trouble ahead.

As a preliminary matter, the dissenting judges took the reference question on convention as asking whether the consent of *all the provinces* is required to amend the constitution where federal-provincial relationships are involved. A reading of the reference makes this clear, despite Saskatchewan's position that a "substantial majority of the provinces" might suffice. In a constitutional reference the Court must answer the question asked, and is "not ... justified in editing the questions to develop a meaning not clearly expressed."[31]

The majority on convention had taken great pains to emphasize that "constitutional conventions, plus constitutional law equal the total constitution of the country,"[32] meaning that if Trudeau proceeded unilaterally he would be violating the constitution. The dissenting judges emphatically deny this:

We cannot, however, agree with any suggestion that the non-observance of a convention can properly be termed unconstitutional in any strict or legal sense, or that its observance could be, in any sense, a constitutional requirement within the meaning of Question 3 of the Manitoba and Newfoundland References. In a federal state where the essential feature of the constitution must be the distribution of powers between the two levels of government, each supreme in its own legislative sphere, constitutionality and legality must be synonymous, and conventional rules will be accorded less significance than they may have in a unitary state such as the United Kingdom.[33]

While this characterization of convention as "non-constitutional" was at variance with the majority view, had such a definition not been disallowed by the Supreme Court, Trudeau could have presented the Joint Address to the Queen for enactment without the imputation that he was acting unconstitutionally.

The dissent proceeds to examine the 22 constitutional amendments obtained since Confederation, including four affecting provincial powers, where unanimous provincial consent was obtained. Formal unanimity alone did not determine the existence of a convention, however. The critical question is whether political actors, in arriving at unanimity, are postulating that unanimity is desirable or even obligatory. Unanimity could be obtained through compulsion, without truly responsible actors deeming it necessary or desirable. This distinction appears in the conclusion of the three dissenting judges: "After examining the amendments made since Confederation and after observing that out of the 22 amendments listed above, only in the case of four was unanimous provincial consent sought or obtained and, even after according special weight to those amendments relied on by the provinces, we cannot agree that history justifies that the convention contended for by the provinces has emerged."[34]

With reference to the fourth principle in the White Paper, to which the majority on convention attached considerable weight, the dissenters are not persuaded of its probative value.[35] The dissent mentions that the rules and principles described in the White Paper are "not constitutionally binding in any strict sense," and that although "[t]he first sentence [in the fourth general principle] pronounces strongly in favour of the existence of the convention," it is contradicted by the third sentence.[36]

The dissent is important in that it emphasizes the political and flexible nature of conventions — that they are defined by political actors, are unenforceable by the courts, and that their development from mere practices or usages requires rigorous demonstration and is not typically the province of courts of law. The dissenters address in sequence all the principal arguments advanced by the majority and make forceful, closely-reasoned reply to each. In the end, however, the majority judgment on convention was decisive in the political sequel to the reference decision. The opinion was crafted in such a way that if the federal government proceeded unilaterally it could be charged with acting unconstitutionally. It was this imperative that prompted the government to negotiate further in order to win over the provinces and thwarted the enactment of the constitutional package in its original form.

Reflecting on the political effect of the majority decision in the mid-1997, Justice McIntyre posed the question of whether Canada is more united and generally better off now, in a constitutional sense, than before the decision on convention. Some argue that the majority decision was poor constitutionalism but good statecraft. They say that in casting the decision as they did, the majority achieved a temporary political breakthrough and preserved a *modus vivendi* for the short run. In the longer term, however, McIntyre considers that the symbolism of English Canada ganging up on Quebec has been exploited by separatist politicians and comprised a division fraught with peril for Canadian federalism. As McIntyre sees it, the manner in which patriation was accomplished has had politically divisive consequences. He regrets the Supreme Court's ruling on convention because it led to further negotiation and compromise, and then to the isolation of Quebec, by facilitating a deal among her potential allies from which she was excluded. What would have been the effect on Canadian federalism had McIntyre's position carried the day? Had Trudeau ignored the ruling on convention and sought enactment in Britain of his constitutional package with eight provinces still opposed, Quebec, as one of the eight, would not have been isolated. If the British Parliament had agreed to pass the amendments in these circumstances, would it have benefited confederation? In both cases, the crucial consent of Quebec would still be lacking.

Would the resultant amendments have possessed political legitimacy? Constitutionalists make a distinction between legal and political legitimacy.[37] An authoritarian government, for example, can impose a new constitution on its citizens, scrupulously observing all the requisite legal norms but acting contrary to the popular will. Can such a constitution endure, particularly if it is not freely accepted by the people and their opposition proved to be intransigent? Political philosophers such as Locke and Rousseau have raised the issue of "consent," which goes to the heart of "majority rule" in modern democratic systems. In the case of Trudeau's 1982 constitutional amendments, legal legitimacy would be satisfied if Parliament in the U.K., who had enacted the B.N.A. Act, also enacted as a final amendment to their own statute the package entrenching the Charter and new domestic amending formulas, thus acceding to the Joint Resolution sent to the Queen by the Canadian Parliament. For the dissenters on convention this would have been a permissible course of action.

The problem, however, is that eight dissenting provinces represent a substantial body of popular opinion in four of the five regions of Canada (excepting Ontario). If Trudeau's unilateral course were taken instead, would the government's "constitutional package," altering as it did the essential character of the parliamentary system, be accepted by the provinces and the people? Would it have true political legitimacy? The federal government might gamble on converting Canadians opposed to the unilateral process by citing its positive results: a Charter of Rights guaranteeing basic rights and freedoms to all Canadians and the final severance of the anachronistic "colonial" link requiring Britain to enact all future amendments to the Canadian Constitution. However, Quebec nationalists could still point to Ottawa's arbitrary course of amending the Constitution without Quebec's consent, and Quebec would remain in the provincial alliance opposing the government's initiative. The charge of "betrayal" levied by Quebec against the other provinces might not exist although, McIntyre argues, Quebecers opposed to Trudeau's amendments could still contend forcefully that the package was imposed on them by central fiat against their will.

Finally, had Trudeau proceeded unilaterally, there is the question of whether or not the British Parliament would have enacted the amendments with governments in four out of five of the regions in Canada opposed.[38] It is McIntyre's opinion that British refusal would have severed Canadian links with Britain and presaged the end of the monarchy. More than 50 years earlier, in 1926, Governor General Lord Byng had precipitated a constitutional crisis when, acting on his reserve powers, he had refused Prime Minister Mackenzie King the dissolution of Parliament requested by the latter. McIntyre emphasizes that over the intervening years Canada's independence and sovereignty have been acknowledged in too many important ways for Britain to refuse a constitutional request forwarded by a Joint Resolution of the Canadian Parliament.

THE CONTROVERSY OVER THE HOUSE OF THE FEDERATION

In 1978, in Bill C-60, Prime Minister Trudeau proposed to substitute a new 118-member House of the Federation for Canada's unelected Senate. Critics claimed the move was undemocratic and anachronistic with few, if any, parallels in the world. In the new body, the federal government proposed that about half the reformed membership represent the provinces, thus changing both the number and proportion of provincial representatives from 1978 levels, while the other half was to be appointed by the federal government. As new provincial governments were elected the composition of the new upper house would shift to represent the changing complexion of provincial politics. The new body would have a limited power to delay legislation compared with the current Senate, which has the same power as the Commons, and would also have a full veto over senior executive appointments to federal institutions when these were designated by Parliament.

The proposal evoked a storm of protest spearheaded by Canada's venerable constitutional authority, Senator Eugene A. Forsey. The government was not only attempting to repeal sections 21 to 36 of the British North America Act, those defining the Senate, along with references to the Senate in certain other sections.[39] It was also trying to do so unilaterally, by ordinary statute, without consulting the provinces whose interests — according to Sir John A. Macdonald and George Brown[40] — the Senate was originally designed to protect. It was the trenchant criticism of Professor William R. Lederman of Queen's University before a parliamentary committee that led the government, initially resolved to simply enact the Bill, to send it up to the Supreme Court to test its constitutionality.

In putting forward this proposal for Senate reform, the federal government contended it had the power to alter the Constitution of Canada pursuant to section 91(1) of the British North America Act. The text gave Parliament the power to alter the Constitution except in designated instances where the Senate was not expressly mentioned.

In the unanimous unsigned opinion by the Court, in which McIntyre concurred, it was held that Parliament did not have the power to alter the Senate in its fundamental aspects. While section 91(1) does define a power to amend "the Constitution of Canada" (except in sensitive areas where safeguards are necessary), the word "Canada" in context refers only to the juristic federal unit, and "is limited to matters of interest only to the federal government."[41] In addition, section 92(1) defines a symmetrical power to amend the constitution of the provinces in matters of interest to them (save for the position of the lieutenant-governor).[42] In over-arching matters that affect the Constitution of both levels of government, the Joint Address procedure prevailing until 1982 was to be followed.[43] The prohibition of federal action was forthright: "[I]t is our opinion that while section 91(1) would permit some changes to be made by Parliament in respect of the Senate as now constituted, it is not open to Parliament to make alterations which would affect the fundamental features, or essential characteristics given to the Senate as a means of ensuring regional and provincial representation in the federal legislative process."[44] The attempt to reconstitute the Senate as the House of the Federation failed. Reform of the upper House must now await a formal amendment pursuant to the amending procedure set out in the Constitution Act, 1982.

THE NEWFOUNDLAND-QUEBEC POWER CONTROVERSY

In 1984 McIntyre spoke for a unanimous Supreme Court in finding The Upper Churchill Water Rights Reversion Act[45] unconstitutional.[46] In 1969 the Churchill Falls (Labrador) Corporation and Hydro-Quebec had entered into a lengthy agreement whereby the latter agreed to purchase virtually the whole output of power produced by Churchill Falls for a term of 40 years, with Hydro-Quebec having the first option to renew for a further 25 years. The price of the power was fixed based on the final capital cost of the project. A plain reading of this contract revealed that, short of a renegotiation of terms by both parties, the Quebec Corporation had an indefeasible right to control massive hydro-electric capacity. It in turn sold huge amounts of power to consumers in New England at a considerable profit and potentially for a term of 65 years.[47] When Premier Joseph Smallwood entered into the contract it seemed to be a bargain. He did not foresee the rising demand for electricity over the coming decades a trend which resulted in an unfairly low fixed price for the utility for a very long period. Soon Newfoundland governments were seeking to renegotiate the price, a difficult initiative because of the fixed contractual terms, or to recoup the energy by statutory means. Much of the argument in the latter case centred on the admissibility of extrinsic evidence that the Reversion Act, while it purported to regulate property and civil rights within the province, actually derogated from or eliminated the extra-provincial rights of Hydro Quebec.[48] McIntyre found this to be the case: "[T]he *Reversion Act* is a colourable attempt to interfere with the Power Contract and thus to derogate from the rights of Hydro-Quebec to receive an agreed amount of power at an agreed price."[49] On its face, the government had simply expropriated all the assets of the Churchill Falls (Labrador) Corporation and made certain provisions for compensating shareholders and creditors (but not the company).[50] The question that McIntyre was answering, however, was whether this was a mere expropriation or a covert plan to break the contract with Hydro-Quebec by rendering provisions for delivering power outside Newfoundland borders ineffective. Was this a "power grab" that was beyond Newfoundland's constitutional ambit? McIntyre found that the legislation sought "to interfere with the rights of Hydro-Quebec outside the territorial jurisdiction of Newfoundland,"[51] and was, accordingly, *ultra vires.*

Quoting texts on conflict of laws,[52] McIntyre concluded that the place of delivery determines jurisdiction. This finding accords with the intention of the parties: "[T]he Power Contract provided that the Courts of Quebec would have jurisdiction to adjudicate disputes arising under it and it is, therefore, the Province of Quebec where enforcement of the contract may be ordered and where the intangible rights under the contract are situate." Newfoundland appeared to be defeated at every juncture: its legislation was colourable and *ultra vires,* and if any contractual dispute arose well into the twenty-first century, it would fall under the jurisdiction of courts in Quebec. This is not to allege that Quebec courts would deal unfairly with such disputes; however, in this vital matter of energy pricing and supply, an issue bearing centrally on Newfoundland's economy, the province appeared, largely because of an improvident contract of its own making, to have little control or input. The dispute continues to the present day: at the time of writing, Newfoundland's Premier Brian Tobin and Quebec's Premier Lucien Bouchard are at an impasse. If one looks at the substance rather than the form of the agreement, it seems that the contending parties are two provinces who signed an energy agreement in 1969 that seemed fair but who were soon overtaken by market forces creating a bonanza for Quebec and a humiliating loss for Newfoundland. Ideally, the parties would negotiate a new contract with fairer terms. Failing that, could the federal government, after consulting the parties, pass legislation under its own interprovincial trade and commerce power, or its peace, order, and good government power, to establish a fairer contract? However desirable, that solution now seems unlikely.

DR. MORGENTALER AND THE ABORTION CONTROVERSY

In a 5-2 decision in 1988 in *R. v. Morgentaler*,[53] the Supreme Court of Canada, with McIntyre and La Forest dissenting, struck down section 251 of the Criminal Code, which permitted therapeutic abortions to safeguard the life and health of the mother when certain prior conditions had been complied with.[54] This 1969 amendment was as an exception to the general prohibition against abortion. It permitted the procedure to be carried out when authorized by therapeutic abortion committees in accredited hospitals, which, in conformity with subsection 4(c) of the amendment,[55] had certified in writing "that in its opinion the continuation of the pregnancy of such female person would or would be likely to endanger her life or health." When a certificate was given to the "qualified medical practitioner" who performed the abortion, it rendered him or her immune from criminal prosecution. If an abortion was performed without a certificate, the doctor and the woman having the procedure were both criminally liable.

In a pre-Charter decision in the mid-1970s,[56] also involving Dr. Henry Morgentaler, the Supreme Court had upheld the constitutional validity of section 251. In that case the accused raised the defences of necessity and reasonable surgical operation under section 45 of the Criminal Code, and the jury returned a verdict of not guilty. The Crown appealed and the Quebec Court of Appeal set aside the acquittal and entered a verdict of guilty. On further appeal by Morgentaler, the Supreme Court of Canada, in a 6-3 decision, upheld the decision of the Court of Appeal. Chief Justice Laskin, along with Judson and Spence, dissented, holding that it must be an unusual case where, after a jury acquittal, a court that has not seen the witnesses or observed their demeanor would substitute its opinion for that of the jury.[57] After remarking on the continuous controversy provoked by the abortion issue in the 13 years since the first decision, Chief Justice Dickson continued: "As Justice McIntyre states in his reasons for judgment at page 138, 'the task of the Court in this case is not to solve or seek to solve what might be called the abortion issue, but simply to measure the content of section 251 against the *Charter*.' It is in the latter sense that the current *Morgentaler* appeal differs from the one we heard a decade ago."[58] As the Chief Justice emphasized, in the earlier appeal Charter norms (such as "security of the person" in section 7) were not yet in existence and could not apply.

All three of the concurring majority opinions held that section 251 conflicted with "security of the person" in section 7 of the Charter, and that the procedures outlined for obtaining a "therapeutic abortion certificate" in section 251(4) violated "fundamental justice," thereby rendering that section of no force or effect. The Chief Justice employed the "purposive" analysis, which afforded "the full benefit of the Charter's protection," as set out in *R. v. Big M Drug Mart.*[59] Invoking by analogy Lamer's reading of "security of the person" in relation to section 11(b) of the Charter, which extended the concept to cover "stress and anxiety,"[60] Chief Justice Dickson said: "If state-imposed psychological trauma infringes security of the person in the rather circumscribed case of section 11(b) it should be relevant to the general case of section seven where the right is expressed in broader terms."[61] Having laid the groundwork for a broad interpretation of "security of the person," Dickson continues,

Section 251 clearly interferes with a woman's bodily integrity in both a physical and an emotional sense. Forcing a woman, by threat of criminal sanction, to carry a fetus to term unless she meets certain criteria unrelated to her own priorities and aspirations, is a profound interference with a woman's body and thus a violation of security of the person. Section 251, therefore is required by the Charter to comport with the principles of fundamental justice.[62]

"Fundamental justice" was denied, because the word "health" in section 251(4) was undefined; its ambiguity rendered the relevant standard for obtaining a therapeutic abortion certificate uncertain. Women were not able to know in advance what standard of "health" would apply to their case.[63] The number of hospitals willing and legally qualified to perform therapeutic abortions was small, and in some areas of the country, Dickson asserted, there were no such hospitals. The search for an available hospital that was ready to perform the procedure would lead to delays that could make abortions surgically more dangerous in that they would be performed closer to the end of the pregnancy. The fair procedure or "due process" requirements of "fundamental justice" were, therefore, not met, and the failure to meet them was so serious that section 251 could not be saved as a "reasonable limit" on rights and freedoms pursuant to section 1.

In their concurring judgment, Beetz and Estey stressed the element of delay: "A pregnant woman's person cannot be said to be secure if, when her life and health is in danger, she is faced with a rule of criminal law which precludes her from obtaining effective and timely medical treatment."[64] They referred to the absence in many hospitals of therapeutic abortion committees, the existence of quotas in other hospitals, and the delays consequent upon both the quota system and the need to obtain the certificate by awkward procedural methods.

In applying section 1, Beetz and Estey found that the primary objective of section 251 was the protection of the fetus. However, section 251 is disproportionate to the objective it purports to serve. Some of the rules it sets out are simply unnecessary, and insofar as they undermine the health of the woman, which Parliament considers of great significance, they are bad. The goal of protecting the fetus is important but safeguarding the life and health of pregnant women is emphasized by section 251(4). In Beetz's words,

I take this parliamentary enactment in 1969 as an indication that, in a free and democratic society, it would be unreasonable to limit the pregnant woman's right to security of the person by a rule prohibiting abortions in all circumstances where her life or health would or would likely be in danger.[65]

The most far-reaching judgment in terms of the extension of abortion rights was made by Madam Justice Bertha Wilson. She said that "a legislative scheme for obtaining an abortion which exposes the pregnant woman to a *threat* to her security of the person would likely violate her right under section 7."[66] She agreed with both Dickson and Beetz, for the reasons they give, that "pregnant women are exposed to a threat to their physical and psychological security under the legislative scheme set up in section 251 and, since these are aspects of their security of the person, their section 7 right is accordingly violated."[67] Under the second, or "fundamental justice" branch of section 7, however, she had to demonstrate that section 251 did not comply with section 7 as a whole. She approached the critical question of whether the requirements of "fundamental justice" were met from both a procedural and a substantive perspective:

[I]f either the right to liberty or the right to security of the person or a combination of both confers on the pregnant woman the right to decide for herself (with the guidance of her physician) whether or not to have an abortion, then we have to examine the legislative scheme not only from the point of view of fundamental justice in the procedural sense but in the substantive sense as well.

On further inquiry, she alone of the members of the Court found abortion rights to be grounded on the right to liberty as well as on the right to security of the person:

[A]n aspect of the respect for human dignity on which the *Charter* is founded is the right to make fundamental personal decisions without interference from the state. This right is a critical component of the right to liberty. Liberty, as was noted in *Singh*, is a phrase capable of a broad range of meaning. In my view, this right, properly construed, grants the individual a degree of autonomy in making decisions of fundamental personal importance.[68]

And it goes without saying, Wilson continues, that in exercising liberty rights in relation to abortion or other matters, "a free and democratic society does not require the state to approve the personal decisions made by its citizens; it does, however, require the state to respect them."[69]

In speaking of a pregnant woman's decision to terminate her pregnancy as a fundamental liberty right of an intimately personal nature, Wilson questions whether any man can appreciate the character and context of such a decision:

It is probably impossible for a man to respond, even imaginatively, to such a dilemma not just because it is outside the realm of his personal experience (although this is, of course, the case) but because he can relate to it only by objectifying it, thereby eliminating the subjective elements of the female psyche which are at the heart of the dilemma.[70]

When one considers that of the nine members on the *Morgentaler* bench only one was a woman, the experiential dimension that Wilson regards as central to weighing the dilemma was largely absent. Even so, the Court found section 251 invalid by a 5-2 majority.

Also, Wilson alone found a parallel source of a woman's right to an abortion is section 2(a) of the Charter, which enshrines the fundamental right of "freedom of conscience and religion." This right guarantees "conscientiously-held beliefs, whether grounded in religion or in secular morality."[71] In applying penal sanctions against a woman for exercising an option based on her right to freedom of conscience and religion, the state is taking sides on the issue of abortion. She saw it as penalizing "one conscientiously held view at the expense of another."[72]

In his dissent, McIntyre, supported by La Forest, saw the essential issue not in terms of the goodness or badness of the existing provisions of section 251, but in terms of whether or not Parliament had the power to pass that section:

[T]he task of the Court in this case is not to solve or seek to solve what might be called the abortion issue, but simply to measure the content of section 251 against the *Charter*. While this may appear to be self-evident, the distinction is of vital importance. If a particular interpretation enjoys no support, express or reasonably implied, from the *Charter*, then the Court is without power to clothe such an interpretation with constitutional status. It is not for the Court to substitute its own views on the merits of a given question for those of Parliament. The court must consider not what is, in its view, the best solution to the problems posed: its role is confined to deciding whether the solution enacted by Parliament offends the *Charter*. If it does, the provision must be struck down or declared inoperative, and Parliament may then enact such different provision as it may decide.[73]

The above passage reflects Justice McIntyre's general approach to Charter interpretation. The Court is not a vehicle for the creation or development of social policy. The proper initiator of social policy is Parliament, which has a specific mandate for that purpose from the Canadian electorate. In the scheme of Canadian government the separation of legislative and judicial powers is imperative: "It is not for the Court to substitute its own views on the merits of a given question for those of Parliament," as McIntyre says. On incendiary contemporary issues such as abortion, judges may be tempted to substitute their own social policy preferences for those of Parliament, but if they do, they are not exercising the self-restraint so essential to their office.

Both Madam Justice Wilson and Chief Justice Dickson infer that under section 7 of the Charter, a pregnant woman has the right to have an abortion.[74] In Dickson's words, the criteria set out in section 251 for obtaining a therapeutic abortion are unrelated to a woman's priorities and aspirations and interfere with the security of her person.[75] This reasoning does not at all commend itself to Justice McIntyre: "All laws ... have the potential," he observes, "for interference with individual priorities and aspirations. In fact, the very purpose of most legislation is to cause such interference. It is only when such legislation goes beyond interfering with priorities and aspirations, and abridges rights, that courts may intervene."[76] He denies outright that "the language of section 7 of the Charter or any other section" confers on women the constitutional right to an abortion.[77] While there is greater specificity in the language of other Charter sections dealing with such controversial matters as mobility rights, language rights, and minority rights, on the question of abortion there is only silence.[78] McIntyre could find no expressed right to abortion in the Charter and considered that the Court should not attempt to pour oil into an empty vessel.

McIntyre quotes an answer to a question put by David Crombie, M.P., to then Minister of Justice Jean Chrétien, as to why drafters of the Charter had preferred the term "fundamental justice" in section 7 to the more American-style "due process of law":

> If you write down the words, "due process of law" here, the advice I am receiving is the court could go behind our [i.e., Parliament's] decision and say that their decision on abortion was not the right one, their decision on capital punishment was not the right one, and it is a danger according to legal advice I am receiving, that it will very much limit the scope of the power of legislation by the Parliament and we do not want that; and it is why we do not want the words "due process of law." These are the two main examples that we should keep in mind.[79]

What the justice minister was talking about here was the question of ambit. Cognizant of the vast range of matters that American courts have recognized as falling within the purview of "procedural" and "substantive" due process,[80] Canadian legislative draftsmen made a deliberate policy choice to use the term "fundamental justice" rather than "due process of law" to qualify the section 7 rights to "life, liberty and security of the person." They considered that the scope of terms like "security of the person" would be narrowed so as not to compass abortion or capital punishment, for example. According to the intentions of the drafters of the Charter, these matters were to be determined through legislative policy in Parliament. As the sequel shows, the judges in the second *Morgentaler* case were not deferential to the legislative intent expressed by Chrétien and did not feel bound by his narrower interpretation of section 7. They took a much broader view of its ambit than the draftsmen had.

I am well aware [McIntyre continues] that there will be disagreement about what was ordained by the *Charter* and, of course, a measure of interpretation of the *Charter* will be required in order to give substance and reality to its provisions. But the courts must not, in the guise of interpretation, postulate rights and freedoms which do not have a firm and reasonably identifiable base in the *Charter*.[81]

Existing law did not, in fact, confer any general right to have or to procure an abortion. It was primarily concerned with protecting the interests of the unborn child, and lifted the criminal sanctions that would otherwise apply only to protect the life or health of the mother.[82] Referring to the great sweep of the due process clause earlier in the century, McIntyre approvingly cites Holmes's caveat about reading constitutional prohibitions too broadly: "Courts should be careful not to extend such prohibitions beyond their obvious meaning by reading into them conceptions of public policy that the particular Court may happen to entertain."[83]

In relation to the problem of access to hospitals that was so emphasized by the majority opinion, McIntyre is utterly unconvinced: "No woman testified that she personally had applied for an abortion anywhere in Canada and had been refused, and no physician testified to his participation in such an application."[84] In fact, the whole focus of the original trial was on the prosecution of several doctors for violating section 251, not on any female person who had been denied an abortion.

Before the first *Morgentaler* decision was handed down in 1975, the writer of a historical survey on abortion in a university law review wrote rather pessimistically of the impending Supreme Court decision: "At this time their decision has not been handed down. One might hope for a dissenting judgment."[85] In the first Morgentaler decision in 1975 there were three dissenters in favour of Dr. Morgentaler and in 1988 there were only two against him. The majority of the Court had discovered in the Charter of Rights the means to invalidate a law that the Court had found legally unobjectionable little more than a decade earlier. McIntyre still can find no justification in the terms of the Charter or other constitutional provision to support women's right to abortion; he agrees with the result of the 1975 decision.

THE *ANDREWS* CASE: EQUALITY RIGHTS

According to Chief Justice Lamer, McIntyre's decision in the *Andrews* case[86] was a major contribution to defining equality rights under the

Charter. Professor Hogg says of *Andrews*: "The principal judgment was written by McIntyre, J, with whom all the other judges agreed as to the interpretation of section 15 and its relationship with section 1."[87] Andrews had initiated proceedings for a declaration that section 42 of the Barristers and Solicitors Act,[88] which made Canadian citizenship a requirement for admission to the practice of law, contravened section 15 (the "equality rights" section) of the Canadian Charter of Rights and Freedoms. A citizen of the U.K., Andrews had taken his law degree at Oxford and satisfied all the requirements for admission to the bar in British Columbia except that of citizenship.

While non-Canadian citizenship is not among the enumerated grounds for discrimination in section 15(1), the qualifying words "in particular" signify that the list is not exhaustive.[89] Andrews had brought himself under section 15(1) by successfully arguing that in requiring "citizenship" as a prerequisite, the Barristers and Solicitors Act had imposed a disadvantage on him that violated section 15.[90] While "citizenship" was not expressly enumerated as a ground it was an analogous ground, and the denial of entry into the legal profession because of non-citizenship was invidious discrimination pursuant to section 15(1).

The two alternative approaches to equality rights not adopted by the Court in *Andrews* were the interpretation of "discrimination," by McLachlin, JA, who spoke for a unanimous British Columbia Court of Appeal, and that of Professor Peter Hogg. According to Madam Justice McLachlin:

[T]he question to be answered under section 15 should be whether the impugned distinction is reasonable or fair, having regard to the purposes and aims and its effect on persons adversely affected. I include the word "fair" as well as "reasonable" to emphasize that the test is not one of pure rationality but one connoting the treatment of persons in ways which are not unduly prejudicial to them. The test must be objective, and the discrimination must be proved on a balance of probabilities: *R. v. Oakes*, ... (applying this test to section 1.) *The ultimate question is whether a fair-minded person, weighing the purposes of legislation against its effects on the individuals adversely affected, and giving due weight to the right of the Legislature to pass laws for the good of all, would conclude that the legislative means adopted are unreasonable or unfair.*[91]

According to McLachlin, it was not *any* legislative distinction that would violate the "non-discrimination" standard in section 15(1) but only those that were "unreasonable or unfair." The test contraposed by Hogg was that *any* legislative distinction should be treated as discrimination in violation of section 15(1).[92]

According to Justice McIntyre, both approaches ignore the proper balance between section 15(1) and section 1. The employment of the McLachlin approach assigns a very limited role to the "reasonable limits" justification in section 1 of the Charter: "She assigns a very minor role to section 1 which would, it appears, be limited to allowing in times of emergency, war or other crises the passage of discriminatory legislation which would normally be impermissible."[93] With the focus on what was "unreasonable or unfair" in the legislative distinctions, the court would be relegating section 1 to a position of relative insignificance. Hogg's approach entailed that any legislative distinction violated section 15(1), thus shifting the analytical task in all cases to section 1. There could hardly be a starker contrast with McLachlin's perspective, but his approach minimizes the importance of section 15(1).

McIntyre adopts a "middle ground" between the two rival positions.[94] His approach emphasizes, in agreement with the text of section 15(1), what is described as the "enumerated or analogous grounds" test.[95] To paraphrase Hugessen, JA, who was quoted approvingly by McIntyre in his judgment,[96] one must not simply ask whether there is a legislative distinction, or whether the impugned category is "unreasonable or unfair," but whether there is discrimination in the pejorative sense of the word, and whether the legislative category is enumerated or analogous to those enumerated.[97]

According to McIntyre's approach,

The analysis of discrimination in this approach must take place within the context of the enumerated grounds and those analogous to them. The words "without discrimination" require more than a mere finding of distinction between the treatment of groups or individuals. Those words are a form of qualifier built into section 15 itself and limit those distinctions which are forbidden in the section to those which involve prejudice or disadvantage.[98]

Using this approach he found Andrews to be a victim of invidious discrimination. As contrasted with the two competing positions, McIntyre's middle way has the merit of adhering more faithfully to the written text of section 15, and in subsequent cases[99] his position, with rare exception, has remained the Supreme Court's position on "Equality."

Under McIntyre's approach the question of whether discrimination is justified is examined under section 1. Here he departed from a majority of the Court, who agreed with McLachlin, that citizenship was unnecessary as a prerequisite for admission to the bar because it did not ensure familiarity with Canadian institutions and customs, which was the rationale for its use. In McIntyre's words, "I would agree with her that the desired results would not be ensured by the citizenship requirement but I would observe at the same time, that no law will ever ensure anything. To abolish the requirement of citizenship on the basis that it would fail to ensure the attainment of objectives would, in my view, be akin to abolishing the law against theft, for it has certainly not ensured the elimination of that crime."[100] In upholding the citizenship requirement under section 1, McIntyre was joined by Lamer. It is somewhat ironic that the classic Supreme Court formulation on "equality rights" was made in a dissent.

R. V. VAILLANCOURT: CONSTRUCTIVE MURDER

In *R. v. Vaillancourt*[101] the Supreme Court was called upon to consider the validity under the Charter of "constructive murder," pursuant to section 213(d) of the Criminal Code.[102] The appellant had been convicted of second-degree murder. He and his accomplice had been attempting to commit armed robbery in a pool hall. The appellant, armed with a knife, had not known that his accomplice possessed a loaded gun. He had remained near the front of the hall while his accomplice went to the back. A struggle occurred and the gun was fired, killing a client in the pool hall. The accomplice fled and was never found. Vaillancourt's evidence was that in a previous armed robbery his own gun had discharged accidentally and since he did not want that to happen again, he had insisted on his accomplice unloading his gun. Before the robbery, Vaillancourt had actually removed the three remaining bullets and placed them in his glove, which the police retrieved at the scene. The appellant testified that at the time of the robbery he was certain his accomplice's gun was unloaded. His counsel argued that there must be subjective *mens rea* for the commission of a crime of such gravity and that he lacked the requisite mental state to commit murder.

The Court majority overruled the judgment of the Quebec Court of Appeal[103] dismissing the accused's appeal from his conviction on second-degree murder. They found that section 213(d) was in conflict with both section 7 of the Charter, which required that liberty not be denied except in accordance with "fundamental justice," and section 11(d), guaranteeing the presumption of innocence. In this case McIntyre was the lone dissenter.

Section 213 sets out instances where "culpable homicide" constituting murder is committed when it occurs during the commission of other specified crimes, "whether or not the person means to cause death to any human being and whether or not he knows that death is likely to be caused to any human being." With particular relevance to this case the section stipulates:

213(d) he uses a weapon or has it upon his person
   (i) during or at the time he commits or attempts to commit the offence, or
   (ii) during or at the time of his flight after committing or attempting to commit the offence, and the death ensues as a consequence.

Where homicide is incidental to the commission of another crime, armed robbery in this case, and is carried out by one of two persons who have formed a "common intention" to commit the crime (section 21(2) of the Criminal Code), both perpetrators are party to the offence whether or not they could foresee the act or its consequences. The question that arises here is whether or not this criminal had the requisite mental state to commit murder when he had taken precautions to ensure that his partner did not have the means to kill and believed his partner incapable of performing such an act. The answer of the Court was that section 213 violated sections 7 and 11(d) of the Charter and was of no force and effect. Vaillancourt must have a new trial. In the words of Lamer, J. (as he then was):

Section 213 will catch an accused who performs one of the acts in paragraphs (a) to (d) and thereby causes a death, but who otherwise would have been acquitted of murder because he did not foresee and could not reasonably have foreseen that death would be likely to result. For that reason, section 213 *prima facie* violates section 7 and 11(d). It is thus not necessary to decide whether objective foreseeability is sufficient for murder as section 213 does not even meet that standard.[104]

Section 213, moreover, cannot be saved by the "reasonable limit" prescription of section 1 of the Charter. Its object was manifestly to deter the use or carrying of a weapon in the commission of certain offences because of the increased risk of death thereby occasioned, but Parliament could simply punish, independently, the use or carrying of such weapons: "It is not necessary to convict of murder persons who did not intend or foresee the death and who could not even have foreseen the death in order to deter others from using or carrying weapons."[105] Justice Lamer also considered that a manslaughter conviction would be a sufficient deterrent to the use or carriage of weapons in these circumstances. The majority, accordingly, abolished the crime of "felony murder," which had existed under the common law and in criminal statutes for centuries.

Mr. Justice McIntyre considered that the majority were too preoccupied with semantics surrounding the word "murder" in section 213:

> The principal complaint in this case is not that the accused should not have been convicted of a serious crime deserving of severe punishment, but simply that Parliament should not have chosen to call that crime "murder." No objection could be taken if Parliament classified the offence as manslaughter or a killing during the commission of an offence, or in some other manner. As I have observed before (see *R. v. Ancio*, [1984] 1 S.C.R. 225, at page 251), while it may be illogical to characterize an unintentional killing as murder, no principle of fundamental justice is offended only because serious criminal conduct, involving the commission of a crime of violence resulting in the killing of a human being, is classified as murder and not in some other manner.[106]

McIntyre also referred to the fact that in Canada the crime of murder had not incurred the death penalty since 1976. He quoted a standard text by Mewett and Manning as follows:

> The policy behind section 213 is to put the risk of killing a victim during the course of the commission of certain offences upon the offender to a higher degree than if it were merely classified as manslaughter. In any case, with the present distinction between murder punishable by death and murder punishable by life imprisonment now abolished, much of the criticism loses its force.[107]

Since "constructive murder" was no longer visited by the death penalty, in making the balance between the right of an accused to a fair trial and the protection of society, McIntyre would have emphasized the latter value more than his colleagues, while sacrificing nothing essential of procedural due process. This approach typified his reasoning in criminal cases.

DOLPHIN DELIVERY: THE SCOPE OF THE CHARTER

Among the important constitutional issues considered in Justice McIntyre's majority decision in RWDSU v. Dolphin Delivery[108] were two main questions: first, whether or not picketing during a lawful strike constituted freedom of expression under section 2(b) of the Charter; and second, the scope of the term "government" in section 32(1), defining the precise types of disputes that were included and excluded from Charter consideration. In other words, did the term "government" in section 32(1) signify that private disputes lacking a governmental element were not subject to the Charter?

In this tangled British Columbia labour dispute the appellant, a Retail, Wholesale and Department Store Union local, was the federally-certified bargaining agent for the locked-out employees of Purolator, an Ontario courier. Prior to the lockout, the respondent, Dolphin Delivery, made deliveries in the province for both Purolator and an associated company, Supercourier. The appellant union applied to the provincial Labour Relations Board for a declaration that Dolphin Delivery and Supercourier were allies of Purolator in their dispute with the appellant union. An affirmative finding would have rendered the picketing of Dolphin Delivery's business premises lawful and empowered its employees not to cross the picket line according to authorization in the collective agreement to that effect. However, since the appellant was a federally-certified union, the provincial Labour Relations Board refused to hear the application, arguing that it lacked jurisdiction. Since the Canadian Labour Code was silent on the issue of the appellant's proposed secondary picketing of a third party to the dispute, the issue fell to a decision at common law. No picketing had yet taken place because Dolphin Delivery obtained a *quia timet* injunction against picketing that was upheld on appeal. The central issue in the dispute was whether the proposed secondary picketing was protected as freedom of expression under section 2(b) of the Charter, and not subject to an injunction to restrain it.

The appeal against Sheppard, LJSC,[109] the Chambers judge, and the Court of Appeal,[110] which upheld his injunction, was then taken to the Supreme Court of Canada. At issue was whether or not the common law principles applied by the Chambers judge in granting the injunction had infringed freedom of expression under section 2(b) of the *Charter*. A finding of infringement would have left the appellants free to engage in secondary picketing against Dolphin Delivery, which Justice McIntyre found to have been correctly identified as a third party to the dispute. The lower court had also found that picketing would have been "tortious" in that its purpose was not only to publicize that a strike was in progress but to induce a breach of contract by Dolphin employees that would harm their company. It was assumed (although no picketing took place), that the demonstration would be peaceful but trade union members and customers who refused to cross the picket line would disrupt the respondent's business.

Justice McIntyre defined the issues as follows:

1. Does the injunction complained of in this case restrict the freedom of expression secured under section 2(b) of the *Canadian Charter of Rights and Freedoms*?
2. Does the *Charter* apply to the common law?
3. Does the *Charter* apply in private litigation?
4. If it is found that the injunction does restrict freedom of information, is the limit imposed by the injunction a reasonable limit in accordance with section 1 of the *Charter*?

It would be appropriate to discuss these four issues in sequence.

First, as he would in *Irwin Toy*,[111] McIntyre makes a strong case for freedom of expression, citing John Milton and John Stuart Mill,[112] Mr. Justice Holmes's dissenting opinion in *Abrams v. United States*,[113] and Canadian authorities such as *Boucher v. The King*,[114] *Switzman v. Elbling*,[115] and *Reference re Alberta Statutes* in support of this right.[116] Both theory and precedent sought to advance freedom of expression as an aspect of parliamentary democracy within the limitations of the implied bill of rights. With certain caveats McIntyre comes down firmly on the side of picketing as a protected form of expression under section 2(b) of the *Charter*:

That freedom, of course, would not extend to protect threats of violence or acts of violence. It would not protect destruction of property, or assaults or other clearly unlawful conduct. We need not, however, be concerned with such matters here because the picketing would have been peaceful. I am therefore of the view that the picketing sought to be restrained would have involved the exercise of the right of freedom of expression.[117]

Having found that peaceful picketing is protected under section 2(b), McIntyre inquires whether an injunction based on the common law tort of inducing a breach of contract (since the other possibly relevant tort of conspiracy to injure had been abolished by Statute in British Columbia), could be sustained as a "reasonable limit" under section 1, thereby upholding the injunction despite the resultant curtailment of freedom of expression.[118]

Observing that the social costs of labour disruptions are great and tolerable only if they further the collective bargaining process, McIntyre adds that some restraint is necessary so that the conflict "will not escalate beyond the actual parties,"[119] and in order to prevent harm to others. He concludes that the injunction is a "reasonable limit" on section 2(b) and can stand.[120]

In answer to the second question, McIntyre invokes the French text of section 52(1),[121] which provides that the Constitution of Canada is the supreme law of the land. He asserts that the translation of the phrase "any law that is inconsistent" as "*de tout autre regle de droit,*" clarifies that the Charter does apply to the common law. For the third question, concerning whether the Charter applies to private litigation, McIntyre finds that the purpose of the Charter is "to restrain government action and to protect the individual," and unless some governmental action was involved there was no intention to apply it to private litigation.[122] The text of section 32(1) of the Charter extends its application to legislatures and governments, the actors to be restrained in protecting individual rights,[123] but not to courts. To regard a court order as an element of government intervention within the scope of section 32(1) would render the Charter applicable "to virtually all private litigation."[124] An undisciplined interpretation of that section would run counter to the guiding purpose of the Charter, which is to protect individuals from arbitrary executive and legislative action rather than from the courts, which one American commentator called "the least dangerous branch" of government.

The *Dolphin Delivery* dispute is a purely private one, with no element of government involvement, and hence is beyond the scope of the Charter:

> In the case at bar ... we have no offending statute. We have a rule of the common law which renders secondary picketing tortious and subject to injunctive restraint, on the basis that it induces a breach of contract. While, as we have found, the *Charter* applies to the common law, we do not have

in this litigation between purely private parties any exercise of or reliance upon governmental action which would invoke the *Charter*. It follows that the appeal must fail.[125]

There has been considerable academic criticism of McIntyre's judgment on the basis that he narrows unduly the application of the Charter; even where there is no governmental involvement, individual rights might still be adversely affected by private action in ways the Charter would address. Yet McIntyre's rationale for limiting Charter rights to government action, based on the text of section 32(1) and the aim of the Charter, seems proper in law. However, governmental *in*action in the face of an offensive curtailment of rights by private means could connote government approbation, and since governments can enact countervailing legislation to remedy abuses, inaction could reasonably trigger the application of the Charter. In view of the academic criticism, and subsequent Supreme Court cases such as *R. v. Rahey*[126] and *British Columbia Employees Union v. AGBC*[127] (see *infra*) which applied the Charter to certain court actions without expressly repudiating *Dolphin Delivery*, it seems that there is a growing judicial inclination to apply the Charter to "courts" as well as "governments," and that McIntyre's position may not stand.

THE RULE OF LAW AND LABOUR STRIFE IN THE BRITISH COLUMBIA COURTS

In *British Columbia Government Employees' Union v. AGBC*[128] the appellant union picketed all the law courts in the province in the course of a legal strike, hoping to reduce court activity to matters of urgency. Persons crossing the picket line were considered to have honoured it if they first procured a pass from the strike committee. Members of the Law Union urged the public to respect the picket line and to encourage lawyers not to cross it except when they possessed a picket pass.[129] Chief Justice McEachern was asked by a member of the Law Union to close the courts and adjourn all civil and criminal procedures "other than for clear emergency situations as may be agreed upon with the B.C.G.E.U. and Operation Solidarity."[130] Instead, he declared that he had a constitutional duty to keep the courts open and issued an *ex parte* injunction on his own motion to that effect.[131] Pursuant to the terms of the final paragraph of the order, the union moved to have his injunction set aside. Their application was supported by the Law Union and opposed by the attorney general of British Columbia.

In issuing the *ex parte* injunction Chief Justice McEachern declared: "The question arises whether it is proper or permissible for anyone, individually or collectively, deliberately or accidentally, or directly or indirectly to interfere with the business of the Courts of justice or to interfere with or impede the absolute right of access all citizens have to the court of justice."[132] He answered this question with an emphatic negative, referring to the thousands of cases in progress every day in provincial courts. Those in custody had a right to apply for bail, and those awaiting trial had a right to have their guilt or innocence determined expeditiously. It was not a question of the dignity of the judges but of the preservation of due process and the need for unrestricted public access to the courts. "The rule of law has not been suspended in this province," he added.[133] The injunction was upheld in a unanimous judgment of the B.C. Court of Appeal, with Chief Justice Nemetz defining the issue as, "whether in a democratic society any person or bodies of persons can restrict the rights of its citizens to enjoy the benefits of the rule of law under the protection of an independent judiciary."[134] Nemetz emphasized that it was not the withdrawal of services by members of the court house staff that gave rise to contempt but rather the picketing activity. The injunction was directed to that form of protest, while the strike itself was unquestionably a perfectly legal one.[135]

In the ultimate appeal, Chief Justice Dickson trenchantly observed, "[I]t would be inconceivable that Parliament and the provinces should describe in such detail the rights and freedoms guaranteed by the *Charter* and should not first protect that which alone makes it in fact possible to benefit from such guarantees, that is, access to a court."[136] It is the hallowed principle of the rule of law that protects access to the courts: "There cannot be a rule of law without access, otherwise the rule of law is replaced by a rule of men and women who decide who shall and who shall not have access to justice."[137]

Upholding the right of the provincial superior court judge to forbid picketing where such activity impeded access to a court house, Dickson, speaking for four colleagues, considered certain Charter arguments advanced by the appellant union. Insofar as the union members' right to liberty under section 7 was limited by the injunction it "constituted a minimal interference with the procedural rights of those who had set out on a deliberate course of action which could only result in a massive disruption of the activities of the courts and consequent interference with the legal and constitutional rights of all citizens of

British Columbia."[138] There was no violation of "fundamental justice," so section 7 need not be considered further. The union's claims under subsections of section 2(d) also failed. And while the injunction's restraint of the right to picket did involve a denial of freedom of expression under section 2(b), a balance had to be sought here between individual values and public and societal values under section 1. In this conflict of values, the societal value of unimpeded access to the courts outweighed the individual value of freedom of expression.[139] The order was therefore justified under section 1.

In a short concurring judgment, Justice McIntyre saw no reason to invoke the "reasonable limits" provision in section 1, since he found no Charter right of the union to be violated. Like the judge who had originally held in *Dolphin Delivery* that picketing during a strike was a protected form of "freedom of expression," he found no parallel between the facts in that case and those in the present dispute. McIntyre held that the conduct here enjoined was clearly unlawful and an infringement of the Charter rights of those whose access to the courts were impeded. *Dolphin Delivery* was altogether different, since the illegality there related only to interference with a contractual right, a tort, the justification against which a "reasonable limit" under section 1 would have to be weighted.[140] This is not a case for balancing, as the other opinion maintains; the question here is more basic: Does any person or group have a Charter right to engage deliberately in conduct calculated to abridge the Charter rights of others? In denying this right, McIntyre emphasizes that no resort to section 1 is necessary: the section need only be invoked when a Charter right is infringed.

CONSUMER PROTECTION AND FREEDOM OF SPEECH

In *Irwin Toy Ltd. v. A.-G. Quebec*,[141] the constitutional validity of sections 248 and 249 of Quebec's Consumer Protection Act[142] was challenged in the Supreme Court by a manufacturer of children's toys. These sections forbade advertisers to direct advertising, regardless of the medium used, at persons under 13 years of age. The legislation assumed that persons in this age group lacked the maturity and judgment to discriminate between truth and falsity in advertising, and that it was not in the public interest to have a vulnerable and suggestible target group exposed to advertising campaigns.

In the majority judgment, Chief Justice Dickson, Lamer, and Wilson agreed that the challenged statutory provisions infringed section 2(b) of the Charter and section 3 of the Quebec Charter insofar as they violated guarantees of freedom of expression. However, they went on to uphold the sections as "reasonable limits" on speech under section 1, and under its Quebec analogue, section 9.1. The majority stated:

> In sum, the evidence sustains the reasonableness of the legislature's conclusion that a ban on commercial advertising directed to children was the minimal impairment of free expression consistent with the pressing and substantial goal of protecting children against manipulation through such advertising. While evidence exists that other less intrusive options reflecting more modest objectives were available to the government, there is evidence establishing the necessity of a ban to meet the objectives the government had reasonably set. This Court will not, in the name of minimal impairment, take a restrictive approach to social science evidence and require legislatures to choose the least ambitious means to protect vulnerable groups.[143]

> Nor were the deleterious effects of the ban on advertising of such magnitude as to outweigh the government's pressing and substantial objective of protecting children against commercial manipulation.[144]

In their joint dissent McIntyre and Beetz emphasized the overriding importance of free speech in a democratic society. McIntyre denies that a case has been made that the welfare of children is at risk because of advertising directed at them. Nor was he impressed with evidence that small children could not distinguish fact from fiction in advertising: "This is hardly surprising: many adults have the same problem. Children, however, do not remain children. They grow up and, while advertising directed at children may well be a source of irritation to parents, no case has been shown here that children suffer harm."[145]

At the conclusion of their dissenting judgment, McIntyre and Beetz made a ringing affirmation of freedom of speech:

> The argument that freedom of speech was dangerous was used to oppose and restrict public education in earlier times. The education of women was greatly retarded on the basis that wider knowledge would only make them dissatisfied with their role in society. I do not suggest that the limitations imposed by sections 248 and 249 are so earth-shaking or that if sustained they will cause irremediable damage. I do say, however, that these limitations represent a small abandonment of a principle of vital importance in a free and democratic society and, therefore, even if it could be shown that some child or children have been adversely affected by advertising of the kind

prohibited, I would still be of the opinion that the restriction should not be sustained. Our concern should be to recognize that in this century, we have seen whole societies utterly corrupted by the suppression of free expression. We should not lightly take a step in that direction, even a small one.[146]

Their dissent takes on added importance when it is recognized that the impugned sections regulate commercial expression, while the central core of section 2(b) relates to political expression.

QUASI-CONSTITUTIONAL DECISIONS

MILITARY JUSTICE AND THE JURISDICTION OF THE CIVIL COURTS

In *MacKay v. The Queen*,[147] McIntyre's concurring judgment upheld section 120 of the National Defence Act.[148] This section provided for the trial of civil offences, including offences under the Criminal Code or any other Act of Parliament, by service tribunals, and McIntyre's judgment was favourably commented upon by Professor Peter Hogg.[149] The appeal was not an attack on the court-martial procedure, which was perfectly valid in a proper military setting, but an assertion by the appellant, Private R.C. MacKay, that the facts of his case required that he be tried in civil court.

MacKay had been convicted by a Standing Court Martial of selling drugs to military personnel on a military base and sentenced to 60 days detention. After his appeal to the Court Martial Appeal Court left his sentence substantially intact, he appealed to the civil courts, arguing that his trial by court martial instead of by a civil judge meant he was being denied the right to equality before the law as set out in section 1(b) of the Canadian Bill of Rights. At issue was whether the accused was suffering inequality before the law because, unlike other Canadians who were not members of the forces, he was charged in a military rather than in a civil court. Insofar as the proceedings in this case were not instituted and conducted by the Attorney General of Canada or of a province, were they *ultra vires* the Parliament of Canada?

Ritchie, with four other judges,[150] held that since the law had been "enacted for the purpose of achieving a valid federal objective,"[151] the distinction the appellant was making between two kinds of justice, one for the military and the other for civilians, was untenable. This opinion was a conclusory rather than a reasoned one because it made no attempt to explain what was meant by the phrase "valid federal objective" or to tie that phrase to the objective of the Act.[152] Laskin, joined by Estey, dissented, holding that when a person was charged with an offence under the ordinary criminal law, he or she was entitled to be tried before a court of justice "separate from the prosecution and free from any suspicion of or dependency on others."[153] A military tribunal did not fit into this category. The appellant had been denied equality before the law under section 1(b) and also the right to be tried before an independent and impartial tribunal under section 2(f). "The result," the Chief Justice said, "is that section 120 of the *National Defence Act* must be held to be inoperative in so far as it subjects members of the armed forces to a different, and, indeed more onerous liability for a breach of the ordinary law as applicable to other persons in Canada who are also governed by that law."[154]

It was McIntyre's judgment, however, that Hogg found "a model of judicial reasoning under an equality guarantee."[155] McIntyre, in contrast with the majority concurring opinion, enunciated a sophisticated test that sharply defined the meaning of "valid federal objective," and also erected a criterion for distinguishing between equality and inequality.

"Equality ... must not be synonymous with mere universality of application,"[156] McIntyre declared. In relation to the meaning of "valid federal objective," the primary consideration was to inquire into the rationale for any inequality created by statute: "The question which must be resolved in each case is whether such inequality as may be created by legislation affecting a special class (the military) is arbitrary, capricious or unnecessary, or whether it is rationally based and acceptable as a necessary variation from the general principle of universal application of law to meet special conditions and to attain a necessary and desirable social objective."[157] Any inequality, he emphasizes, must have been "created rationally in the sense that it is not arbitrary or capricious and not based upon any ulterior motive or motives offensive to the provisions of the *Canadian Bill of Rights*."[158]

Applying the above criterion, McIntyre upheld the validity and appropriateness of the charge of trafficking under the Narcotic Control Act (as administered by a service tribunal) levelled against MacKay. The needs of the military were not limited to punishing service offences such as desertion, cowardice in the face of the enemy, or drunkenness on duty, but covered as well general laws, material elements of which were service-related. In this case the offence was not one in which the military element was purely incidental, such as arson committed by a soldier on leave in a civilian area. It was the sale of drugs by a soldier to other servicemen on a military base: the transaction related integrally to the military. The technique of "reading down" a broad statutory provision in the interest of constitutional validity is also apparent here. In other words, were it not for the military elements in the fact situation — trafficking on a military base to servicemen — the defendant's argument that he should have been tried in civil rather than military court would have had more force.

MANDATORY RETIREMENT AND PROVINCIAL HUMAN RIGHTS

In the *Etobicoke* case,[159] McIntyre was called upon to decide whether an Ontario municipality's policy, set out in a collective agreement, properly required a deputy fire chief and a fire captain to retire at age 60. Section 4(1)(b) of the Ontario Human Rights Code[160] prohibited discrimination on the basis of age (between 40 and 65 years), unless a younger age was a *bona fide* occupational qualification and requirement for the position.

Professor Bruce Dunlop, who acted as a board of inquiry, decided that the compulsory retirement age amounted to a refusal to employ the two firemen, contrary to section 4(1)(b) of the Code. He rejected the employer's defence that compulsory retirement at age 60 constituted a *bona fide* occupational requirement within section 4(b) of the Code.[161] He ordered the reinstatement of the appellants, provided that they continue to possess the physical and mental capacities required for their work, along with compensation for loss of earnings from the date of compulsory retirement to the date of reinstatement.[162] An appeal was allowed by the Divisional Court (with Cory, J., dissenting), which accepted the *bona fide* occupational test propounded by Professor R.S. McKay in another case, the appeal being upheld by the Ontario Court of Appeal.[163] When Professor Dunlop reheard the case to decide the amount of compensation to be paid by the employer, the latter argued that Dunlop had applied the wrong test, while Dunlop maintained that his test and McKay's test were essentially the same.[164]

Justice McIntyre agreed that there was no significant difference in the tests applied by Dunlop and McKay, and saw no serious objection to their characterization of the subjective element of the test — that defining a *bona fide* occupational requirement. McIntyre proceeded to propound the test:

To be a *bona fide* occupational qualification and requirement a limitation, such as a mandatory retirement at a fixed age, must be imposed honestly, in good faith, and in the sincerely held belief that such limitation is imposed in the interests of the adequate performance of the work involved with all reasonable dispatch, safety and economy, and not for ulterior or extraneous reasons aimed at objectives which could defeat the purpose of the *Code*. In addition it must be related in an objective sense to the performance of the employment concerned, in that it is reasonably necessary to assure the efficient and economical performance of the job without endangering the employee, his fellow employees, and the general public.[165]

As far as the first or subjective branch of the test was concerned, there was no evidence that the employer's motives "were other than honest and in good faith in the sense described."[166] However, according to McIntyre, the objective test to be satisfied required more adequate evidence than the opinions advanced:

I am by no means entirely certain what may be characterized as "scientific evidence." I am far from saying that in all cases some "scientific evidence" will be necessary. It seems to me, however, that in cases such as this, statistical and medical evidence based upon observation and research on the question of aging, if not in all cases absolutely necessary, will certainly be more persuasive than the testimony of persons, albeit with great experience in fire-fighting, to the effect that fire-fighting is a "young man's game." My review of the evidence leads me to agree with the board of inquiry. While the evidence given and the views expressed were, I am sure, honestly advanced, they were, in my view, properly described as "impressionistic" and were of insufficient weight.[167]

An added contention by the respondent that the parties could change the retirement age and establish their own "*bona fide* occupational requirements in their collective agreement," was rejected. For reasons of public policy contracting out was impermissible and contracts to this effect were void as a matter of public policy.[168] Accordingly, McIntyre allowed the appeal with costs, and reinstated the order of the board of inquiry.

ADVERSE EFFECT DISCRIMINATION AND MINORITY RIGHTS

In this important case on adverse effect or "non-facial" discrimination, McIntyre delivered the opinion of the Supreme Court upholding the complaint of Theresa O'Malley (Vincent) against the respondent, a department store.[169] The appellant alleged discrimination on the basis of religious creed contrary to section 4(1)(g) of the Ontario Human Rights Code.[170]

The appellant was first employed by the respondent store in Quebec City in 1971. After moving to Kingston, Ontario, she worked full-time at that location in the ladies' wear department from 1975 to 1978. From the point of view of sales, the busiest time of the week was Thursday evening to Saturday evening. It was a condition of employment that full-time sales clerks would work on Friday evenings on a rotating basis, and on two Saturdays out of three. In October 1978, the complainant became a member of the Seventh Day Adventist Church, which holds, as a matter of faith, that the Sabbath, from sundown Friday to sundown Saturday, must be strictly observed. There was no question of the *bona fide* intention of O'Malley's conversion or of the store's employment policy.[171]

When O'Malley informed the store manager of her conversion and its consequences in terms of work on weekends, he advised her that she would be discharged if she could not work on Saturdays. Later that month she was offered part-time employment, and she accepted. In doing so she lost full-time employment status, however, and was rehired on a contingent basis only.

In due course, O'Malley's complaint came before the Ontario Human Rights Commission, the Board of Inquiry being conducted by Professor Edward J. Ratushny. He held that section 4(1)(g) of the Code demanded an interpretation prohibiting "not only employment conditions which are on their face discriminatory, but also those which, though innocuous in their terms, could result in discrimination against a particular employee or group of employees."[172] In dealing with the second point, Ratushny held "that the duty of the employer was to accommodate the position of the complainant unless 'undue hardship' would result."[173] He went on to say, however, that the department store had not acted unreasonably in the steps it had taken to accommodate the complainant after learning that the general condition of her employment was incompatible with her religious observance.[174]

Subsequent appeals by the appellant to the Ontario Divisional Court and the Court of Appeal were both dismissed. In the latter forum Lacoursière, JA, dismissed the appeal, holding that there could be no breach of the anti-discrimination provision in the Ontario

Human Rights Code unless the employer intended to discriminate on one of the prohibited grounds. There was clearly no such intention in the case at bar. Lacoursière concluded by saying: "For these reasons I agree with the majority of the Divisional Court that an intention to discriminate is an essential requirement for a contravention of section 4(1)(g) of the Code prior to the proclamation of the amendment."[175]

In the ultimate appeal to the Supreme Court, McIntyre, distinguished between a case of direct discrimination, where an offending provision is embedded in the very terms of the statute and must be struck down (citing *Etobicoke*), and indirect discrimination, where the law is not on its face repugnant but its effect on a person or persons may be, perhaps as it relates to the performance of a job, and a different approach is called for. The rule is not to be struck down as invalid or inoperable but its effect on the complainant must be considered and he or she must be accommodated, as far as possible, by the employer. This ordinarily requires some adjustment in working conditions so as to eliminate the non-facial religious discrimination. In such cases the Code must be applied flexibly to protect the rights of employees. A compromise is necessary between these rights, and the employer's to proceed with the lawful conduct of business. The Code was not intended to accord rights to one party at the direct expense of another. American courts have also approached this problem with a "duty to accommodate" on the part of the employer,[176] short of undue hardship.

In O'Malley, and pursuant to *Etobicoke*, the onus is on the plaintiff to establish adverse effect discrimination, here on the basis of creed. Once it is shown that the offending rule is rationally connected to the performance of a job, the employer must show that reasonable steps to accommodate the employee's working conditions have been taken, meaning those open to the employer without incurring undue hardship.[177]

Theresa O'Malley had been required by her employer to work part-time from October 1978 to July 1979. She voluntarily relinquished full-time employment after the latter date, and sought no compensation for the subsequent period. McIntyre allowed the appeal and directed the respondent to pay her, as compensation, the difference between her earnings as a part-time employee from October 1978 to July 1979 and the amount she would have earned full-time during that period.[178]

FREEDOM OF RELIGION IN THE WORKPLACE

The test developed by Justice McIntyre in 1982 in *Etobicoke* was applied three years later by him in *Re Bhinder and C.N.R. Co.*[179] Here he spoke for the court majority in finding that the appellant, K.S. Bhinder, a Sikh, could be dismissed by the respondent railway for refusing to wear a hard hat, which was required in his job classification. Bhinder was an electrician who worked in the Toronto coach yard where all employees were required to wear hard hats at work. Bhinder's religion forbade him to wear anything on his head except a turban. Bhinder was informed by letter in December 1978 that there were no exceptions to the hard hat rule and that unless he complied he would not be permitted to work. His dilemma was a real one. He was not prepared to work other than as an electrician, and there were no positions for electricians where the wearing of a hard hat was not required. Accordingly, his employment with the CNR was terminated on December 5, 1978.

When he applied to the Canadian Human Rights Commission, alleging discrimination on the basis of religion, the tribunal established by the Commission found that the CNR had engaged in a discriminatory practice contrary to the Canadian Human Rights Act,[180] and awarded Bhinder $14,500 for loss of salary and ordered his reinstatement. However, in the resultant appeal the Federal Court of Appeal set aside the tribunal's decision, referring the matter back to that forum on the basis that the rule requiring Bhinder to wear a hard hat was not a discriminatory practice within the meaning of the Act.[181] From that decision, Bhinder appealed to the Supreme Court of Canada.

At first instance, the Canadian Human Rights Commission held that when the railway adopted its hard hat rule it did so without discriminatory intent against Sikhs, and that in refusing to obey Bhinder was honestly following the dictates of his religion. While the rule applied to all employees, it had a discriminatory effect against Bhinder because of his religion. In his case, the hard hat rule was not a *bona fide* occupational requirement under section 14(a) of the Act and, accordingly, the CNR had a duty to accommodate Bhinder's position, short of undue hardship to the company, which had not been shown. It was conceded that without the hat Bhinder would face a greater likelihood of injury, but if he was willing to assume the small extra risk and there was no greater danger to others because of his decision, he should be excepted from the rule.[182] In allowing the railway's appeal, Heald, J, in the Federal Court of Appeal held that only intentional discrimination was forbidden by the Act and since the hard hat rule was applied to everybody, it was not discriminatory. Any different effect on Bhinder was unintentional and incidental.[183]

Referring to the tribunal's finding that a working condition (wearing the hard hat) was not a *bona fide* occupational requirement in Bhinder's case, McIntyre found that since the requirement was meant to apply to an occupation and not to an individual, it was not susceptible to individual exceptions.[184] In his words, "This must refer to a requirement for the occupation, not a requirement limited to an individual. It must apply to all members of the employee group concerned because it is a requirement of general application concerning the safety of employees. The employee must meet the requirement in order to hold the employment. It is, by its nature, not susceptible to individual application."[185]

Referring to the holding in *Etobicoke* that the rule under the Ontario Human Rights Code was non-discrimination, and discrimination the exception, McIntyre held this to be equally true of the Canadian Human Rights Act. The interpretative approach is to apply provisions prohibiting discrimination liberally and to construe exceptions narrowly, but where section 14(a)[186] applies in cases of *bona fide* occupational requirements, there is no discrimination: "To conclude then that an otherwise established *bona fide* occupational requirement could have no application to one employee, because of the special characteristics of that employee, is not to give section 14(a) a narrow interpretation; it is simply to ignore its plain language."[187] McIntyre disagreed with that part of the Federal Court of Appeal's judgment that said that the Act extended only to intentional discrimination; he found that it applied also to adverse effect discrimination. In a similar case in Britain, special legislation was passed to exempt Sikhs from wearing safety helmets while riding motorcycles.[188] Whether that should be done in Canada was a question for the legislature rather than the Court.

Dickson and Lamer both dissented, holding that section 14(a) should not be interpreted so widely as to defeat the purposes of the Act. Where a *prima facie* case of discrimination was shown, as here, the employer had a duty to reasonably accommodate the subject of the discrimination.[189]

The two foregoing cases on "adverse effect" or "non-facial" discrimination arrive at different results while acknowledging the duty to accommodate those subject to discrimination in the workplace. Because of the tenets of her religion, Mrs. O'Malley, was exempted from a Sunday-observance requirement that did not correspond with her faith, while Mr. Bhinder, a Sikh, was not exempted from wearing the safety helmet required in his job description. McIntyre based these different treatments on the clear wording in the different statutes which applied to each case. In the absence of a valid statutory impediment, it seems that the "duty to accommodate" would apply.

MCINTYRE'S METHODOLOGY

The foregoing cases all suggest that McIntyre has had a major influence on Canadian constitutional jurisprudence. His approach to constitutional decision making was marked by his respect for the separation of powers between the judiciary and the political branches of government, and buttressed by habitual self-restraint. Unless there was a clear conflict between a challenged law and an entrenched constitutional provision, his practice was to let the law stand. Constitutional constraints on government action should apply only when their existence could be clearly demonstrated. In the *Patriation* case,[190] where the rule on convention affirmed by the Court majority was not demonstrated to his satisfaction, he would have allowed Trudeau's amendment package to go forward to Westminster. On the other side of the ledger, when the federal government proposed fundamental changes in the structure of the Senate without provincial consent,[191] he agreed with a unanimous Court that Parliament could not enact this law unilaterally. In the latter case there was no question that reconstituting the Upper House without the consent of the provinces would be unconstitutional.

The same careful approach is exhibited in his dissent in the *Morgentaler* case,[192] where, as Professor F.L. Morton has observed, he questioned the very jurisdiction of the courts to decide the abortion issue: "The abortion issue, he noted, dealt with the respective rights of women and the unborn, none of whom were present in the case. The appellants were all doctors charged with conspiracy to violate the Criminal Code. None of the doctors could claim they had been denied a therapeutic abortion."[193] While expressing no personal opinion on the abortion issue, McIntyre could find no constitutional grounds for invalidating the impugned provision of the Criminal Code, which he would have let stand.

By delimiting the scope of "governmental action" in section 32(1) of the Charter in *Dolphin Delivery*,[194] he would have relegated many private legal actions beyond the range of Charter review. He held in this case that the term "government," applied to the executive and legislative arms but not to the courts. Some critics see a modification of this rule in more recent cases,[195] although *Dolphin Delivery* has never been expressly overruled.

March 1999 saw an important reconsideration of the test for "equality rights" advanced by McIntyre in the *Andrews* decision, in *Law v. Canada*.[196] Justice Iacobucci held for a unanimous Supreme Court that the ultimate focus of the test should be shifted to an emphasis on "human dignity." In *Law* the Court rejected an age discrimination claim by a 30-year old widow who alleged she was denied equality rights when she was refused a survivor's pension under the Canadian Pension Plan because of her young age. The Court declared that a claimant in an equality rights' case generally chooses the "comparator group" to be used as a standard for determining whether the differential treatment amounts to discrimination. They stated that a claim could be based on one ground or a confluence of grounds. Human dignity was described in part as meaning that "an individual or group feels self-respect and self-worth. It is concerned with physical and psychological integrity and empowerment. Human dignity is harmed by unfair treatment premised upon personal traits or circumstances which do not relate to individual needs, capacities or merits. It is enhanced by laws which are sensitive to the needs, capacities and merits of different individuals, taking into account the context underlying their differences." *Law* is essentially a development of *Andrews,* retaining the main characteristics of the latter's definition of equality rights while placing greater emphasis on the deprivation of human dignity that results in discriminatory treatment of an individual or group.

While "human dignity" is at the core of the revised test for equality rights, the unanimous judgment in *Law*, certainly a complex one, shows signs of the melding together contributions from a number of judges, past and present. "Human dignity" is now the hallmark, not only of equality rights, but of human rights legislation generally, and it remains to be seen how effectively such a broad concept, even with the elaboration supplied in these judgments, can be applied in practice.

Justice Iacobucci adds: "This is one of the rare cases contemplated in *Andrews supra*, in which differential treatment based on one or more of the enumerated or analogous grounds in section 15(1) is not discriminatory. It is important to identify such cases through a purposive analysis of section 15(1), in order to ensure that analysis under section 15(1) does not become mechanistic, but rather addresses the true social, political and legal context underlying each and every equality claim."[197]

NOTES

1. Now the "Constitution Act, 1867."
2. The *Globe and Mail* [Toronto], March 30, 1978, 7.
3. Letter and memorandum of Hon. Howard Ferguson, *The Toronto Globe*, Sept. 20, 1930, in R.M. Dawson, *Constitutional Issues in Canada, 1900-1931* (London: Oxford University Press, 1933), 28-34; and see, K.C. Wheare, *The Statute of Westminster and Dominion Status* (Oxford, London, 5th ed., 1953).
4. H.W.R. Wade "Amendment of the Constitution of Canada" (unpublished memorandum, Nov. 24, 1980), 8-9; see also, *The Kershaw Report*, first report from the Foreign Affairs Committee [Sir Anthony Kershaw, chairman] (Great Britain: House of Commons, 1980-81), 1xi, which makes a similar argument in favour of the provinces in the current dispute.
5. See the indirect reference to these provinces in *Re: Resolution to Amend the Constitution of Canada* [1981] 1 S.C.R. 765.
6. Freedman, C.J.M., Matas and Hall, JJ.A, for the federal government and O'Sullivan and Huband, JJ.A, for the provinces; see *Ref. re: Amendment of the Constitution of Canada (No. 1)*, (1981) 117 D.L.R. (3d), 1 (Man. C.A.).
7. Mifflin, C.J.N., Morgan and Gushue, JJ.A, for the provinces; *Ref. re: Amendment of the Constitution of Canada (No. 2)*, (1981) 118 D.L.R. (3d), 1 (Nfld. C.A.).
8. Crete, C.J.Q., Owen, Turgeon, and Belanger, JJ.A, for the federal government and Bisson, JA, for the provinces; *Ref. re: Amendment of the Constitution of Canada (No. 2)*, (1981) 120 D.L.R. (3d), 385 (Que. C.A.).
9. *Ref. re: Amendment of the Constitution* [1981] 1 S.C.R. 753.
10. Chief Justice Laskin and Justices Dickson, Beetz, Chouinard, Lamer, Estey, and McIntyre; Justices Martland and Ritchie dissented.
11. *Ref. re: Amendment of the Constitution* [1981] 1 S.C.R. 773.
12. The majority consisted of Justices Martland, Ritchie, Dickson, Beetz, Chouinard, and Lamer; Chief Justice Laskin and Justices Estey and McIntyre dissented.
13. *Re: Authority of Parliament in Relation to the Upper House*

[1980] 1 S.C.R. 54. Mr. Justice Goldie's statement was made to the writer in an interview in Vancouver in 1996.
14. *Ref. re: Amendment of the Constitution* [1981] 1 S.C.R. 808.
15. *Ibid.*, 815.
16. *Ibid.*, 830.
17. *Ibid.*, 835-36.
18. *Ibid.*
19. *Ibid.*, 840.
20. *Ibid.*, 846.
21. *Ibid.*, 847-48.
22. *Ibid.*, 880.
23. *Ibid.*, 881.
24. *Ibid.*, 882.
25. *Ibid.*, 883.
26. *Ibid.*, 883-84.
27. As set out *ibid.* at 899, the mentioned principle is as follows:

    The fourth general principle is that the Canadian Parliament will not request an amendment directly affecting federal-provincial relationships without prior consultation and agreement with the provinces. This principle did not emerge as early as others but since 1907, and particularly since 1930, has gained increasing recognition and acceptance. The nature and degree of provincial participation in the amending process, however, have not lent themselves to easy definition.

28. *Ibid.*, 900 (emphasis added).
29. *Ibid.*, 909.
30. *Ibid.*, 849.
31. *Ibid.*, 851.
32. *Ibid.*, 883-84.
33. *Ibid.*, 852.
34. *Ibid.*, 867.
35. *Ibid.*, 870.
36. *Ibid.*, 870-71.
37. See, e.g., B.L. Strayer, *The Patriation and Legitimacy of the Canadian Constitution* (Cronkite Memorial Lectures, College of Law, University of Saskatchewan, 1982).
38. A delegation of provincial opponents of the patriation package had gone to London to ask British parliamentarians not to enact the amendments, at least until broader provincial consent was obtained.
39. *Re: Authority of Parliament in Relation to the Upper House* [1980] 1 S.C.R. at 59.

40. *Ibid.*, 66-67.
41. *Ibid.*, 70.
42. *Ibid.*, 72.
43. *Ibid.*, 60 ff.
44. *Ibid.*, 77-78.
45. 1980 (Nfld.), c. 40.
46. [1984] 1 S.C.R. 297, 335.
47. *Ibid.*, 305.
48. *Ibid.*, 332.
49. *Ibid.*, 333.
50. *Ibid.*, 325.
51. *Ibid.*, 335.
52. *Ibid.*, 334; the texts cited are Castel, *Canadian Conflict of Laws*, vol. 2 (Toronto: Butterworths, 1980), 347; and, Dicey and Morris, *The Conflict of Laws*, vol. 2 (London: Stevens & Sons, 10th ed., 1980), 553.
53. [1988] 1 S.C.R. 30.
54. See the *Criminal Law Amendment Act, 1968-69*, S.C., 1968-69, 17-18 Eliz. II, c. 38, s. 18.
55. *Ibid.*
56. *Morgentaler v. The Queen* (1975) 53 D.W.R. (3d) 161 (S.C.C.).
57. *Ibid.*, 181.
58. *R. v. Morgentaler* [1988] 1 S.C.R. at 46.
59. [1985] 1 S.C.R. 295, 344.
60. In *Mills v. The Queen* [1986] 1 S.C.R. 863, cited by Dickson, C.J.C. [1988] 1 S.C.R. 30.
61. *R. v. Morgentaler* [1988] 1 S.C.R., 55.
62. *Ibid.*, 56-57.
63. *Ibid.*, 68-69.
64. *Ibid.*, 90.
65. *Ibid.*, 126.
66. *Ibid.*, 162.
67. *Ibid.*, 163 and 173.
68. *Ibid.*, 166.
69. *Ibid.*, 167.
70. *Ibid.*, 171.
71. *Ibid.*, 179.
72. *Ibid.*
73. *Ibid.*, 138.
74. *Ibid.*
75. *Ibid.*, 142.

76. *Ibid.*
77. *Ibid.*, 143.
78. *Ibid.*
79. *Ibid.*, 144.
80. *Ibid.*, 138.
81. *Ibid.*, 136.
82. *Ibid.*, 134.
83. *Ibid.*, 139.
84. *Ibid.*, 150.
85. J.P. Maksymiuk, "The Abortion Law: A Study of *R. v. Morgentaler*," in (1974-75) 39 *Sask. L.R.* 259 at 284.
86. *Law Society of British Columbia v. Andrews* [1989] 2 W.W.R. 289 (S.C.C.).
87. Peter W. Hogg, *Constitutional Law of Canada*, 4th student edn. (Toronto: Carswell, 1996), 907.
88. R.S.B.C. 1979, c. 26; s. 42(a) reads, "The benchers may call to the Bar of the Province and admit as a solicitor of the Supreme Court,
    a) a Canadian citizen with respect to whom they are satisfied that he ..."
89. *Re: Andrews and Law Society of B.C.* [1986] 27 D.L.R. (4th) 600, 610 (B.C.C.A.).
90. His action was dismissed at trial before Taylor, J., in the Supreme Court of British Columbia [1986] 1 W.W.R. 252, 66 B.C.L.R. 363, 22 D.L.R. (4th) 9, but the lower court judgment was reversed on appeal to the Court of Appeal [1986] 4 W.W.R. 242; 2 B.C.L.R. (2d) 305; 27 D.L.R. (4th) 600, in a judgment written by McLachlin, JA (as she then was).
91. *Re: Andrews and Law Society of B.C.* [1986] 27 D.L.R. (4th) 600, 609-10 (B.C.C.A.).
92. Peter W. Hogg, *Constitutional Law of Canada*, 2nd edn. (Toronto: Carswell, 1985), 799-801.
93. *Law Society of British Columbia v. Andrews* [1989] 2 W.W.R., 312.
94. Hogg, *Constitutional Law*, 4th student edn., 968.
95. *Ibid.*
96. *Law Society of British Columbia v. Andrews* [1989] 2 W.W.R., 312-13; see the excerpt cited by McIntyre from Hugessen, JA, in *Smith, Kline and French Laboratories v. Can. (A-G.)* [1987] 2 F.C. at 367-69.

97. *Law Society of British Columbia v. Andrews* [1989] 2 W.W.R., 313.
98. *Ibid.*
99. Hogg, *Constitutional Law*, 4th student ed., 968, and see the cases cited there in ftn. 77. But see the discussion of *Law v. Canada* (1999) 170 D.L.R. 4th, 49, *infra* at 145.
100. *Ibid.*, 320.
101. [1987] 2 S.C.R. 636.
102. R.S.C. 1970, c. C-34.
103. (1984), 31 C.C.C. (3D) 75.
104. [1987] 2 S.C.R. 659.
105. *Ibid.*, 660.
106. *Ibid.*, 663.
107. *Ibid.*, 664; see, A.W. Mewett and M. Manning, *Criminal Law*, 2nd edn. (Toronto: Butterworths, 1985), 544-45.
108. [1986] 2 S.C.R. 573.
109. [1983] B.C.W.L.D. 100, granting an interlocutory injunction.
110. [1984] 3 W.W.R. 481.
111. [1989] 1 S.C.R. 927.
112. [1986] 2 S.C.R. 583.
113. 250 U.S. 616 (1919), at 630.
114. [1951] S.C.R. 265 at 288.
115. [1957] S.C.R. 285 at 306.
116. [1938] S.C.R. 100 at 138.
117. [1986] 2 S.C.R. 588.
118. *Ibid.*, 588-90.
119. *Ibid.*, 591.
120. *Ibid.*, 592.
121. 52(1) La Constitution du Canada est la loi Suprême du Canada: elle rend inopérantes les dispositions incompatible *de toute autre regle de droit*. *Ibid.*, 593 (emphasis added).
122. *Ibid.*, 593.
123. *Ibid.*, 598-59.
124. *Ibid.*, 600.
125. *Ibid.*, 603-04.
126. *R. v. Rahey* [1987] 1 S.C.R. 588.
127. *British Columbia Government Employee's Union v.* A.G.B.C. [1988] 2 S.C.R. 214.
128. [1988] 2 S.C.R. 214.
129. *Ibid.*, 221.
130. *Ibid.*

131. *Ibid.*, 221-22.
132. *Ibid.*, 223; see *Ex parte injunction* [1983] 6 W.W.R. 640 (B.C.S.C.).
133. *Ibid.*, 224.
134. (1985) 20 D.L.R. (4th) 399 at 401, as quoted in *ibid.*, at 227.
135. *Ibid.*, 228.
136. *Ibid.*, 229.
137. *Ibid.*, 230.
138. *Ibid.*, 246.
139. *Ibid.*, 248.
140. [1988] 2 S.C.R., 251-52.
141. *Irwin Toy Ltd. v. Quebec (Attorney-General)* [1989] 1 S.C.R. 927.
142. R.S.Q., c. P-40.1 (previously S.Q. 1978, c. 6).
143. [1989] 1 S.C.R. 999.
144. *Ibid.*, 1000.
145. *Ibid.*, 1007.
146. *Ibid.*, 1008.
147. [1980] 2 S.C.R. 370.
148. R.S.C. 1970, c. N-4.
149. Hogg, *Constitutional Law of Canada*, 2d edn., at 793.
150. Martland, Pigeon, Beetz, and Chouinard.
151. [1980] 2 S.C.R. at 391.
152. Hogg, *Constitutional Law*, 2d edn., at 793.
153. [1980] 2 S.C.R. at 380.
154. *Ibid.*, 386.
155. Hogg, *Constitutional Law*, 2d edn., at 793.
156. [1980] 2 S.C.R. at 406.
157. *Ibid.*
158. *Ibid.*, 407.
159. *Ontario Human Rights Commission v. Etobicoke* (1982) 132 D.L.R. (3d) 14.
160. R.S.O. 1970, c. 318 (now R.S.O. 1980, c. 340).
161. *Ontario Human Rights Commission v. Etobicoke*, 16.
162. *Ibid.*
163. *Re: Ontario Human Rights Commission and City of North Bay* (1977) 81 D.L.R. (3d) 273 (Ontario Divisional Court) and 92 D.L.R. (3d) 544 (Ont. C.A.).
164. *Ontario Human Rights Commission v. Etobicoke*, 17.
165. *Ibid.*, 20.
166. *Ibid.*

167. *Ibid.*, 23.
168. *Ibid.*, 23-24.
169. *O'Malley v. Simpson Sears* [1985] 2 S.C.R. 536.
170. R.S.O. 1980, c. 340.
171. *O'Malley v. Simpson Sears* [1985] 2 S.C.R. 539-40.
172. *Ibid.*, 542-43.
173. *Ibid.*, 543.
174. *Ibid.*, 543.
175. *Ibid.*, 544-45.
176. *Ibid.*, 552-53; see *Reid v. Memphis Publishing Co.*, 468 F. 2d. 346 (6th Cir. 1972); and *Riley v. Bendix Corp.* 464 F. 2d.1113 (5th Cir. 1972), both cited by McIntyre.
177. *Ibid.*, 558.
178. *Ibid.*, 560.
179. (1986) 23 D.L.R. (4th) 481, 494.
180. 1976-77 (Can.), c. 33.
181. (1986) 23 D.L.R. (4th), 495.
182. *Ibid.*, 497.
183. *Ibid.*
184. *Ibid.*, 500.
185. *Ibid.*
186. The section mentioned reads as follows:
    14. It is not a discriminatory practice if:
    a) any refusal, exclusion, expulsion, suspension, limitation, specification or preference in relation to any employment is established by an employer to be based on a *bona fide* occupational requirement.
187. (1986) 23 D.L.R. (4th), 500.
188. *Ibid.*, 501-02.
189. *Ibid.*, 486.
190. *Ref. Re: Amendment of the Constitution* [1981] 1 S.C.R. 753.
191. *Re: Authority of Parliament in Relation to the Upper House* [1980] 1 S.C.R. 54.
192. *R. v. Morgentaler* [1988] 1 S.C.R. 30.
193. F.L. Morton, *Morgentaler v. Borowski, Abortion, The Charter and the Courts* (Toronto: McClelland & Stewart, 1992), 239.
194. RWDSU *v. Dolphin Delivery* [1986] 2 S.C.R. 573.
195. Hogg, *Constitutional Law of Canada*, 1998 student edn., at section 34.2(f), 682-85.
196. *Law v. Canada* (1999) 170 D.L.R. 4th, 1 (S.C.C.).
197. *Ibid.*, 49.

VI

CRIMINAL AND OTHER DECISIONS

CRIMINAL

- The Supreme Court Overrules Itself
- Acquittal by Inadvertence
- Conviction by Circumstantial Evidence
- Mandatory Minimum Sentences and Importation of Narcotics
- Medical Treatment of Children and Freedom of Religion
- The Exclusion of Evidence for Investigative Malfeasance
- Soliciting for the Purpose of Prostitution
- Bilingualism on the Prairies

OTHER

- Loss of Consortium by a Wife
- Gymnastics Gone Awry
- "Heritage Property" and Due Process for Landowners
- Are Catholic Teachers Bound by Doctrinal Requirements?

METHODOLOGY

SOME LEGAL OBSERVERS considering McIntyre's criminal law decisions have concluded that he was excessively concerned with the promotion of law and order. However, close colleagues on the court such as Justices Antonio Lamer and Bertha Wilson, with whom he worked on the friendliest terms, acknowledge that his cautionary advice to colleagues has had a salutary effect on the Court. He would often dissent in criminal cases, but his presence on the Supreme Court at a critical time prevented the tribunal from adopting more unbalanced positions in that area. He was always mindful of the need to balance liberty of the person with the state's interest in security. His reputation as a "conservative" jurist, especially among academics, needs to be reconsidered. He was conservative insofar as he respected tradition and common law norms, but he was also the author of some of the most liberal decisions in Canadian jurisprudence, such as his well balanced dissent on the question of capital punishment in *Miller and Cockriell* (which was overruled by more "liberal" judges), and his eloquent indictment of the abuse of prosecutorial discretion in *Rourke*. Indeed, if one takes the sum total of his majority and dissenting opinions, they compare favourably with those of his colleagues who are perceived as legal liberals.

CRIMINAL CASES

THE SUPREME COURT OVERRULES ITSELF

In *R. v. Ancio*,[1] McIntyre held for the Court that *R. v. Lajoie*,[2] a former decision of the Supreme Court, should be overruled. He demonstrated that in a proper case, where the Court so desires, it is not bound by its own prior decisions but can reverse itself in order to dispense with a rule that is no longer appropriate. The Supreme Court has also held that it is no longer bound by Privy Council decisions.[3] This position accords with decisions taken in the U.K. where, in a "practice note" in 1966, Lord Chancellor Gardiner said that the House of Lords was not necessarily bound by its own past rulings, and in the United States, where the Supreme Court has never considered itself so bound.

In *Lajoie* it was held that a conviction for attempted murder could be sustained where the Crown had shown that the accused either attempted to kill the potential victim, or intended to cause bodily harm that he knew was likely to cause death, or was "reckless" whether death ensued or not. In dismissing the Crown's appeal and confirming the Ontario Court of Appeal's order for a new trial, McIntyre, declared,

> The *mens rea* for attempted murder is, in my view, the specific intent to kill. A mental state falling short of that level may well lead to conviction for other offences, for example, one or other of the various aggravated assaults, but not to a conviction for an attempt to murder. For these reasons it is my view that *Lajoie* should no longer be followed.[4]

Thus, McIntyre affirmed that a person cannot "intend" to commit those statutorily defined unintentional killings described in sections 212 and 213 of the Code. Ritchie, J, who was part of the 1974 majority in the Lajoie case, dissented, holding that case still to be controlling.

ACQUITTAL BY INADVERTENCE

In one of the more bizarre cases in which McIntyre gave the judgment of the Court, the accused found himself to be the unexpected beneficiary of a misconception of the judicial process by the jury. In *Head v. R.*,[5] Hrabinsky, J, had carefully instructed the jury that it could find the accused, who was charged with attempted murder, guilty on that charge or on certain lesser included offences. During their deliberations, the jury returned to ask the judge to give them further instructions with respect to included offences.[6] The court record, as set out in Lamer's judgment, clarifies the dilemma that eventually came before the Supreme Court:

Court Clerk:	How say you, is the prisoner guilty or not guilty?
Foreman:	The prisoner is not guilty.
Court Clerk:	Harken to your verdict as the Court records it, you find the prisoner not guilty.
Foreman:	Yes.
Court Clerk:	And so say you all.
Jurors:	Yes.
The Court:	Ladies and Gentleman of the Jury, I thank you for your careful attention given to this case and the care you took in reaching your decision. *You are free to leave,* but you must return on Monday, October seventeenth at ten a.m. Thank you again. If you wish to stay in the courtroom, you may, if you want to move into the courtroom. (Emphasis in original.)

The trial judge then turned to the accused and told him that he had been found not guilty and that he was discharged. The clerk of the court then said, "Court is adjourned until ten o'clock Monday morning." The following conversation then took place between the judge and the foreman of the jury:

The Court: Oh, just a moment, the jury foreman, did you wish to say something?

Foreman: Well, when we discussed this we thought we could find the defendant not guilty of the charge as laid, but guilty of a lesser charge, is that right?

The Court: Well, I believe I'm *functus officio*. That means I have nothing further. That is why I spelled out very clearly to you the various things that you were to find. However, I'll hear submissions from counsel.[7]

By the time this colloquy had taken place between the foreman of the jury and the judge, one of the jurors had gone past the bar and was in the body of the courtroom. Mr. Justice Hrabinsky then said that in his opinion he was "*functus*" or without jurisdiction, the acquittal of the accused having been formally announced and the jury discharged. The Crown could, he said, have a remedy by way of appeal, entailing a new trial if it was successful.

On appeal to the Saskatchewan Court of Appeal,[8] Tallis and Vancise, JJ.A, said that Hrabinsky, J, was in error in applying the doctrine of "*functus officio*." The verdict was not complete, since the jury had not dealt "with all possible verdicts open to them on the indictment."[9] Hall, JA, in dissent, said that the accused was acquitted of the principal charge and all included offences; to have him stand trial afterward for any of the included offences would place him in double jeopardy.

In an incisive eight-page judgment, McIntyre allowed the appeal and restored the acquittal:

[T]he charge to the jury was adequate, both as to the principal offence and as to the included offences. When the jury returned its verdict, the foreman gave a clear anc (*sic*) completely unambiguous verdict of acquittal and it was acknowledged according to the accepted practice, by each member of the jury. The jury had been charged once on included offences and had returned to the courtroom after commencing deliberation for further instruction. It was then in these circumstances a reasonable conclusion on the part of the trial judge that the jury had considered the included offences and that the jury's verdict was intended to be a full acquittal, including the principal and any included offences. Even in these circumstances, it might have been wiser for the trial judge to inquire ... respecting included offences, but I cannot say it was reversible error on his part to do as he did and discharge both the prisoner and the jury.[10]

Such a misconception by the jury must be exceedingly rare. Instead of being punished for a lesser included offence, as the jury apparently intended, the accused in this case walked free. As McIntyre said, "[I]f there is any consolation in a situation such as this, I suppose it can be said it is better to err in favour of the accused if one is to err."[11]

CONVICTION BY CIRCUMSTANTIAL EVIDENCE

In *R. v. Yebes*,[12] the appellant had been found guilty of the second-degree murder of his two adopted children. Justice McIntyre was called upon to interpret section 613(1)(a)(i) of the Criminal Code allowing a court of appeal to set a conviction aside "where it is of the opinion that the verdict should be set aside on the ground that it is unreasonable or cannot be supported by the evidence." The key question here concerned the criteria a court would apply to determine that the verdict was unreasonable or unsupported by the evidence.

The appellant, Thomas Yebes, a hairdresser, and his wife, Elvira, lived in Surrey, near Vancouver, with their two daughters, who were born in 1971 and 1973. They were concerned with the plight of children in the poorer countries of the world and in 1977 began procedures to adopt two Chilean boys. In 1979 the children arrived in Canada to reside with the Yebes family with a view to formal adoption. The boys were unruly and did not fit easily into their new home and in July 1981, the couple sought psychiatric assistance to try to resolve the domestic conflict occasioned by the presence of the boys in the house. In September of the same year, at about the time the adoption was finalized, the couple agreed to a trial separation of three to six months. As the burden of supporting two households fell to Mr. Yebes, financial difficulties ensued. The couple thought of reconciliation, but Mrs. Yebes did not think she could manage with the boys and suggested that they be readopted. On inquiry Mr. Yebes learned that readoption would entail delay and many difficulties, and he asked a family support worker to furnish him with a letter saying that the boys could not be readopted. He hoped to persuade his wife to accept the boys by showing her this letter so that the family could be reunited. This was the state of affairs on February 23, 1982, when the death of the boys occurred.

At that time, pressure was mounting on Mr. Yebes to move back with his wife, because the lease on his town house was expiring at the end of the month. Both parents had planned a supper for the whole family at the town house that evening. Later, after Mrs. Yebes and her two daughters had departed, Mr. Yebes put the boys to bed and put on a stereo headset so that he could listen to music in bed. He fell asleep, only to be awakened by a noise which he thought might be the boys going to the bathroom or a neighbour in an adjoining townhouse. He went back to sleep. He was later aroused a second time by the smell of smoke, and, on going downstairs to the utility room, found the two boys dead on a burning mattress. They were covered and apparently had made no move to escape. He then called the police.[13]

At trial, a fire expert testified that the fire had been set deliberately. It had not started at a single location and spread, but had started in three separate locations. Moreover, it could not have been set solely by the butane lighter that was found on the premises. Further expert evidence revealed that the two boys were dead before the fire began. The investigating pathologist ruled out fire as the cause of death, but could not determine the exact cause because of the damage caused to the bodies by the flames.[14]

Evidence at the trial disclosed an event that had occurred on February 7, 1982, about two weeks before the death of the boys. That night, Mr. Yebes had phoned the police, complaining of a fire in the boys' bedroom. When they arrived, police found evidence of a fire and a candle on a plate. The boys said the fire had been caused by a "monster." The investigating officer, however, found no evidence of entry through the doors or windows. He concluded that the boys had been playing with fire and had fabricated the story of the monster to avoid reprimand.[15] Mr. Yebes testified at the trial that he could not recall specifically locking the front door on the night they died. When the police sergeant arrived, however, the door was unlocked, as Mr. Yebes was apparently aware, given that instead of going downstairs to let him in, he shouted to the officer, "In here! In here!"[16]

The appeal to the British Columbia Court of Appeal was dismissed, with Hutcheon, JA, dissenting, clearing the way to the Supreme Court. According to McIntyre the main grounds of appeal were: (1) that the

Court of Appeal failed to apply the correct test for section 613(1)(a)(i) of the Code where the evidence against the appellant was entirely circumstantial; and (2) that the Court erred in failing to consider the absence of Mrs. Yebes, a material witness, in determining whether the verdict was one that a properly instructed jury, acting judicially, could reasonably have rendered.[17] In summarizing the onus that the appellant had to satisfy, McIntyre said,

As a general proposition, the verdict at trial will stand where there is evidence before the jury going in proof of all elements of the offence and where the trial judge has properly charged the jury on all matters of law which arise in the case and has made such references to the evidence as may be necessary to facilitate the application of the law to the facts. However, section 613(1)(a)(i) of the *Criminal Code* provides an additional basis for the challenging of the verdict at trial. A court of appeal may allow an appeal against a conviction where it is of the opinion that the verdict should be set aside on the ground that it is unreasonable or cannot be supported by the evidence.[18]

McIntyre concluded that there was evidence before the jury from which it could reasonably find that the boys were dead before the fire occurred and that they did not die from natural causes. There was evidence that the fire was deliberately set and that Yebes had both motive and opportunity to kill the boys.[19] Concerning the question of access to the town house, he observed, "There is no evidence of the presence of any other persons, save the two boys, in the town house that evening. Only the unlocked front door could raise a question as to exclusive opportunity. I am of the view that there was evidence before the jury upon which a properly charged jury could reasonably have reached the conclusion that Yebes had exclusive opportunity to kill the boys."[20] As to the failure of the Crown to call Mrs. Yebes, that was not a critical element. There was no evidence or suggestion that she was present when the deaths occurred or that she had any knowledge of the tragedy. "What could Mrs. Yebes add to the narrative?" McIntyre asks. "The whole tragic history of these children and this family was put before the court by other witnesses."[21]

MANDATORY MINIMUM SENTENCES AND IMPORTATION OF NARCOTICS

Whether or not the mandatory minimum seven-year sentence for importing narcotics into Canada provided by section 5(2) of the Narcotic

Control Act was "cruel and unusual treatment or punishment," and thus contrary to section 12 of the Charter, was the issue in *R. v. Smith*.[22] The majority of the Court found for the appellant, who had returned to Canada from Bolivia with seven and a half ounces of 85 to 90 percent pure cocaine secreted on his person. He pleaded guilty to importing a narcotic contrary to section 5(1) and was sentenced to eight years in the penitentiary. The British Columbia Court of Appeal dismissed an appeal from the sentence imposed by Wetmore, Co. Ct. J, and overturned the latter's ruling that section 5(2) of the Act was a contravention of section 12 of the Charter.[23]

Lamer, J, and Dickson, CJ, found that a mandatory minimum sentence was not in and of itself cruel and unusual. "For example," Lamer notes, "a long term of penal servitude for he or she who has imported large amounts of heroin for the purpose of trafficking would certainly not contravene section 12 of the *Charter*, quite the contrary. However, the seven-year minimum prison term of section 5(2) is grossly disproportionate when examined in light of the wide net cast by section 5(1)."[24] The section in question covers substances with varying degrees of danger to life and human health and ignores the issue of the quantity imported. Such indiscriminateness breaches the "minimal impairment test": there is no need to sentence small offenders to the mandatory minimum time in order to deter more serious ones.[25]

McIntyre's dissent commences by his recognizing that there is an air of unreality about the appeal because the issue of "cruel and unusual punishment" under section 12 of the Charter does not emerge clearly from the facts of the case. The trial judge found that the minimum mandatory sentence of seven years laid down in section 5(2) of the Narcotic Control Act violated the Charter, yet he imposed a sentence of *eight* years on the appellant for importing a narcotic with a "street value" of between $126,000 and $168,000. The judges who considered the case in the lower courts were of the opinion that the long sentence was entirely appropriate.

Reviewing the criteria set out by Tarnopolsky in his article "Just Deserts or Cruel and Unusual Treatment or Punishment? Where Do We Look for Guidance?,"[26] McIntyre is largely in agreement with their definition but finds they can be stated more succinctly:

A punishment will be cruel and unusual and violate section 12 of the *Charter* if it has any one or more of the following characteristics:

1) The punishment is of such character or duration as to outrage the public conscience or be degrading to human dignity;

2) The punishment goes beyond what is necessary for the achievement of a valid social aim, having regard to the legitimate purposes of punishment and the adequacy of possible alternatives; or,
3) The punishment is arbitrarily imposed in the sense that it is not applied on a rational basis in accordance with ascertained and ascertainable standards.[27]

McIntyre finds that all three of these criteria have been met by section 5(2) of the Act. With respect to the third criterion, the appellant's contention was that under section 5(2) of the Act, the minimum sentence must be imposed by the trial judge "without regard to the type or amount of the narcotic imported or exported, nor its intended use, nor to the criminal history or background of the accused." McIntyre disagrees. The appellant is really arguing that the trial judge's discretion should be unfettered, and that the arbitrariness of the mandated procedure pursuant to section 5(2) results in a violation of the "cruel and unusual" standard in section 12. McIntyre cannot accept this proposition. "It would under the guise of protecting individuals from cruel and unusual punishment unduly limit the power of Parliament to determine the general policy regarding the imposition of punishment for criminal activity. It would, in effect, constitutionally entrench the power of judges to determine the appropriate sentence in their absolute discretion."[28]

This statement shows McIntyre's sensitivity to the separation of powers between the legislature and the judiciary. There could be cases where a mandatory minimum sentence in relation to a specific offence is unreasonable or "cruel and unusual," but this is not one of them. The courts should be more compliant with the legislature when the latter sets a lower limit for sentencing specified criminal acts.

MEDICAL TREATMENT OF CHILDREN AND FREEDOM OF RELIGION

In *R. v. Tutton*,[29] McIntyre was called upon to decide a case where the accused parents of a five-year-old diabetic son, acting from religious motives, refused to supply him with insulin. Had they shown a wanton and reckless disregard for the lives and safety of other persons within the meaning of section 202 (the "manslaughter" provision) of the Criminal Code?

In this case the appeal by the Crown from an Ontario Court of Appeal decision[30] setting aside the conviction by Salhany, Co. Ct. J, sitting with a jury, was dismissed, and a new trial ordered. The judgments in this case, which generally set aside the conviction and ordered a new trial,[31] struggled with the appropriate test for section 202 of the Code: should it be an objective or a subjective one? McIntyre considered that in construing the section, which grounded liability on either "doing anything" or "failing to do anything," there was no real difference between commission and omission, and that the authorities[32] dictated that an objective test should be applied. The test was not made in a vacuum: "The decision must be made on a consideration of the facts existing at the time and in relation to the accused's perception of those facts."[33] It would not involve an investigation of malice, for example, since that would involve the Court in an exploration of a subjective state of mind, but would posit a standard of "reasonableness" with regard to the conduct allegedly breaching the section.

The parents of the diabetic boy were good parents who, apart from the allegations in the present case, had always provided affectionate care and the necessities of life to their son. They were sincere members of a religious sect, and the mother believed that God would miraculously cure her boy, as communicated to her in a dream, even in the absence of further medical treatment. She decided to withdraw insulin and told her husband of her decision a day later. He agreed. The child died shortly afterward whereupon the parents were charged with manslaughter. Were the parents negligent? McIntyre stressed in his judgment the necessity of coming to such a determination by objective criteria:

In the case at bar, then, the assertion of the Tuttons that they believed a cure had been effected by Divine intervention and that insulin was not necessary for the preservation of the child's life would have to be considered by the jury. The jury would have to consider whether such a belief was honest and whether it was reasonable. In this, they would be required to consider the whole background of the case. They would have to take into account the experience of the Tuttons with the child's illnesses; the fact that they had seen the result of the withdrawal of insulin on one occasion and that they had been informed of its necessity for the continued care of the child: and, that Mrs. Tutton had received some formal instruction or training in dealing with diabetes and diabetics. They would, as well, have to consider whether the belief in a miraculous cure leading to the conclusion that insulin and medical care were not required, though honest, was reasonable. Upon these facts and all others concerning the matter which were revealed in the evidence, the jury would be required to decide whether the refusal of insulin and medical attention represented a marked and significant departure of the standard to be observed by reasonably prudent parents.

I would dismiss the appeal and confirm the direction for a new trial.[34]

From the time of Bracton in the thirteenth century, there has been a strong current of English common law, represented more recently in the thought of Oliver Wendell Holmes, Jr., toward the establishment of an objective standard of criminal and tort liability. Whether or not a subjective state of mind is manifest in overt acts, it is the concrete acts, rather than the subjective state, on which legal liability should rest. McIntyre's judgment is a strong example of the common law preference for an objective standard.

THE EXCLUSION OF EVIDENCE FOR INVESTIGATIVE MALFEASANCE

Unlike certain other national declarations of right, the Charter enables judges to extend appropriate remedies to those whose rights and freedoms have been violated (s. 24(1)), and authorizes them to exclude evidence when it is improperly obtained, and "would bring the administration of justice into dispute" (s. 24(2)). The latter subsection does not require the exclusion of *all* evidence improperly obtained, but only where its admission would breach the above-mentioned standards.

The first major test of the "reach" of subsection 24(2) occurred in the case of *R. v. Therens*,[35] when the Supreme Court considered the case of a motorist in Moose Jaw whose vehicle swerved out of control and collided with a tree. The police took Therens to the police station for a breathalyzer test, but did not inform him of his right to counsel as required by section 10(b) of the Charter. They did not consider it necessary to give Therens the warning because section 10(b) applied only "on arrest or detention." At the time he was taken to the police station he had not been arrested and the police did not believe — and there was a pre-Charter precedent to support them[36] — that he had been "detained." When the breathalyzer test was administered, it was found that the quantity of alcohol in his blood exceeded the limit of "80 milligrams of alcohol in 100 milliliters of blood" set by section 236(1) of the Criminal Code.[37]

Both lower courts concurred that the accused's Charter right to counsel in section 10(b) had been infringed by the failure of police to advise him of the right to counsel before the blood test, and that because of this violation the certificate of analysis recording the accused's blood level should be excluded as evidence under Charter subsection 24(2). Moreover, since the test was the only incriminating evidence in the case and its admission "would bring the administration of justice into disrepute," the lower courts considered that they had no recourse but to dismiss the charge.

By a 6-2 majority (with Ritchie, J, not participating and Le Dain and McIntyre, JJ, dissenting), the Supreme Court upheld the two lower Saskatchewan courts,[38] holding that while Therens had not been "arrested" at the relevant time, he had been "detained" by police and consequently should have been advised by them of his right under section 10(b) "to retain and instruct counsel without delay."

In Chromiak, conversely, "this Court unanimously held that a person who complied with a demand pursuant to section 234.1(1) to accompany a police officer and submit to a roadside breath test was not detained within the meaning of section 2(c) of the *Canadian Bill of Rights*."[39] The Crown argued vigorously that the rule in *Chromiak* should be followed in *Therens*, with the result that the latter subject's compliance with the police request would signify that he was not "detained," there would be no violation of his rights, and the certificate of analysis would be admissible. While dissenting, Le Dain held that *Chromiak* was not conclusive on the issue under the Charter, and the majority agreed with him. The Charter was a constitutional instrument whose entrenched provisions differed fundamentally from those in the Canadian Bill of Rights. In Le Dain's words,

> In considering the relationship of a decision under the *Canadian Bill of Rights*, to an issue arising under the *Charter*, a court cannot, in my respectful opinion, avoid bearing in mind an evident fact of Canadian judicial history, which must be squarely and frankly faced: that on the whole, with some notable exceptions, the courts have felt some uncertainty or ambivalence in the application of the *Canadian Bill of Rights* because it did not reflect a clear constitutional mandate to make judicial decisions having the effect of limiting or qualifying the traditional sovereignty of Parliament. The significance of the new constitutional mandate for judicial review provided by the *Charter* was emphasized by the Court in its recent decisions in *Law Society of Upper Canada v. Skapinker* [1984] 1 S.C.R. 357, and *Hunter v. Southam Inc.* [[1984] 2 S.C.R. 245].[40]

In addition, section 10(b) of the Charter on the right to counsel went beyond the analogous provision in section 2(c)(ii) of the Canadian Bill of Rights, stipulating "that anyone arrested or detained had a right to be informed of the right to counsel." This phrase evinced a more expansive view of the right to counsel than that contained in the Bill. It would be incorrect, accordingly, to take the *Chromiak* case as determinative of the meaning of "right to counsel" in the Charter.

Both the majority and the minority agreed that Therens's section 10(b) right to be informed of his right to counsel had been violated. Where they differed was that the majority considered that this violation triggered the provision in section 24(2) excluding the blood analysis certificate, whereas the minority did not. In Estey's words: "Here the police flagrantly violated a *Charter* right without any statutory authority for so doing. Such an overt violation as occurred here must, in my view, result in the rejection of the evidence thereby obtained."[41] In the dissent, Le Dain laid emphasis on the *Chromiak* case:

In view ... of the judgment of this Court in *Chromiak*, the police officer in this case was in my opinion entitled to assume in good faith that the respondent did not have the right to counsel on a demand under s. 235(1) of the *Criminal Code*. Because of this good faith reliance, I am unable to conclude, having regard to all the circumstances, as required by section 24(2) of the *Charter*, that the admission of the evidence of the breathalyzer test in this particular case would bring the administration of justice into disrepute.[42]

In a very short concurring judgment, McIntyre declared,

The exclusion of such evidence is not automatic. It must be excluded only where it is established that its admission, having regard to all the circumstances, would bring the administration of justice into disrepute. In my view, that is not established here. The exclusion of the evidence in the circumstances of this case would itself go far to bring the administration of justice into disrepute.[43]

After the majority decision in *Therens* there was widespread concern among Canadian prosecutors that the American Miranda[44] rule had migrated north, and that their work would be made more onerous by having to exclude probative evidence gathered in a manner contrary to prescriptions in section 24. To some extent their fears have been justified, yet the extent to which their work has been made more difficult remains unresolved. Efficiency and due process do not always sit easily together.

SOLICITING FOR THE PURPOSE OF PROSTITUTION

In *R. v. Whitter*,[45] McIntyre spoke for a unanimous nine-member Supreme Court in upholding lower court decisions[46] that allowed appeals from two Vancouver women accused of soliciting for the purpose of prostitution. Their appeals once more raised questions about the meaning of the term "solicit" in section 195.1 of the Criminal Code, which reads,

Soliciting
195.1   Every person who solicits any person in a public place for the purpose of prostitution is guilty of an offence punishable on summary conviction.

It is not prostitution but solicitation in a public place that constitutes the offence.

In the 1978 precedent case,[47] Spence, J, held that the word "solicit" as used in section 195.1 of the Criminal Code did not connote a simple offer of availability for prostitution. Conviction required an element of persistence or pressure. A streetwalker who simply winked and asked a potential customer if he or she "wanted some company" would not be guilty of the offence. It was necessary, apparently, to actively pursue a prospective customer and repeat the request in order to come within the terms of this definition.

The pattern of conduct of the two women who were arrested, Whitter and Galjot, was remarkably alike. The former on Granville Street and the latter on West Georgia Street in Vancouver had approached a number of men before they unwittingly accosted undercover police officers and indicated their availability and willingness to engage in sex. No evidence was tendered in either case of what the accused said to the men they spoke to before they made advances to the police officers, nor was there any evidence in the latter case that "would import the element of persistence or pressure required for a Solicitation."[48] The Crown argued that quite apart from the words spoken in any particular case the cumulative approaches, when taken together, signified pressing and persistent conduct. The Court unanimously rejected this argument. In McIntyre's words,

The respondents were charged in the words of the section with "soliciting a person." From the evidence adduced it was abundantly clear that the person, in each case, was the police officer named in the evidence. To convict, the Crown then had to show, in addition to her offer of her services as a prostitute, an element of persistence or pressing conduct in the presentation of that offer. This, the Crown admittedly did not do, and in my view, evidence that she approached others cannot for the reasons I have endeavoured to outline, supply the deficiency.[49]

Prostitution was on the rise in Canada, especially in urban centres, and McFarlane, JA, who dissented in the Court of Appeal, said that the parliamentary intention here was to "abate a social nuisance and inconvenience caused by the practice of soliciting for prostitution in public."[50] McIntyre replied, however, that if that was the case the enactment did not sufficiently give effect to that intention, "and renders compliance with the terms of the enactment and achievement of any such parliamentary intention impossible. If change is desirable in this respect, it is my view that legislative action would be necessary."[51] Municipalities found it increasingly difficult to secure convictions for solicitation under the "pressing and persistent" requirement, and sometimes enacted their own by-laws, as in the case of Calgary and Montreal. These penalized persons offering sexual services for sale within civic boundaries as a measure of "street control," and the Supreme Court struck them down in the mid-1980s as colourable encroachments on federal criminal law.[52] As McIntyre said, if legislative action was required then it would have to be accomplished in Parliament.

Parliament did enact new legislation to combat the problem of street prostitution in 1985.[53] The relevant section 213(1)(c) reads as follows:

                    Offence in Relation to Prostitution

213(1)   Every person who in a public place or in any manner communicates or attempts to communicate with any person

  (c)   stops or attempts to stop any person or in any manner communicates or attempts to communicate with any person for the purpose of engaging in prostitution or of obtaining the sexual services of a prostitute is guilty of an offence punishable on summary conviction.

The new provision successfully withstood a Charter challenge[54] that it infringed freedom of expression in section 2(b), or that it was void for vagueness or violated "fundamental justice" in section 7.

In upholding the new law Chief Justice Dickson examined the tangled historical background:

> It is legitimate to take into account the fact that earlier laws and considered alternatives were thought to be less effective than the legislation which is presently being challenged. When Parliament began its examination of street soliciting, it was presented with a spectrum of views and possible approaches by both the Fraser Committee and the Justice and Legal Affairs Committee. In making a choice to enact s. 195(1)(c) as it now reads, Parliament had to try to balance its decision to criminalize the nuisance aspects of street soliciting and its desire to take into account the policy arguments regarding the effects of criminalization of any aspect of prostitution. The legislative history of the present provision and, in general, of legislation directed to street solicitation is both long and complicated. The legislative scheme that was eventually implemented and has now been challenged need not be the "perfect" scheme that could be imagined by this court or any other court. Rather, it is sufficient if it is appropriately and carefully tailored in the context of the infringed right. I find this legislation meets the test of minimum impairment of the right in question.[55]

McIntyre was in the process of leaving the Supreme Court when this decision was made and took no part in it. A strong dissent to the validity of the new law was made by Wilson, J, who argued that it criminalized one aspect of prostitution, which was an otherwise legal activity: "Such a broad prohibition as to the locale of the communication would seem to go far beyond a genuine concern over the nuisance caused by street solicitation in Canada's major centres of population. It enables the police to arrest citizens who are disturbing no one solely because they are engaged in communicative acts concerning something not prohibited by the Code."[56] Madam Justice Wilson was here raising the question of whether Parliament should penalize a commercial activity that, however unsavoury it appeared to the public, fell within the sphere of "victimless crimes," and was resorted to by persons who often had little other choice of livelihood.

BILINGUALISM ON THE PRAIRIES

In an important decision on bilingualism in Saskatchewan and Alberta, the Supreme Court decided 6-2 in *R. v. Mercure*,[57] in February 1988, that section 110 of the Northwest Territories Act,[58] as continued in force in Saskatchewan by section 16 of the Saskatchewan Act,[59] authorized the use of both the English and the French before the provincial courts and legislature, and made mandatory the printing of all provincial laws in both languages. The decision also applied to Alberta, section 110 having been continued also by the Alberta Act.[60]

Although Mr. Justice McIntyre was not the author of the relevant judgment, he did concur in the dissenting judgment of Estey, J;[61] the decision is interesting in that the two judges having the closest connection with Saskatchewan disagreed with the majority. This would not affect the law, of course, but it is instructive that they shared the same historical and legal perspectives in coming to their result.

The case arose in 1980, when Father André Mercure, a Battleford priest and a dedicated supporter of bilingualism, was charged and convicted in English only for a speeding violation that infringed section 139(4) of the Vehicles Act.[62] According to Roger Lepage, Father Mercure's counsel, his client so believed that the provincial Constitution required the use of French in statutes and pleadings, that he attempted to create a test case. He raced his car up and down the street in the vicinity of the police station until they, perhaps reluctantly, finally laid a charge against him.

Father Mercure argued that the laws of 1891 and 1905 required all provincial statutes to be printed in both languages, failing which they would be invalid. If he was right (as proved to be the case), all unilingual English statutes in Saskatchewan and Alberta from 1905 to 1988 would be invalid until retroactive French editions were prepared or the requirement was legally dispensed with. When Father Mercure died in 1986 with his appeal in progress, the Supreme Court ordered that the "intervening" French cultural associations be named as principal parties so that proceedings could continue.

The appellant partially succeeded in the first instance, when Judge Deshaye of the provincial court considered it sufficient for a party to legal proceedings to speak through an interpreter. He held that the language requirement should be applied not to provincial "laws" enacted after 1905, but only to pre-existing territorial "ordinances."[63] The appeal to the Saskatchewan Court of Appeal came to substantially the same conclusion.[64]

Speaking for a six-judge majority,[65] Mr. Justice Gerard La Forest quoted Chief Justice John Marshall's admonition to his colleagues in *M'Culloch v. Maryland* to remember "that it is a *constitution* that we are expounding."[66] Such a document should be given a broad and liberal construction.[67]

Section 110 of the 1891 Northwest Territories Act set out that, "[e]ither the English or the French language may be used by any person in the debates of the Legislative Assembly of the Territories and in the proceedings before the courts; and both those languages shall be used in the records and journals of such Assembly; and all ordinances made under this Act shall be printed in both languages."[68] Section 16(1) of the Saskatchewan Act continued territorial laws in effect "so far as they are not inconsistent with anything contained in this Act, or as to which this Act contains no provision intended as a substitute therefor."[69] The 1905 Saskatchewan Act was silent on language rights.

La Forest held for the Court that bilingualism had been continued in force by the Saskatchewan Act, either by section 16(1) or by the combined effect of sections 16(1) and 14 (another transitional provision). In so holding he laid strong emphasis on the character of the right in question:

If human rights legislation can be said to be fundamental or almost constitutional, it is at least equally true of the legislation at issue here; for many years it was entrenched, so far as the inhabitants of the area to which it applied were concerned, since it could only be removed by Parliament, not the local legislature, something, it will be remembered, Parliament had refused to do. It formed part of the basic law of a vast area of this country from the earliest days of the founding of the nation and is rooted in a deeply sensitive reality recognized by the Canadian Charter of Rights and Freedoms, which among our fundamental values set forth that English and French are the official languages of this country (s. 16(1)).[70]

While La Forest, held that bilingualism was required by the combined effect of the two foregoing statutes, he drew back from endorsing appellants' argument that section 110 now had entrenched status. Sections 16(1) and 14 provided that laws continued under the Saskatchewan Act could be repealed by the legislature.[71] Unlike section 23 of the Manitoba Act,[72] the analogous Saskatchewan provision was not entrenched: "Accordingly, the legislature may resort to the obvious, if ironic, expedient of enacting a bilingual statute removing the restrictions imposed on it by s. 110 and then declaring all existing provincial statutes valid notwithstanding that they were enacted, printed and published in English only."[73] This, in due course, the Saskatchewan legislature proceeded to do; the Language Act[74] so enacted was the only bilingual statute ever passed in the province.

In his dissent, concurred in by McIntyre, Mr. Justice Estey explores in great detail the legal, historical, legislative, and other ramifications of the issue of bilingualism in the provinces of Saskatchewan and Alberta:

> There was no constitutional impediment or restriction, unlike the situation resulting from the presence of s. 23 of the Manitoba Act, 1870, to the new province exercising its free legislative will under s. 92 of the Constitution Act, 1867, as regards the use of language in the legislature and the courts. Indeed, Parliament acting under its authority to establish new provinces under s. 2 of the Constitution Act, 1871, might well have made reference in the Saskatchewan Act to section 133 of the Constitution Act, 1967 [referring to bilingualism in certain federal institutions], or might have inserted a clause comparable to s. 23 of the Manitoba Act, 1870. It did neither. It would be unusual to find in the light of all this that s. 110 has by an indirect and convoluted process somehow been introduced into the Constitution of Saskatchewan.[75]

Section 3 of the Saskatchewan Act, moreover, applies the antecedent British North America Acts to the new province as if it had been one of the provinces originally united, endowing it with full powers to establish its own legislature and courts without any express fetter on language rights.[76] Consequently, when it proceeded to create a unilingual legislature and court system it was acting within its jurisdictional competence.

Estey bolstered his argument by referring to the constitutional division of powers between the provinces and the federal government. Under section 92(14) of the Constitution Act, 1867, the provinces, including Saskatchewan, acquired legislative power to establish and provide for the administration of its own court system. In addition, section 16(2) of the Saskatchewan Act foresaw that the new province would abolish the Supreme Court of the Northwest Territories. The result was clear: "Section 110 of the North-West Territories Act cannot reasonably be read so as to have the effect of altering by inference this constitutional division of powers provided for in both the Constitution Act, 1867, and the Saskatchewan Act from the very beginning of the province. Nor could it have such effect in law."[77]

The majority judgment is broader and more ringing in its deduction from principle, but the dissent of Estey and McIntyre is more closely reasoned. It seemed to McIntyre that no intention was discernible in the province's founding statute that the bilingualism of the pre-existing territories was to be continued: in his opinion, Saskatchewan was to be free to prescribe the language or languages in which it would transact official business.

OTHER DECISIONS

LOSS OF CONSORTIUM BY A WIFE

In *Woelk v. Halvorson*[78] McIntyre spoke for a unanimous Supreme Court bench in a relatively rare case of a wife suing for the loss or impairment of consortium of her husband, following serious injuries sustained by him in an automobile accident in Alberta, in February 1975. The couple had been happily married for a number of years but as a result of this accident, involving severe injuries to the husband's head and spleen, he underwent a personality change that, along with his debilitating injuries, substantially deprived her of his affection and company.

That the longstanding right of action for loss of consortium was usually brought by a husband in respect to injuries to his wife can be seen from the description of the cause of action by Sir William Blackstone in the mid-eighteenth century: "[I]f the beating or other maltreatment be very enormous, so that thereby the husband is deprived for any time of the company and assistance of his wife, the law gives him a *separate* remedy by an action upon the case for this ill usage, *per quod consortium amisit*, in which he shall recover a satisfaction in damages."[79] In more contemporary terms, as in the case decided by Justice McIntyre, the action can be brought by either spouse for the loss of the company, society, affection, and aid of the injured partner by reason of the wrongful action of a third person.

The couple succeeded at trial, where the husband's general damages for pain and suffering were assessed at $30,000, with special damages fixed in excess of $14,000 (the latter award was not in contention on appeal). The wife's damages for loss of consortium were set at $10,000. On appeal to the Alberta Court of Appeal, the husband's general damages were reduced to $15,000 and the award to the wife was reduced drastically to $100.[80] The legal validity of the Court of Appeal's so reducing damages was the key issue on appeal to the Supreme Court of Canada.

There was little question of the severity of the husband's injuries:

The physical injuries suffered by the husband consisted of a left frontal skull fracture, extending into the temporal area with approximately a 2 mm. separation but no displacement; a brain concussion with loss of consciousness for five days; a rupture of the spleen which required emergency surgery and removal; a laceration of the forehead which required 16 sutures; and a severe swelling of the eyelids.[81]

The judgment goes on to describe the grave physical consequences of the injuries in terms of double vision, headaches, dizziness, loss of balance, a drooping of the left eyelid, and acute depression. The effect of the injuries on the wife's enjoyment of the marital state was significant:

The wife who was formerly happily married and secure in a well-established home, now finds herself married to one whose behaviour she described as that of a "zombie" who has withdrawn from almost all participation in family life. She is left with the burden of family cares and problems with practically no assistance from her husband. Her children prefer to go to their grandparents in their free time, rather than remain in the home. She works, and has actually extended her working hours from what they were formerly, in order to remain away from home for longer periods of time. Her participation in church activities has been greatly curtailed because of her husband's unwillingness to participate. She said that she had considered divorce but, up to the date of trial, her religious scruples had dictated against that step. She gave evidence, accepted by the trial judge, that she can no longer find any help or comfort in the society of her husband, her marriage has become a burden, and the home has ceased to be the happy one it once was.[82]

The common law position, as reflected in Blackstone, was that an action for loss of consortium was only maintainable by a husband. This may have had its origin in the feudal notion that a husband had a "property right" in his wife's person. The English case of *Best v. Samuel Fox & Co. Ld.*[83] held that "a married woman, whose husband had been injured by the negligence of another, had no cause of action against the negligent person for loss or impairment of consortium resulting from such negligence."[84] In Alberta, however, the common law position had been changed by section 35 of the Domestic Relations Act,[85] which extended a right of action for loss of consortium to either spouse.

The Supreme Court of Canada, speaking through McIntyre, restored the higher damages awarded to the plaintiffs at trial. Despite his judicial restraint, it is evident that McIntyre considered the reduction in the wife's damages from $10,000 to $100 to be gravely excessive:

> It is my view that, the Legislature having created the right of the wife to damages and having omitted any restriction on damage awards, the courts must endeavour to assess the damage realistically, according to the evidence in each case. The Legislature did not intend, in my view, to perpetuate an action leading only to insignificant recovery, nor can it be said that it regarded the remedy as anomalous.[86]

Moreover, the Court of Appeal was in error, in that after finding the trial judge had not acted upon a wrong principle and that there was no lack of evidence to support his conclusion, they had nonetheless proceeded to draw entirely different conclusions from this evidence and to reduce the award of damages. "Weighing and evaluating the evidence," McIntyre held, "lies fully with the province of the trial judge and, where there is evidence to support a finding which he has made, the fact that the Court of Appeal would have preferred to accept other evidence to the contrary, leading to a different finding, will not justify interfering with the trial judge's conclusion."[87]

McIntyre's judgment in this case is a thoroughly contemporary and scrupulous interpretation of the law as it increasingly reflects and recognizes women's rights.

GYMNASTICS GONE AWRY

In *Myers v. Peel County Board of Education*[88] McIntyre delivered the judgment of the Court allowing an appeal from a judgment of O'Driscoll, J, in the Court of Appeal of Ontario.[89] The appellant was a 15-year-old member of the grade eleven physical education class who broke his neck while performing a gymnastics exercise at the Erindale Secondary School, under the Peel County Board of Education.

On the day of the accident, the grade twelve teacher responsible for physical education was ill and not in school, and it was necessary for the grade eleven teacher, W.W. Jowett, to supervise both gym sessions, which took place at the same time. The appellant and a classmate named Chilton asked the permission of Jowett to leave the gymnasium to go to the exercise room to practise manoeuvres. Permission was granted, as it usually was in such cases. The number of boys practising at the same time was unclear, with estimates by witnesses varying from six to eight (according to Jowett), to fifteen (according to the appellant). As was usual, Chilton was acting as the appellant's "spotter," assisting him on the rings and, in the event of a fall, catching him or making contact to break a fall. When the appellant had finished his manoeuvre and dismounted from the rings, the spotter, considering the workout finished, turned and moved away. The spotter's evidence was that he had no forewarning the appellant was going to attempt a difficult new manoeuvre, and that he saw "out of the corner of his eye," the appellant falling on his head. The appellant testified that he had told the spotter he was going to do a "straddle dismount," and he assumed the spotter would be there to help him. The trial judge did not accept this evidence, however. The appellant had never attempted such a dismount before, and as the result of a bad fall, broke his neck.

The trial judge found that the attempted manoeuvre was suitable for someone of the plaintiff's age and condition with proper coaching. He found the defendants liable on two grounds, however: (1) they had not provided the degree of supervision that was needed; and (2) there was insufficient protective matting beneath the rings at the time of the accident. He rejected the defendant's evidence of *volenti non fit injuria*, and the matter of voluntary assumption of risk by the plaintiff was not pursued in the Supreme Court. He found the defendant 80 percent liable and the plaintiff 20 percent. In the Ontario Court of Appeal, Arnup, JA, overruled the trial judge, considering that neither a different type of matting nor the presence of a teacher in the exercise room would have precluded the accident. Blair, JA, dissented, supporting the trial judge.

After carefully reviewing the evidence, McIntyre reversed the decision of the Court of Appeal, finding the original decision of the trial judge supportable. He considered the standard of care exercised by school authorities in such cases to be that of "a prudent parent," as described in *Williams v. Eady*,[90] with allowances made for "modern times because of the greater variety of activities conducted in schools, with probably larger groups of students using more complicated and more dangerous equipment than formerly."[91] He found this standard had not been met in the present case. There was no doubt that the injury was foreseeable; indeed, it was foreseen. McIntyre explained:

Against this background, I am unable to conclude that a prudent parent would be content to provide as protective matting only the two and one-half inch compressed slab mats when other and more protective mats could be obtained. I am also unable to conclude that, considering the nature of the activity which was contemplated in the gymnastics course, a prudent parent would have been content to have his son permitted to depart from the gymnasium into a room where there would be no adult supervision to practise gymnastic manoeuvres on the rings which could involve the straddle dismount with its potential dangers.[92]

McIntyre allowed the appeal, leaving intact the findings of contributory negligence against the appellant and the apportionment of damages in the trial court.

"HERITAGE PROPERTY" AND DUE PROCESS FOR LANDOWNERS

Speaking for a four-judge majority[93] with Estey, dissenting, McIntyre allowed an appeal by church officials against an attempt by the City of Ottawa to prevent them from demolishing a building protected by the Ontario Heritage Act.[94] The statute required municipal consent for demolition of heritage properties, but this consent to demolish was deemed to be granted in the absence of notice from the City within 90 days of the application date. The appellants were not given notice in the form required by section 34(2) of the Act, and proceeded to partially demolish the building. The City then obtained an injunction restraining further demolition.

Central to this appeal was the issue of whether notice had been given in due form. The lower courts held that even if section 34(2) had not been complied with by the City in its exact terms, the church trustees had learned of City Council's decision as it was incorporated in a municipal by-law passed within the required period. The respondents argued that the word "deemed" in section 34(2) should be construed to mean "deemed until the contrary is proved,"[95] and that as a matter of fact the trustees were cognizant of council's decision.

At the heart of the case was the right at common law for a property owner to deal with his property as he wished. Although such a right may be regulated by the sovereign in the public interest, where the state was imposing statutory restrictions on individual property rights those restrictions had to be observed formally in order for them to be effective.

While conceding the important goals of the Act in conserving, protecting, and preserving the heritage of Ontario, McIntyre declared for the Court that such goals must be balanced with a due regard for property rights:

> It is equally evident, however, that the Legislature recognized that the preservation of Ontario's heritage should be accomplished at the cost of the community at large, not at the cost of the individual property owner, and certainly not in total disregard of the property owner's rights. It provided a procedure to govern the exercise of the municipal powers, but at the same time to protect the property owner within the scope of the *Act* and in accordance with its terms.[96]

Canvassing the authorities on interpretation of statutes along with the effect of the Ontario Interpretation Act,[97] section 10 of which provided that "every Act shall be deemed to be remedial," and hence should be construed liberally to achieve its purpose, McIntyre added that, even so, the property owner's rights should be respected:

> I am not of the view, however, that in order to give effect to what is taken to be the purpose of the statute it is open to the court of construction to disregard certain provisions of the *Act*. The whole *Act* must be construed. It must be construed to give effect to the purpose above described but also to have regard for many provisions of the *Act*, particularly sections 34 and 67, the purpose of which is to protect the interests of the landowner concerned. To ignore these provisions or to read them down to where they are deprived of any real significance, is not to construe the statute but to decline to assign any meaning to certain of the words that were used by the Legislature.[98]

Estey, dissented on the basis that appellants had "notice," in an empirical sense, and that the requisite knowledge of council's intention could be inferred from the notice: the deeming provision in section 34(3), moreover, should be construed as "deemed to be so until the contrary is proved."[99]

ARE CATHOLIC SCHOOL TEACHERS BOUND BY DOCTRINAL REQUIREMENTS?

The duty of Catholic teachers to conform to the religious tenets of the Church while teaching within the Catholic Public School System of Vancouver was in dispute in a 1985 case, in which McIntyre spoke for the Court.[100] The employment of Mrs. Caldwell was not renewed because, contravening two rules of the Catholic Church, she married a divorced person, and in a civil ceremony. In the eyes of the Church, a divorced person is still married.

In February 1978, the respondent Stuart, the school principal, learned of the marriage. After interviewing Mrs. Caldwell, who admitted the facts, he informed her that her teaching contract for the following school year would not be renewed. At the end of the school year she lodged a complaint, alleging discrimination by the school authorities on the basis of marital status and religion, and dismissal without reasonable cause. The complaint was heard by a Board of Inquiry set up under the British Columbia Human Rights Code,[101] which dismissed Mrs. Caldwell's complaint.[102] An appeal by way of a stated case pursuant to section 18 of the Code was allowed by the British Columbia Supreme Court,[103] but that decision was reversed in a further appeal to the Court of Appeal.[104]

The director of the British Columbia Human Rights Code joined the proceedings as an appellant, supporting Mrs. Caldwell, while the attorney general of British Columbia was a respondent, seeking restoration of the Board of Inquiry's order dismissing Mrs. Caldwell's complaint. The principal objection made by the director and Mrs. Caldwell was upon the Board's conclusion that this was a case where religion and marital status could be considered as *bona fide* qualifications under section 8(1) of the Code, despite their specific inclusion in section 8(2)(a) as factors that could not be reasonable cause for a dismissal from employment.

Section 8 of the Code extended to every person "the right of equality of opportunity based on *bona fide* qualifications in respect of his occupation or employment," and protection from dismissal without reasonable cause.

In commenting this statutory provision, McIntyre said,

Ordinarily a person who is academically qualified and duly licensed by the proper authority, would certainly possess the *bona fide* qualifications for employment as a teacher in the public school. I am in complete agreement with the proposition that if Mrs. Caldwell had been employed in a secular or public school and had been dismissed because of her marriage, she would have the full protection of section 8 and be entitled to reinstatement. This result may not always follow and particularly in cases related to denominational schools. As has been pointed out, the Catholic school is different from the public school.[105]

According to McIntyre, it was incorrect to focus in this case on subsection 8(2), which provided that neither religion nor marital status can be reasonable causes for dismissal. Rather, the issue was whether, by losing a *bona fide* qualification in respect of her occupation, she had also lost the right conferred by subsection 1. In McIntyre's words, "[T]he Church depends not so much on the usual form of academic instruction as on the teachers who, in imitation of Christ, are required to reveal the Christian message in their work and as well in all aspects of their behavior."[106] The teachers in the Catholic system taught by precept and example and, in that her marriage with a divorced person in a civil ceremony conflicted with basic teachings of the Church, Mrs. Caldwell had lost a *bona fide* qualification for employment within the system. The doctrinal requirement was part of a Catholic teacher's contract of employment.[107]

Applying the test that he developed in *Ontario Human Rights Commission et al. v. Borough of Etobicoke*[108] concerning the test to establish a *bona fide* qualification for employment, McIntyre found that the Church's requirement in the case at bar satisfied both branches of the test. The first, or subjective, requirement was met, because "at no time in these proceedings has it been suggested that the motives of the school authorities were not honest and in good faith or that the requirement of religious conformance was not imposed solely to promote the objects of the school. No ulterior motive has been shown or even suggested."[109] In connection with the second, or objective, branch of the *Etobicoke* test, McIntyre held that the requirement of religious conformity by Catholic teachers, objectively viewed, was reasonably necessary to assure the accomplishment of the objectives of the Church in operating a Catholic School system.[110]

Finally, section 22 of the Code permitted a religious or educational institution whose primary purpose was the promotion of the interests or the welfare of an identifiable group with a common religion to grant a preference to members of that group.[111] This section had been satisfied by the action of the school authorities. "In failing to renew the contract of Mrs. Caldwell, the school authorities were exercising a preference for the benefit of members of the community served by the school and forming the identifiable group by preserving a teaching staff whose Catholic members all accepted and practiced the doctrines of the Church."[112] In so deciding McIntyre was defining the central core of Catholic education. Had Mrs. Caldwell been reinstated, and if the result were generalized, it might have opened the way for two co-existing public school systems, instead of one public system and one parochial system.

MCINTYRE'S METHODOLOGY

As a jurist who held the common law in high regard, McIntyre always sought to put present legal problems in a context that emphasized the historical foundations of the law. In doing this he would give due weight to the inception of the Charter in 1982, but his whole outlook bespoke a body of legal doctrine extending back to its English origins many centuries ago. He gave less significance to 1982 as a watershed year than did such colleagues as Dickson, Lamer, and Wilson, since he regarded the Charter itself, and particularly the "legal rights" provisions from sections 7 to 14, as crystallizing former common law concepts. It followed that he was less likely than most of his colleagues to use the Charter to invalidate common law norms. When he was dealing with traditional criminal law concepts, torts, and property rights, his reliance on the common law was manifest. He remained scrupulously respectful of the lower court "record" of the cases on appeal and rarely, if ever, made inferences from the record that were not fully supportable. He stated the salient facts clearly, and enunciated the law with economy and precision. On a court where many decisions rendered during his time were both lengthy and complicated, his own were noted for their brevity and lucidity.

NOTES

1. [1984] 1 S.C.R. 231.
2. [1974] S.C.R. 399.
3. See Hogg, *Constitutional Law of Canada*, 3rd edn., 1992, section 8.7 at 220, where instances of the Supreme Court's overruling Privy Council decisions are given in *Re: Agricultural Products Marketing Act* [1978] 2 S.C.R. 1198 at 1234 and 1291, and in *Re: Bill 30 (Ontario Separate School Funding)* [1987] 1 S.C.R. 1148 at 1190-96.
4. [1984] 1 S.C.R. 251.
5. [1986] 2 S.C.R. 684.
6. *Ibid.*, 687.
7. *Ibid.*, 696.
8. (1984) 13 C.C.C. (3d) 198.

9. [1986] 2 S.C.R. 697.
10. *Ibid.*, 692.
11. *Ibid.*, 696-97.
12. [1987] 2 S.C.R. 168.
13. *Ibid.*, 171-74.
14. *Ibid.*, 175-76.
15. *Ibid.*, 177.
16. *Ibid.*, 177-78.
17. *Ibid.*, 180.
18. *Ibid.*, 180-81.
19. *Ibid.*, 186.
20. *Ibid.*, 190.
21. *Ibid.*, 191.
22. [1987] 1 S.C.R. 1045.
23. *Ibid.*, 1052.
24. *Ibid.*, 1077.
25. *Ibid.*, 1080.
26. (1978), 10 *Ottawa L. Rev.* 1.
27. [1987] 1 S.C.R. 1097-98.
28. *Ibid.*, 1105.
29. [1989] 1 S.C.R. 1392.
30. (1985) 18 C.C.C. (3d) 328.
31. See Wilson, J, at 1403 and Lamer, J (who largely agrees with McIntyre) at 1434.
32. Citing Cory, JA, for the Ontario Court of Appeal in *R. v. Waite* (1986) 28 C.C.C. (3d) 326, which was approved by the Supreme Court of Canada in *R. v. Tutton* [1989] 1 S.C.R. 1392 at 1436.
33. [1989] 1 S.C.R. 1416.
34. *Ibid.*, 1433-34.
35. [1985] 1 S.C.R. 613.
36. *Chromiak v. The Queen* [1980] 1 S.C.R. 471.
37. The facts are stated [1985] 1 S.C.R. 627-28, in the dissenting judgment of Le Dain, J.
38. *R. v. Therens* (1982) 70 C.C.C. (2d) 468 (Sask. Prov. Ct.), per Judge Alastair J. Muir, and *R. v. Therens* (1983) 5 C.C.C. (3d) 409, (Sask. C.A.), Tallis, JA, writing for the majority with Bayda, CJS, Hall and Cameron, JJ.A, concurring, and Brownridge, JA, dissenting.
39. [1985] 1 S.C.R. at 631, per Le Dain, J, dissenting.

40. *Ibid.*, 638-39.
41. *Ibid.*, 621.
42. *Ibid.*, 653.
43. *Ibid.*, 622-23.
44. *Miranda v. Arizona*, 384 U.S. 436 (1966).
45. *R. v. Whitter* [1981] 2 S.C.R. 606.
46. (1980) 54 C.C.C. (2d) 539.
47. *Hutt v. The Queen* [1978] 2 S.C.R. 476.
48. *R. v. Whitter* [1981] 2 S.C.R. 609.
49. *Ibid.*, 612.
50. *Ibid.*
51. *Ibid.*
52. *Westendorp v. R.* (1983) 144 D.L.R. (3d) 259 (Calgary), and *Goldwax v. City of Montreal* [1984] 2 S.C.R. 525 (Montreal).
53. An Act to amend the Criminal Code (prostitution), R.S.C. 1985, c. 51 (1st Supp.), the amendment having received royal assent on 20 December 1985.
54. *Ref re Criminal Code Sections 193 and 195(1)(c)* [1990] 4 W.W.R. 481 (S.C.C.).
55. *Ibid.*, 493.
56. *Ibid.*, 555.
57. *R. v. Mercure* [1988] 1 S.C.R. 234 (S.C.C.).
58. R.S.C. 1886, c. 50, as amended by S.C. 1891, c. 22, s. 18.
59. S.C., 1905, c. 42.
60. 4-5 Edw. VII, c. 3, s. 16.
61. *R. v. Mercure* [1988] 2 S.C.R. 577 (S.C.C.). 57, 584.
62. R.S.S. 1978, c. V-3 (now repealed).
63. *R. v. Mercure* [1981] 4 W.W.R. 435 (Sask. Prov. Ct.).
64. [1986] 2 W.W.R. 1 (Sask. C.A.).
65. Dickson, CJC, Beetz, Lamer, Wilson, Le Dain, and La Forest, JJ. Chouinard, J, took no part in the judgment.
66. *M'Culloch v. Maryland*, 17 U.S. (4 wheat) 316 at 407 (1819).
67. *R. v. Mercure* [1988] 1 S.C.R. 234 at (S.C.C.) 627.
68. S.C. 1891, c. 22, s. 18.
69. S.C. 1905, c. 42.
70. *R. v. Mercure* [1988] 1 S.C.R. 234 (S.C.C.) 633-34.
71. *Ibid.*, 635.
72. See *Ref re Manitoba Language Rights* [1985] 1 S.C.R. 721.
73. *R. v. Mercure* [1988] 1 S.C.R. 234 (S.C.C.) 642.
74. S.S. 1988-89, c. L-6.1.

75. *R. v. Mercure* [1988] 1 S.C.R. 234 (S.C.C.) 597.
76. *Ibid.*, 597.
77. *Ibid.*, 609.
78. *Woelk v. Halvorson* [1980] 2 S.C.R. 430.
79. William Blackstone, *Commentaries on the Laws of England*, facsimile of the first edition of 1765-69, vol. 3 (Chicago and London: University of Chicago Press, 1979), 140.
80. (1980) 106 D.L.R. (3d) 726, [1980] 1 W.W.R. 609.
81. *Woelk v. Halvorson* [1980] 2 S.C.R. 433.
82. *Ibid.*, 434.
83. [1952] A.C. 716.
84. *Woelk v. Halvorson* [1980] 2 S.C.R. 437.
85. R.S.A. 1970, c. 113, as amended by (1973) Alta., c. 61, s. 5(16).
86. *Woelk v. Halvorson* [1980] 2 S.C.R. 439.
87. *Ibid.*, 436.
88. [1981] 2 S.C.R. 21.
89. (1978) 5 C.C.L.T. 271. (Ont. C.A.).
90. (1893) 10 T.L.R. 41.
91. [1981] 2 S.C.R. 31-32.
92. *Ibid.*, 32-33.
93. *The Trustees of St. Peter's Evangelical Lutheran Church, Ottawa v. Ottawa* [1982] 2 S.C.R. 616.
94. 1974 (Ont.) c.122, now R.S.O. 1980, c. 337.
95. *The Trustees of St. Peter's Evangelical Lutheran Church, Ottawa v. Ottawa* [1982] 2 S.C.R. 621.
96. *Ibid.*, 624.
97. R.S.O. 1980, c. 219.
98. *The Trustees of St. Peter's Evangelical Lutheran Church, Ottawa v. Ottawa* [1982] 2 S.C.R. 626.
99. *Ibid.*, 640.
100. *Re: Caldwell and Stuart et al.* (1985) 15 D.L.R. (4th) 1 (S.C.C.).
101. R.S.B.C. 1979, c. 186.
102. *Re: Caldwell and Stuart et al.* (1985) 15 D.L.R. (4th) 1 (S.C.C.) 7.
103. 114 D.L.R. (3d) 357 (B.C.S.C.).
104. 132 D.L.R. (3d) 79 (B.C.C.A.).
105. *Re: Caldwell and Stuart et al.* (1985) 15 D.L.R. (4th) 1 (S.C.C.) 11.

106. *Ibid.*, 13.
107. *Ibid.*, 15.
108. *Ibid.*, 5.
109. *Ibid.*
110. *Ibid.*, 17.
111. *Ibid.*, 18.
112. *Ibid.*, 22.

VII

THE CHARTER OF RIGHTS AND FREEDOMS

IN HIS 1835 WORK, *Democracy in America,* Alexis de Tocqueville observed: "Scarcely any political question arises in the United States which is not resolved, sooner or later, into a judicial question. Hence all parties are obliged to borrow in their daily controversies, the ideas, and even the language peculiar to judicial proceedings." One wonders if this statement could not also apply to Canada since the adoption of the Charter in 1982. Hardly a week passes without mention in the media of some court tackling an important social issue. Our political vocabulary is replete with references to the language of the Charter: "equality rights," "life, liberty and security of the person," "Aboriginal and treaty rights," "language rights," and so forth. Former Premier Allan Blakeney of Saskatchewan, whose views of law and legislation coincide with McIntyre's, refers to the "judicialization of politics" now underway. Professors Cairns and Laforest, from their academic perspective, reflect on Trudeau's calculations in putting forth the Charter, and speculate on the nature and ultimate effects of the legal conflicts it has inspired. What influence has the Charter had on Canadian unity? With judges now making important policy decisions, should we not know more in advance of elevation about their values and biases? Do we need a judicial confirmation process similar to that in the United States? McIntyre has doubts about the advisability of adopting a review process, and counsels judges to be restrained when exercising their new and discretionary Charter powers. In its worst expression, the Charter can be used by politicians to defer, sometimes for years, politically sensitive decisions on the pretext of "letting the courts decide." This raises very basic questions of accountability and the appropriate relationship between courts and legislatures.

While he has never been an opponent of the Charter, McIntyre agrees with former Chief Justice J.O. Wilson that an entrenched enumeration of rights and freedoms tends to entangle courts in political decision making and may ultimately give rise to conflicts with governments. Wilson also felt there was a risk that the traditional supremacy of Parliament might be displaced by the growing hegemony of the courts. Once the Supreme Court has defined an entrenched guarantee in the Charter, legislators, government administrators, and others have less room to manoeuvre, and adjudication can lead to inflexibility.

McIntyre prefers the term "legal system" to the more frequently used contemporary term "justice system." In many cases — perhaps a substantial majority — the courts are struggling with technical problems of law that are not classifiable under the term "justice." In many such cases judges invoke the Charter to apply standards that are inappropriate. McIntyre believes that the Charter should not be resorted to simply because it's there; it should be used only when it is necessary. Unlike most of his colleagues, he did not view the new Charter as a revolutionary departure in Canadian law. It did not create new rights; these existed already. What the Charter did was to guarantee them and place them beyond the reach of the legislature to change. But essentially, all the rights were already there.

Because of his careful approach to decision making, and his reluctance, on grounds of principle, to invoke the Charter as often as did his colleagues, McIntyre has been described as a judicial conservative. While he dislikes labels, he would not reject such an ascription if it signified respect for tradition and a careful, principle-grounded approach to deciding cases. He also never attempted to stretch the evidentiary record or make factual assumptions not borne out by the "case" submitted to the Court. Other judges are not always so careful. And against the allegation of undue conservatism he can cite the cases of *Miller and Cockriell*[1] and *Rourke*[2] in the British Columbia Court of Appeal, and *O'Malley*[3] and *Andrews*[4] in the Supreme Court of Canada (in the latter he formulated the definition of "equality rights" still used with modifications, by the Supreme Court), which compare in liberality of spirit with any of the judgments drafted by his colleagues. And even where he found against the appellants in human rights cases, as in *Bhinder*[5] and *Caldwell*,[6] he spoke for the Supreme Court and substantiated his reasons carefully, demonstrating cogently why the claimed rights must be rejected. Some of his reputation as a judicial conservative rests on his dissent in *Morgentaler*,[7] where he disagreed with the majority's more liberal concessions on abortion rights, but that case, too, is entirely consistent with his whole judicial attitude. He considered in that case that Parliament had jurisdiction to pass the therapeutic abortion provision in the Criminal Code, and that no Charter provision justified the majority result.

McIntyre's former law partner Lloyd George McKenzie contends that McIntyre has been described as conservative because in method he is a "rationalist"; he organizes his thought and justifications for solving legal problems in a rational way. McKenzie says, that using the terms "liberal" and "conservative" to describe judges became current during Franklin Roosevelt's "New Deal," when the president was seen to appoint "liberal" judges to the U.S. Supreme Court to overcome obstruction to his social program from the more hidebound "conservatives" on the bench. Not many judges, McKenzie adds, can explicate as well as McIntyre does the philosophical framework that informs his judgments. What is confused with "conservatism" is his ability to articulate and justify the progression of his thought. In contrast, McKenzie regards "liberal" judges as freethinkers. They tend to spurn the past. They develop particular attitudes to a particular set of problems in an ad hoc manner but their thought does not "flow from a framework." McIntyre has sometimes criticized younger academics and judges for tendentious reasoning; in their desire to legally support a favoured result they distort the law. An agenda of this kind can harm the legal system by creating incoherence in legal doctrines.

McIntyre's respect for tradition can be seen in his approach to Charter rights. Except for democratic or voting rights, which derive from the Constitution Act, 1867, and language rights, which at least in part have the same source, the other important categories, such as fundamental freedoms, legal rights (or what the Americans call "due process"), mobility rights, and equality rights all stem from pre-existing common law.[8] Aboriginal rights are *sui generis*, emanating from treaties and longstanding Aboriginal customary practices.

Mr. Justice McKenzie's observation that McIntyre explicates his reasoning in relation to a framework refers to the interpretation of Charter provisions in relation to the common law rights from which they derive. For example, in the *Morgentaler* decision on abortion rights, while the concurring majority opinion invoked "security of the person" in section 7 to strike down section 251, McIntyre found nothing in the concept that would lead to that result. "Security of the person" connoted such things as the right to live undisturbed in one's home or freedom from arbitrary arrest; nowhere was it previously invoked as grounds for declaring that laws allegedly inducing "state-imposed psychological trauma" were of no force or effect. The court majority were unwarrantably extending the reach of the concept, McIntyre believed. This did not mean that his view of the law was a static one. In interpreting Charter provisions he would take the common law as supplying the essential "core" definitions of the various rights and freedoms and make certain extensions along their "perimeter" where necessary. What was added, however, always had to be related to what was already there.

McIntyre thinks that judges are now making law, in many cases without regard to the proper boundary separating the judicial and legislative spheres, and are tending to disregard the residual legislative supremacy that has continued to have force since 1982. He readily concedes that the separation of powers is not as strong in Canada as in the United States, where it is constitutionalized. However, in Canada, especially recently, there has been a growing separation between the courts and the political branches of government, and a strengthening tradition of judicial independence. What distinguishes Canada from the United States is the fusion of the executive and the legislature in Parliament, with the principle of responsible government requiring the executive to maintain the confidence of the legislature on important issues in order to remain in power. In the United States no amount of executive-legislative discord will, by itself, topple a government.

The peril implicit in the new constitutional order is that judges, armed with newly-entrenched powers, will be increasingly tempted to use them to strike down laws enacted by Parliament and the legislatures, thus replacing the rule of legislators with the rule of judges. That this prospect is not a mere fancy can be seen from the confrontation between the U.S. Supreme Court and the Roosevelt administration when the judges, before 1937, tried to emasculate Roosevelt's New Deal. Fresh from his overwhelming victory in the 1936 election, Roosevelt introduced a "court-packing" plan to diminish the power of the court to obstruct social legislation. He proposed that for every existing judge who reached the age of 70 and failed to retire (there being no compulsory retirement age), he would appoint a new judge, up to a maximum of 15 on the former 9-member court. In one of his "fireside chats" he appealed to the nation to support his proposal for judicial reform:

Last Thursday I described the American form of government as a three-horse team provided by the Constitution to the American people so that their field might be plowed. The three horses are, of course, the three branches of government — the Congress, the executive, and the courts. Two of the horses are pulling in unison today; the third is not. Those who have intimated that the President of the United States is trying to drive that team overlook the simple fact that the President, as Chief Executive, is himself one of the three horses.[9]

Roosevelt's purpose in enlarging the court was to appoint judges sympathetic to his administration's social policy. Yet, despite popular sympathy with the President, a strong consensus developed among influential opinion-makers and voters that his cure was too radical. Even liberal opinion in the United States turned against him, and Roosevelt was forced to abandon his plan. Had he succeeded, despite the postulated system of co-equal powers, the executive would have attained such dominance over the judiciary that the letter's independence might have been seriously impaired. Instinctively, the American people realized this and resisted his proposal.

Judges are at a disadvantage when they are drawn into controversy with the executive, because, by convention, they conceive it to be their duty not to speak out on political issues. This convention is not always observed. In Canada, when Justice Tom Berger of the Supreme Court of British Columbia criticized Prime Minister Trudeau's denial of Quebec's veto power and the temporary removal of the "Aboriginal rights" section from the draft Charter in 1981, he so incurred the displeasure of Chief Justice Laskin and the Canadian Judicial Council that he later felt obligated to resign.[10]

When Roosevelt made his frontal attack on the Supreme Court in 1937, Chief Justice Charles Evans Hughes strongly defended the institution he led and helped sway public opinion in its favour. At the same time he exerted his judicial leadership and persuaded his colleagues not to invalidate Roosevelt's statutes in so sweeping a manner as formerly. As the older Supreme Court judges retired, the president appointed lawyers who supported him and gradually was able to attain his majority while Chief Justice Hughes's diplomacy avoided further conflict. The court was saved.

The seeds for a comparable conflict are sown in Canada. Canadian judges are at the same time more powerful and more vulnerable than their brethren in the United States. In the United States the Supreme Court (like other federal courts), adjudicates issues of federal law, while the state courts deal exclusively with state law, except where a federal or constitutional issue arises, in which case the dispute may be transferred to the federal system. This happens relatively infrequently.

In Canada, the Supreme Court is a final appellate court of general jurisdiction; it can hear *all* matters of provincial and federal law. Its jurisdiction is plenary. However, the Canadian tribunal has not the same status as the U.S. Supreme Court. It does not owe its existence to a constitutional instrument[11] and, despite its enhanced powers, is still, arguably, subsidiary to the political branches of government. The Court was established by statute in 1875, pursuant to section 101 of the Constitution Act, 1867, enabling Parliament to "provide for the Constitution, Maintenance and Organization of a General Court of Appeal for Canada, and the Establishment of any additional courts for the better Administration of the Laws of Canada."[12] There is, strangely, no guarantee of the existence of the Supreme Court as an institution in the Constitution, although section 41(d) of the Constitution Act, 1982, requires the unanimous consent of Parliament and the provinces to alter "the composition of the Supreme Court of Canada." Arguably, a new Supreme Court of Canada could be constituted with new judges as long as its "composition" (the ratio of Quebec to non-Quebec judges) remained constant. This could be done by statute, whereas a constitutional amendment would be needed in the United States to substantially alter or abolish the Court.

Even before the Charter, a confrontation between the courts and Parliament could have developed in Canada over Conservative Prime Minister R.B. Bennett's New Deal social program, which was modelled on Roosevelt's. Chronic unemployment, crop failure, and severe restrictions on world markets had devastated the Canadian economy. Bennett's brother-in-law, W.D. Herridge, had served as Canadian minister to the United States during the early New Deal years, and knew such influential architects of Roosevelt's social reform program as Dean Acheson, Raymond Moley, and A.A. Berle. From Washington he plied the prime minister with a barrage of letters pleading of the inception of a similar program in Canada, both to counter the ravages of the Depression and as a means to achieve Bennett's electoral salvation. Bennett, whose Conservatives had suffered a series of by-election reverses, was irked by Herridge's constant entreaties but receptive to his basic message. In January 1935, in five ground-breaking radio broadcasts aired nation-wide, he announced the creation of a New Deal package which would essentially overhaul Canadian capitalism. To a startled electorate, the image of an affluent entrepreneur and corporation lawyer advocating what many former supporters regarded as socialism precipatated a crisis in the Conservative party. While

Bennett's conversion to left-wing politics seemed unreal to his erstwhile adherents, the opposition Liberals, led by Mackenzie King, who propounded governmental non-intervention or "laissez-faire," were horrified. In the 1935 general election campaign, King represented Bennett's New Deal as a massive federal assault on provincial jurisdiction, and the premiers, who were by now virtually all Liberal, echoed these sentiments. With Bennett's defeat, MacKenzie King sent his proposed legislation to the Supreme Court by way of a constitutional reference to determine its validity. The Court and the Judicial Committee eviscerated the Canadian New Deal in 1936-37. King was not unhappy when the judges declared his rival's social legislation unconstitutional, although he later became concerned about the implications of their decision for future federal jurisdiction.[13] The new federal Liberal government had used the courts to invalidate much-needed legislation on unemployment insurance, enlightened labour standards, and the establishment of effective marketing agencies by producers of natural products. All of these necessary Depression measures were sacrificed on the altar of the constitutional division of powers between Ottawa and the provinces. Incidental effects were to curtail federal jurisdiction to enact future social programs, as well as to undermine its treaty-implementing power.

Even right-wing Conservatives such as C.H. Cahan, one of Bennett's former ministers, were deeply critical of the British Privy Council's invalidation of almost all of the New Deal statutes, and Cahan actually presented a Bill in Parliament to abolish overseas appeals (a campaign which finally succeeded in 1949). Bennett criticized the legal reasoning of the Judicial Committee, but the fate of his legislation was sealed. The Liberals, and particularly Mackenzie King, were satisfied that their new government did not have to implement an opponent's reform program, which had figured as a manifesto, albeit a muted one, in the 1935 general election.

When Mr. Justice McIntyre recalls the prophetic reservation of Chief Justice Wilson concerning the Charter, specifically that its entrenchment would involve the courts in political decisions to an unacceptable extent, he is saddened by its accuracy. At first he thought this hazard could be avoided if judges exercised self-restraint. He attempted to reassure members of the British Columbia bar, many of whom were unenthusiastic about the new Charter, that it would not have a revolutionary impact. He gave the Charter measured support because it promoted rights and freedoms on both the federal and the provincial levels, but he never viewed it as an instrument for displacing or eclipsing common law norms. As time passed, with a court majority led by strong Charter proponents such as Chief Justice Dickson and Justices Wilson and Lamer, McIntyre grew increasingly apprehensive that the decisions of the Court were moving in a distinctly political direction. When he arrived on the Court he was resolved to engage in consensus decision making, but the gulf between himself and his colleagues on Charter issues was such that he dissented frequently. Inevitably, the trend toward politicization provokes comparison with the U.S. Supreme Court.

It is fashionable in the United States to categorize judges as either models of self-restraint, such as Oliver Wendell Holmes and Felix Frankfurter, or as judicial activists, such as Earl Warren, William O. Douglas, William Brennan, Thurgood Marshall, and the younger Hugo Black. The former tend to defer more to the legislature, upholding challenged legislation unless there is a clear conflict between an impugned law and the Bill of Rights. The latter are more prone to strike down what they regard as illiberal laws in the interest of promoting human rights and due process. The individual judge's view of institutional priorities is important here. No one would deny that Holmes was as liberal as his more activist colleagues, he simply thought that the legislature rather than the court should take the lead in promoting rights issues. The same could be said for McIntyre in Canada. In the terms of the social Darwinism of his day, Holmes regarded the nation as a vast laboratory where the Congress and 48 state legislatures were enacting myriad, often contradictory laws. Gradually, amid this welter of legislation, the better laws, those reflecting more successful social experiments, would be reinforced and emulated and the inferior ones discarded. This was the legal equivalent of the principle of "survival of the fittest," yet Holmes also considered that these laws should be generated not by courts but by legislatures. Not all adherents of judicial restraint, of course, agreed with this philosophy.

Between these poles, one evincing a preference for court-generated, the other for legislature-generated policy making, there is a spectrum of intermediate positions, and the approach of individual judges may shift depending on the case. In the U.S. Supreme Court, so-called swing judges such as Lewis F. Powell are seen as being situated in the strategically important "neutral centre" of the court. Especially in close 5-4 decisions they can incline the court one way or another. Counsel will often direct arguments at, and attempt to engage in dialogue with, these "centrist" judges, since they are more likely to change their positions than those whose legal views are relatively fixed.

CONFIRMATION OF JUDICIAL NOMINEES BY THE U.S. SENATE

In the United States, the importance of the Supreme Court in the governmental process renders the appointment of federal judges the very stuff of national politics. In presidential election campaigns, when Richard Nixon, Ronald Reagan, or Bob Dole spoke of appointing "strict constructionists" to the Supreme Court, they had an institutional paradigm in mind. They may not be appointing judges known for their self-restraint so much as those who support conservative social policy, a bias which may take as activist a direction as liberal policy in that judges may actively discourage attempts to disturb the legal status quo.

Presidential candidates are mindful the need to gain and hold the support of the Senate judiciary subcommittee and the Senate as a whole, so as to have their judicial nominees confirmed. Senators Joseph Biden and Orrin Hatch have both had to consider the nominees of a president from the opposing party, a Republican president in Biden's case and a Democratic one in Hatch's. Much political discussion and probing occurs — almost always unsuccessfully — toward discovering a prospective judge's views on issues that might come before the court in future. Nominees are subjected to the most intense scrutiny of their personal lives and professional qualifications, and do not always secure confirmation.

When President Lyndon Johnson nominated a sitting Justice, Abe Fortas, for the chief justiceship near the end of his second term, there were allegations that Fortas, a very able jurist, was involved in a conflict of interest and he voluntarily withdrew from the process. Johnson had no time to make another nomination before the 1968 presidential election. Instead of Fortas, President Nixon's nominee, Warren Burger, was confirmed to succeed Earl Warren as Chief Justice. However, two of Nixon's other nominees, Clement Haynesworth and Harrold Carswell, were rejected by the Senate, as was Reagan's nominee, Robert F. Bork. When Clarence Thomas was nominated by Bush, charges of sexual impropriety directed against him by Professor Anita Hill resulted in a protracted and controversial debate, and in the end he was confirmed by only a few votes. In the cases of Bork and Thomas, the Democratic Senate majority had strong reservations about the generally conservative views of both men, in addition to personal factors. Bork was unquestionably able but his academic writing for law journals had revealed his conservative legal philosophy so trenchantly that it soured his relationship with liberal leaders in the Senate. Someone with similar views who had expressed them more equivocally and less prolifically might have been confirmed.

LEGISLATIVE CONFIRMATION FOR JUDGES IN CANADA

The Supreme Court in Canada has historically occupied a more subordinate position than its American counterpart, but with the adoption of the Charter in 1982 it has come to wield substantial, quasi-political power in areas of jurisdiction more extensive than the U.S. Supreme Court. For example, the American Court reviews questions of state law only when a federal constitutional issue arises, whereas, as a "general court of appeal," the Canadian Supreme Court can entertain any matter of provincial or federal law. This more ample accretion of decision making power signifies that, potentially, no law in Canada is immune to review by the Court, while in the United States, many laws are beyond the scope of the Supreme Court.

Given the existence and reach of the Charter, should legislative confirmation of Canadian judicial nominees be required before their appointment to the Supreme Court? McIntyre considers that these appointments have not been political in the past and sees no necessity for changing the current appointing system. His opinion coincides with that of the Canadian Bar Associations's Committee on the Appointment of Judges in Canada, which reported in 1985: "Parliament should not play a role in the selection or appointment of federal judges. It is neither necessary nor desirable for the legislative branch to be involved. It is contrary to the Canadian tradition for the appointment of judges to be subjected to a Congressional-type process of public examination and review."[14] To admirers of the common law like McIntyre, the appeal to tradition is powerful, but in the age of the Charter, which involves judges at all levels in social policy making, a persuasive argument can be made in favour of a legislative confirmation process in Canada. What did the Canadian public really know about any of the recent appointees to the Supreme Court before their nomination by the federal cabinet? What were their social backgrounds, their career patterns, their values and biases? The Canadian Bar Association's committee finding was reached after extensive consultation with judges and lawyers in every province in Canada and with foreign legal experts. Generally, they regarded the American confirmation process as unduly political and unfocussed on objective legal merit. It intruded too much into private life and detered superior candidates from presenting themselves.

Despite these apparent drawbacks there is not much evidence that superior American candidates for judicial appointment have been deterred by the president's constitutional mandate to secure "the advice and consent of the Senate" prior to appointing Supreme Court judges. In one celebrated confirmation process in 1937, it was revealed that one of President Franklin Roosevelt's nominees, Hugo Black, had been a member of the Ku Klux Klan in Alabama. After Roosevelt assured the Senate of Black's current "progressive" views, he was confirmed and became a leading member of the Court, and particularly championed First Amendment freedoms. The Senate judiciary committee is known for its close interrogation of nominees, and for the latters' tendency to hedge when asked questions on controversial matters such as abortion or affirmative action, on the ground that these might come before the court and should not be prejudged. Nevertheless, before nominees are confirmed or rejected, the American public knows much more about their opinions and backgrounds than the Canadian public does concerning their future judges.

Two dissenters from the view of the Canadian legal establishment, which opposes legislative confirmation, are Ron Basford, a minister of justice under Trudeau, and Svend Robinson, an M.P. for the federal New Democratic Party. They both favour a scrutiny of nominees by legislative committee, on grounds that a new openness is needed in the Charter era. Because judges exercise unprecedented power in human rights issues, the public has a right to know more about their character and opinions, their legal philosophy, their commitments, and their professional lives. People have a right to inquire into any racial, religious, or gender biases that might deflect a nominee from deciding human rights issues impartially. Mr. Robinson thinks that a more open process would encourage the selection of women and minority group members, thereby making courts more representative of Canadian society. In Canada this debate continues. On the occasion of Mr. Justice McIntyre's retirement in 1989, Professor F.L. Morton of the

University of Calgary cited the plethora of legal cases involving "abortion, mandatory retirement, immigration, the political activities of unions, censorship of pornography, anti-hate literature, bilingual education and a mind-boggling host of section 15 equality issues," then posed the question: "Does it really make sense that we know absolutely nothing about the judges who will make these decisions until they are appointed?"[15] On the other side, Professor Ian Hunter of the University of Western Ontario questioned whether judicial review would be of any real use: "Such hearings will prove ineffective because only two kinds of questions may be put to a prospective nominee: irrelevant questions which will be answered but are a waste of time, and relevant questions, which any prospective judge worth his salt will decline to answer."[16] In the latter category Professor Hunter included all questions on matters before the court and those up for judicially examination after the nominee's appointment.

Former Saskatchewan Premier Allan E. Blakeney foresees the eventuality of a Canadian legislative confirmation process for judges.[17] Because of the enormous scope of federal judicial authority, which in Canada involves all aspects of federal and provincial law, such a process could lead to the establishment of a separate constitutional court in Germany, or more recently, South Africa. The extensive scope for review in Canada seems to require a wider range of judicial skills and also, perhaps, separate intermediate appellate courts. Blakeney recognizes that while the U.S. Supreme Court serves as a single, final, appellate tribunal, it also has a narrower jurisdiction because it does not consider nearly as many "civil law" matters (most of which are finally disposed of by state courts) as its Canadian counterpart.

McIntyre would disagree with Blakeney and others on the need for legislative confirmation and also on the establishment of a constitutional court or new intermediate appellate forum between provincial Courts of Appeal and the Supreme Court of Canada. He believes that the nomination process would become unduly politicized if a confirmation process were adopted, and considers that there are too many appeals in the existing system. As courts become more involved in social policy issues, however, the pressure will probably increase for a Canadian legislative confirmation process for judges.

REVISITING THE CHARTER

According to McIntyre's analysis, the isolation of Quebec toward the end of the bargaining over patriation, and the entrenchment of the

Charter in November 1981, did more harm than good to the cause of Canadian unity. For reasons described earlier,[18] he regarded the majority opinion on constitutional convention as mischievous and unnecessary. The issue of "convention" addressed by the majority was not legal but political, and should have been left to the political actors to decide. It did not fall appropriately within the ambit of judicial review. When the court majority resolved to split the issues into legal and conventional segments, deciding the former in favour of Ottawa and the latter in favour of the provinces, the parties were driven back to the bargaining table to negotiate a compromise enabling the amendment package to proceed to Westminster with the support of "a substantial majority of the provinces." It was in those final sessions that the rift between Quebec and the other parties, with all its fateful consequences, occurred.

Ironically, in setting out his proposal for an entrenched enumeration of rights in October 1980, Prime Minister Trudeau thought that he was honouring a promise he had made to Quebec in the May 1980 referendum on "sovereignty-association," in that the "constitutional renewal" so effected would promote national unity. Trudeau, Justice Minister Jean Chrétien, and provincial Liberal leader Claude Ryan had promised the Quebec electorate that in return for their rejecting "sovereignty-association," the province's constitutional needs would be seriously addressed. On May 20, 60 percent of Quebec voters rejected the proposal. A constitutional task force jointly led by Chrétien and Saskatchewan Attorney General Roy Romanow, toiling throughout the summer of 1980, proved abortive, and in the following October, with the breakdown of further negotiations, Trudeau decided to proceed unilaterally. He announced his intention to do so on October 2 on national television. The federal government was supported only by Ontario and New Brunswick, with the other eight provinces eventually arguing in the Supreme Court of Canada that Trudeau's proposal was unconstitutional.

A wide ideological gulf separated the two Québécois negotiators, Trudeau and Lévesque, in the federal-provincial sessions, and some wonder whether they could ever have agreed on a constitutional package. Like Diefenbaker before him, Pierre Trudeau was a believer in "One Canada," and the foe of any narrow, inward-looking nationalism, in Canada or elsewhere. His cosmopolitan background included classes under Joseph Schumpeter at Harvard and Harold Laski at the London School of Economics. His adversary, René Lévesque, had been

Liberal minister of natural resources in the early 1960s, when the government had nationalized Hydro-Quebec. He was disposed to challenge authority. He had discontinued his studies at Laval University's law school when a future Supreme Court of Canada judge, Louis-Philippe Pigeon, had told him to put out the cigarette that he was smoking in class. He left the classroom and never returned. He later became a widely admired documentary journalist with Radio Canada. Still later, this fervent nationalist served two terms, from 1976 to 1984, as Parti Québécois premier of Quebec. As the dispute over patriation developed in the months after October 1981, the animosity between Lévesque and Trudeau became increasingly bitter.

Former Premier Blakeney, a leading participant in the 1980-82 constitutional dispute, contends that as negotiations unfolded the premiers were unaware of the level of bitterness dividing Lévesque and Trudeau. On one occasion, Blakeney attended a dinner at 24 Sussex Drive, where Trudeau was accompanied by one federal minister and all the other guests were premiers:

We were talking about the Constitution and Trudeau and Lévesque began to get into a real slanging match. And they began to use quite insulting language, as is their wont. They were speaking in French and as they glanced around the table they could see that the premiers weren't able to follow it, so they switched to English, belaboring and insulting each other so that we could get the full benefit of it. It is so uncharacteristic, because the rest of us were uniformly polite; we may have been a little sharp at times, if we had a point to make.

This personal rancor did not bode well for a future agreement.

As the dispute continued, Trudeau assured the other nine premiers that he could speak as effectively for Quebec as Premier Lévesque. If it proved impossible to secure Lévesque's consent to the constitutional package, Trudeau would speak for the province in his place. In the election of 18 February 1980, which returned Trudeau to power after the brief career of Prime Minister Joe Clark, he won almost every seat in Quebec. According to Trudeau's mathematics,

Let's remember that the members of Parliament from Quebec had voted in favor of the 1982 Constitution by 72 to 2 (vote of December 2, 1981). And the members of the legislative assembly from Quebec had voted 70 to 38 that they could not "accept the plan for repatriating the Constitution" (vote of December 1, 1981). If I am not mistaken, this makes a total of 72 delegates who did not accept the 1982 Constitution and a total of 111 who did accept it. What an amazing power play that was: one that was accepted by 60 percent of Quebec's elected representatives.[19]

Citing a different vote in the Quebec National Assembly on another resolution, Professor Guy Laforest disputes Trudeau's arithmetic.[20]

While McIntyre, like Trudeau, inclined toward a centralist vision of federalism, he has doubts in hindsight about the latter's wisdom in promoting a Charter of Rights. Although McIntyre has Saskatchewan roots and represented British Columbia on the Supreme Court, he refers to the much denser populations of Ontario and Quebec which, along with their vibrant industries and rich resources, he considers entitles them to extra weight in federal-provincial councils. While he dislikes the present trend of Charter interpretation by the courts, he certainly hopes that the ultimate effect of the Charter will be positive. Early on he loyally defended the Charter to B.C. legal audiences, some of whom considered the document alien to Canadian legal traditions, but later he became apprehensive about how the courts were applying Charter provisions. He now questions whether a reasoned assessment of the Charter's worth can really be made at this time; it might take half a century before a firm conclusion as to its true value can be hazarded.

Ostensibly, Trudeau put forward his package to fulfil his promise to Quebec voters that if they voted against sovereignty association he would bring about "constitutional renewal" for Quebec. Did he achieve that purpose or did he seriously misread public opinion? Historically, Quebec premiers have opposed centralization and sought to reinforce "provincial autonomy" to further local values. The 1956 *Tremblay Report*,[21] for example, which represented Premier Duplessis' constitutional thinking, likened federalism to a pyramid in which a wide range of social and economic functions would be carried out at the base by local organizations like municipalities, cooperatives, credit unions, and churches. The federal government, at the peak of the pyramid, should assume responsibility only for those functions that could not be performed at lower levels. Such a concept, especially as interpreted by Duplessis, would favour local over national jurisdiction in most areas. The theory behind this constitutional model was that decision making is best undertaken by those persons and groups most affected by the outcome. The call for decentralization by contemporary Canadian premiers has much the same flavour.

In contrast to the above view, Professor Laforest, citing Peter H. Russell and other constitutional scholars, regards the 1982 Charter as having a nationalizing influence. By enhancing the power of the centralist Supreme Court of Canada, it tends to homogenize laws and universalize social policy. Once the Supreme Court has made a decision, it applies throughout the country, including Quebec.[22] In matters of language, sections 16 to 23 of the Charter promote "national standards" rather than provincial control.[23] The concept of citizenship it advances is one where rights inhere to individuals by virtue of their membership in a national community.[24] The Québécois have regarded Canada in terms of two concurrent majorities, one in the broader nation-state and the other in Quebec, each charged with promoting its own interests, and each (preferably) leaving the other alone. However, Trudeau, in his struggle to have the Charter endorsed, appealed to a large number of minority groups, women, and Aboriginal peoples, who later acquired constitutional status in that instrument. They tended to become buffers between the individual and the state. Laforest cites Alan Cairns to the effect that the Charter circumvents duality, substituting for it a political culture of "constitutional minoritarianism":[25]

According to Cairns, these various minorities benefit from a contagion effect: each gain obtained by one encourages the others to follow suit, reinforcing the general system of constitutional minoritarianism. Buttressed by their new rights, they will continue to fight relentlessly and passionately. As Cairns points out, they speak of "shame, pride, dignity, affront, inclusion and exclusion, humiliation and recognition." None of this bodes well for the principle of two majorities.[26]

In enlisting ethnic groups, feminists, Aboriginal communities, and others as allies, it was as if Trudeau were attempting to establish a "counterweight" to the formerly strong powers of the provinces, particularly Quebec. Although the prime minister spoke of "people's rights" or a "people's package," his proposal, according to Laforest, in no way represented "popular sovereignty"; the groups assisting him were cleverly manipulated from above to achieve *his* goals.[27]

For his part, McIntyre foresaw that the newly-empowered groups mentioned by LaForest and Cairns would use the Charter to promote special interests. It was easier for these groups to achieve their purposes through litigation than to appeal for action to often unresponsive majoritarian governments, but the result could also be more socially divisive.

In effect Trudeau promised the Quebec electorate constitutional renewal[28] in return for rejecting sovereignty-association in the 1980 referendum, then effected his promise by creating a Charter that defined human rights in *universal* terms. Is that instrument more assimilationist, even subversive, than not? Both the Québécois and Aboriginal peoples are more concerned with their respective cultural heritages, rooted in the land and nurtured by local tradition and historical experience, than they are with universalist documents. Very similar guarantees to those in the Charter are found in Quebec Charter of Human Rights, but that locally-produced instrument is more subject to local interpretation. The Québécois are also aware that Trudeau, the bestower of rights, invoked the War Measures Act — the very negation or these rights — in the FLQ crisis in October 1970.

Nevertheless, when Laforest contends that the 1982 Charter did not reflect "popular sovereignty" in Quebec, and that it was imposed on an unwilling province by an insensitive federal government, his arguments require close scrutiny. The hope of enshrining rights in the Constitution was pervasive throughout the country at the beginning of the 1980s and was as popular in Quebec as elsewhere. In the 1980 "Beige Paper" setting out the constitutional proposals of the Quebec Liberal Party, an extensive national rights charter was advocated that in some ways ran in advance of the present Charter. Their Charter covered virtually all the rights entrenched in 1982, and its proponents at the time were adamant that there be no "notwithstanding clause" to undermine the enumerated rights through majority vote in provincial legislatures.[29] Thus, a substantial body of thought in Quebec already existed to support the concept of a strong national rights Charter. Moreover, two months after the Charter was proclaimed into law on April 17, 1982, when Canadians were asked in a national opinion poll[30] if "in the long run, our Constitution will be a good thing for Canada," 57 percent of respondents said it was a good thing and 14 percent said it was not, a ratio of four-to-one in favour. In Quebec 49 percent said it was good and 16 percent disagreed, or a ratio of three-to-one in favour of the Constitution. (In both cases, those saying they "did not know" made up the difference to 100 percent.) These figures do not support Laforest's perception of imposed alien values by an arbitrary central government.

McIntyre's argument that, in the long run, the Supreme Court's judgment in the *Patriation* case, by dispensing with Quebec's consent, facilitated that province's isolation and worsened its relations with the rest of Canada, is a cogent one. After 1982 nationalist stalwarts in the Parti Québécois could say, "This is a Constitution not of our making." When Prime Minister Mulroney's two attempts to repair the damage and reintegrate Quebec into the constitutional framework — Meech Lake (1987-90) and the Charlottetown Accord (1992) — both failed, Quebec nationalists could maintain with force that their alienation was all the greater, even though Quebec voters had rejected the Charlottetown initiative in the 1992 referendum. Looked upon cumulatively, the whole linked succession of constitutional endeavour, beginning in 1980-82, provided ample grounds for the separatist outcry. Moreover, it was the centralizing "people's Charter" that was adopted and the two provincial rights instruments that miscarried. The latter were designed to appease Quebec, and Laforest emphasizes that many influential Quebec intellectuals see the Charter despite its incidental good effects, as a centralizing document running counter to their province's historic interests. McIntyre's question can be repeated here: Has Canadian unity really been promoted by the Supreme Court's judgment on "convention" and the entrenchment of the Charter?

Has the Canadian federation passed the point where constitutional events will lead, inexorably, to the breakup of the country? Have we as a nation encountered our constitutional nemesis? Blakeney suggests that the die was cast by October 1980, when Trudeau put his package on the table and said he was ready to proceed unilaterally. With that initiative a public expectation was created that was difficult to counteract. In Blakeney's words,

I would have thought it would have been very difficult to reverse after that [October 1980] without everyone making a strenuous effort: to reverse gracefully. It seemed to me then that we had to come out with something. But I remember expressing this view to the group. The public will somehow get the visceral feeling that this political system cannot produce any agreement. I didn't care in a personal sense how we looked as politicians. I wasn't going to lose any votes about it in Saskatchewan. If there was no final agreement between federal and provincial governments that's got to be bad in the long run. Somehow we've got to bring some closure to this thing.[31]

In Blakeney's estimation there had emerged at the premiers' meeting a sense of inevitability or irreversibility that propelled the participants onward.

The Supreme Court's decision of September 1981 was a Pyrrhic victory for both sides: Ottawa won on "law" but the provinces won on "convention." McIntyre believes that in arriving at their decision the majority ignored certain precedents where constitutional amendments had been made over the protest of one or other of the provinces. He, Laskin, and Estey, in their dissenting judgment, took these into account: "Only in four cases has full provincial consent been obtained and in many cases the federal government has proceeded with amendments in the face of active provincial opposition. In our view it is unrealistic in the extreme to say that the convention has emerged."[32] On convention they were outmaneuvered by the majority who held that "a substantial measure of provincial consent,"[33] unquantified, was necessary to secure a constitutional amendment affecting provincial powers. The Quebec Court of Appeal[34] and the Supreme Court of Canada[35] later held that Quebec did not have to be one of the provinces forming part of that substantial majority. Had the Supreme Court decided that Quebec's consent was necessary, of course, patriation and the Charter would not have been possible unless Quebec changed its position.

The majority judgment on convention made necessary a further federal-provincial constitutional conference, in November 1981, if the newly mandated "measure of provincial consent" was to be achieved. With eight provinces opposed to the federal government package, Trudeau could not say that that standard had been met, and he reluctantly agreed to new negotiations. At the conference in Ottawa he had to make costly concessions in order to secure the consent required. "Some things were given up," he said later, "in order to constitutionalize the amending process. The things I gave up — some of them made me sad."[36]

The surrender that elicited the most criticism was the insertion of a "notwithstanding" clause in section 33 of the Charter, which enabled Parliament or the provinces to override fundamental freedoms, legal rights, and equality rights enumerated in the document. Blakeney concedes that the premiers of the three prairie provinces, himself along with Premier Peter Lougheed of Alberta and Premier Sterling Lyon of Manitoba, were the main proponents of the override. Lyon was implacably opposed to the Charter and sought a means for legislatures to reassert their jurisdiction by overriding it. Blakeney and Lougheed preferred not to have a Charter but saw some merit in it, and wanted to impress on the courts that they, the courts, were not in the law-making business. Blakeney reported another reason for adopting the override; that was to make the Charter more acceptable to Quebec. He was told by the Saskatchewan jurist D.K. MacPherson that the measure would spark "an ongoing dialogue between the legislatures and the courts" as to their respective spheres of operation.[37] The notwithstanding clause was anathema to civil libertarians because it allowed legislatures to take away rights that not only were laid down as universal, but which had been declared to exist and apply in specific cases. An example of this may be the right to "freedom of expression," denied in Quebec's language laws for its anglophone minority, and upheld by the provincial courts.[38] The potential for dispossessing vulnerable minority groups of rights in this manner was regarded as particularly odious, because such groups would have difficulty making a case against the use of the clause in a majoritarian legislature. Why, then, did the main opposition to the clause come from the prairies? Perhaps it could be regarded as an expression of Western populism, which tended to esteem legislatures and distrust courts.

Another compromise Trudeau was forced to make was to substitute the Vancouver constitutional amending formula (preferred by the dissenting provinces, and requiring concurrence by at least two-thirds of the provinces having an aggregate total of half the Canadian population) for the Victoria formula. The prime minister's preference needed the weighted concurrence of provinces in the Western and Atlantic regions, with vetoes for Ontario and Quebec. McIntyre contends the Victoria formula is more realistic, since the density of population and industrial might of the two central provinces should be recognized. This amending formula was resisted by other provinces because it entailed single-province vetoes. Also surrendered was Trudeau's popular referendum device to break future logjams between Ottawa and the provinces over controversial amendments. Some of the premiers opposed this proposal because they thought Ottawa could manipulate public opinion by deciding unilaterally the timing and wording of the referendum.

The decision not to entrench "property rights" in the Charter was also controversial. Blakeney thinks there was no great enthusiasm for this provision during the Charter debate, even among the more conservative premiers. Lyon, the "parliamentary sovereigntist," was the most right-wing of all the premiers, but he opposed the Charter on principle and wanted it weakened rather than strengthened by incorporating new provisions. In the age of positive or interventionist states, all the premiers considered that a "property" provision would make government work more onerous. Opponents thought it would be cited in the courts against laws dealing with expropriation, taxation, environmental protection, income redistribution, marketing standards, and other areas of social policy. There was no way to know in advance what a court might consider "property." If the government claimed airspace above an apartment building adjacent to an airport for "flightway clearance," for example, was that an expropriation for which compensation was due? Or if a utilities commission set the rate for power at too low a figure, could the owner of the utility sue the commission and demand that it raise rates to an "economic level," because there had been a confiscation of its property by the government?

Judge McIntyre sees valid arguments for both sides of the question and does not take a strong position either way. He is aware that many people fear the entrenchment of property rights. Since the mid-nineteenth century there has been a strong public perception that "property rights" can be used to oppress people. Especially since the Great Depression there is a shared view among government leaders that such rights, when entrenched, also interfere with the development of social policy. If McIntyre were opposed to entrenchment, the reason he would give is that the constitutionalization of such rights would result in undue rigidity. All rights have to be limited. Instead of protecting property rights by entrenchment it is preferable to do so by way of legislation, as in the Saskatchewan Human Rights Code,[39] which is more flexible than formal and more likely to be kept up to date.

The debate on property rights was closely allied to the controversy over procedural and substantive due process in section 7 of the Charter. Asked whether certain sections of the Charter were "empty vessels" that judges could fill at will, Blakeney cited sections 7 and 15. Federal draftsmen had gone to great lengths to avoid the American doctrine of "substantive due process" by discarding the term "due process" altogether and substituting the term "fundamental justice" in section 7. Their purpose was to limit judges to remedying defective procedure in criminal and punitive processes and prevent them from going into the intrinsic merits of statute law, which was not perceived to fall within their jurisdiction. American cases interpreting the phrase "due process of law" in the fourteenth amendment made Canadian drafters cautious. One of the leading U.S. cases on substantive due process was *Lochner v. New York*,[40] in which a New York statute prohibited bakery employees from working more than 60 hours in any one week or over 10 hours in a day. The state contended that this law was a valid exercise of police power to protect workers' health, but the U.S. Supreme Court ruled that it was an unconstitutional interference with freedom of contract, a "liberty" protected in the fourteenth amendment. The decision was not concerned with procedure but went into the actual merits of the legislation. Canadian drafters sought to circumvent forays by the courts into the jungle of substantive due process by carefully choosing their words.

Blakeney is the politician whose constitutional views most closely resemble those of McIntyre, although McIntyre saw some limited applicability for the concept of "substantive due process," which Blakeney rejected outright. McIntyre invoked the concept only once[41] in his decade on the Court, and it is clear from his general approach that he would use it very sparingly, and only in exceptional cases. Above all, Blakeney and McIntyre saw judicial self-restraint as desirable and necessary, and they shared a centralist vision of federalism, which Blakeney also considered obliged the federal government to aid provinces suffering adversity, as in the case of Saskatchewan in the 1930s. They also both admired the common law tradition, and had serious reservations about how the Charter was being applied by the courts.

In discussions prior to the Charter's adoption, politicians were assured by federal officials that by using the words "fundamental justice" instead of "due process of law" they had avoided the danger of substantive interpretation. In Blakeney's words,

We had arguments about this [section 7]. Is this procedural, or is it substantive due process, to use the American term? "Oh no, this is procedural." Do we all agree? Barry [now Mr. Justice Strayer], are you clear that this doesn't include any element of substantive due process? "Oh no, no, there's no doubt about that." Everybody agreed on what they thought it meant, and regrettably everybody did not include the Supreme Court, who gave their own interpretation to it, which I would characterize as in forty elements of substantive due process.[42]

Barry Strayer, who was assistant deputy minister (public law) in the Department of Justice, gave essentially the same testimony in a 1985 Supreme Court case, *Re B.C. Motor Vehicle Act*.[43] Concerning the term "fundamental justice" in section 7, he said, "[I]t in our view does not cover the concept of what is called substantive due process, which would impose substantive requirements as to the law in question."[44] In that case, section 94(c) of the B.C. Motor Vehicle Act[45] created an absolute liability offence with mandatory imprisonment for the offence of driving on provincial roads without a valid licence, even if the driver did not know his licence had been suspended. Guilt was established on proof of driving without a licence. The province was obviously attempting to reduce the numbers of highway accidents, but there was also an issue of whether morally innocent persons, those who were not aware that their licences had been suspended for administrative reasons, should be forced to serve a mandatory minimum jail term. The law here, of course, seemed to be bad, not for any procedural reason, but bad in substance. Lamer, J (as he then was), found that there was an element of "fundamental justice" that went beyond procedural due process; its principles "were not limited solely to procedural guarantees."[46] Although she came to the same result, Wilson, J, doubted whether the dichotomy between substance and procedure "should be imported into section 7 of the Charter."[47] That, however, was the effect of her judgment. In a very short concurring judgment, admirable in its lucidity, McIntyre said,

I agree that "fundamental justice," as the term is used in the *Charter*, involves more than natural justice (which is largely procedural) and includes as well a substantive element. I am also of the view that on any definition of the term "fundamental justice" the imposition of minimum imprisonment for an offence in respect of which no defence can be made, and which may be committed unknowingly and with no wrongful intent, deprives or may deprive of liberty and it offends the principles of fundamental justice.[48]

If the Supreme Court wished to get rid of this statutory provision, it had to do so on "substantive" grounds. In doing so, however, they were entering uncharted waters, and the ultimate consequences of this plunge were unforeseeable. Despite the caveats of Lamer and Wilson, there could be no question that an element of "substantive due process" was attributable to section 7. As to Mr. Strayer's testimony to the contrary, Lamer said that the intentions of individual drafters of the Charter would be given little weight. The court would decide for itself the meaning of Charter provisions:

[T]he *Charter* is not the product of a few individual public servants, however distinguished, but of a multiplicity of individuals who played major roles in the negotiating, drafting and adoption of the *Charter*. How can one say with any confidence that within this enormous multiplicity of actors, without forgetting the role of the provinces, the comments of a few federal civil servants can in any way be determinative?

Were this Court to accord any significant weight to this testimony, it would in effect be assuming a fact which is nearly impossible of proof, i.e., the intention of the legislative bodies which adopted the *Charter*. In view of the indeterminate nature of the data, it would in my view be erroneous to give these materials anything but minimal weight.[49]

With this approach, any vestige of Borkean "original intent" was gone. The positive aspect of the judgment was that the intentions of the drafters would not become a strait-jacket for future generations. The negative aspect was that the court would enjoy unfettered leeway in determining what the broad terms of the Charter meant.

In rare cases, both the Supreme Court of Canada and its counterpart in the United States must decide whether or not to invalidate an iniquitous law, one that may be unobjectionable from a procedural point of view but evil in substance. These cases raise vexing questions and involve consideration of the degree of wickedness inherent to an impugned law. Former U.S. Solicitor General Archibald Cox dilates on the long heritage of "substantive due process" in Anglo-American law:

American jurists, with a few exceptions, have always accepted the view that the concept of due process of law, like the words "the law of the land" in Magna Carta, puts some liberties and some property interests beyond the power of government, thus embodying in the Fourteenth Amendment at least a portion of the heritage that we traced from natural law, Lord Coke and "the rights of Englishmen." Lawyers call the concept "substantive due process" to distinguish it from "procedural due process" also required by the amendment.[50]

Despite the most diligent efforts of Canadian government officials to avoid any implication of "substantive due process" in drafting the Charter, their precautions came to naught. The Supreme Court in its wisdom is empowered to decide when and where such a concept could be invoked to strike down laws that are inherently bad. The danger here is that assertions of this power may involve judges in a quasi-legislative role. So far it has been rarely used, but future use could bring the court into conflict with Parliament and the provincial legislatures.

Because "property rights" have not been entrenched in the Charter, it is unlikely that they will be used (as in the United States) for the protection of "property interests."

Although Blakeney now considers his worst fears concerning the Charter to be, as yet, unfulfilled, he still foresees problems ahead, both for courts and for legislatures. Like McIntyre, he sees the legal rights provisions (sections 7-14) of the Charter as a codification of common law rights of the accused, and as such unexceptionable. He has more concerns about the fundamental justice (section 2) and equality rights (section 15) provisions, which he fears may encroach on the legislative prerogative. He would be very worried if the concept of "substantive due process" was applied extensively in future cases, because the courts would then be overinvolved in legislation. He is anxious not only about a "politicization of the courts," i.e., when they make decisions that are essentially political, but also about a "legalization of politics," when the legislatures are constantly looking over their shoulder to see whether the courts agree with what they are doing. In his opinion, the latter happens in the United States all the time. If public pressure is put on a state legislature to pass a law that it knows will not stand the test of time, it may still comply with the public will, knowing that in the end the courts will strike it down. Whatever the target of public distress — mugging in the streets, child molestation, funding for abortion, or hard-core pornography — the enactment of a law prone to protracted judicial review is often used as a stratagem in place of a thorough-going political solution. If the courts invalidate the law in due course, politicians can still say, "It's not our fault, we tried." In the meantime the problem may have passed from the public eye. Something like this happened in Canada when Doug Lewis was minister of justice. He pleaded that he could not enact a revised abortion law until the Supreme Court spoke definitively on the issue. In that case he was confronted by two implacably opposed groups, and any solution he proposed other than non-action would be met with stiff opposition. In the end, the government did nothing. In its worst expression, this kind of institutional interchange can lead to shameless buck-passing.

During the debate on the Charter, Blakeney raised the question of why a Charter was needed when Canada already had a Bill of Rights. McIntyre has also asked the same question. The rights and freedoms defined in the Charter were essentially set out in the Bill of Rights and could have been fully enforced, at least within areas of federal jurisdiction. In fact it was not enforced because no one took the Bill of Rights seriously, and while Blakeney did not know why this was so, he did not think negotiators "should convulse the country to convince the judges" in a national debate on the Charter.[51] McIntyre feels that if the Canadian Bill of Rights were applied on the federal plane and the various human rights codes were applied provincially, the statutory protection of human rights would be as extensive as necessary.

As discussed above, McIntyre disliked the tendency of some of his Supreme Court colleagues to invoke Charter provisions broadly, and without concrete justification, simply to achieve desired results. For McIntyre the reasoning process by which an end was reached was of great importance, and the law should neither be distorted, nor the facts manipulated, to attain a specific result, however desirable, if the means to that end were legally or procedurally unsound. When distortions are introduced into law to such a purpose, the law loses its coherence and becomes more difficult to define. Above all, the courts should avoid the temptation to indulge in "social engineering," to use Roscoe Pound's term, by substituting their policy views for those of Parliament or the provincial legislatures. Eventually, this switch would lead to conflict between the judicial branch and various governments, and entangle the judges politically. In some cases, politicians have encouraged this confusion of roles by using Charter litigation to delay decisions they found embarrassing to take, with the refrain: "Let the courts decide; we're not sure what the legal situation is." Once the courts had spoken on sensitive topics, politicians can then acquiesce, thus absolving themselves of responsibility for social policy. In such cases the Charter, indeed, the Canadian Constitution, could become a device for passing the buck. A very real question arises as to whether such proceedings belong in a democracy. They raise very basic issues of legal and political accountability.

NOTES

1. (1976) 63 D.L.R. (3d), 193 (B.C.C.A.).
2. [1975] 6 W.W.R. 591 (B.C.C.A.).
3. [1985] 2 S.C.R. 536 (S.C.C.).
4. [1989] 2 W.W.R. 289 (S.C.C.).
5. (1986) 23 D.L.R. (4th), 481 (S.C.C.).
6. (1985) 15 D.L.R. (4th), 1 (S.C.C.).
7. [1988] 1 S.C.R. 30.
8. Cf. Stephen Brooks, *Canadian Democracy*, 2nd edn. (Toronto:

Oxford University Press, 1996), 273. The Table in Professor Brooks's work outlines the provenance of the various Charter provisions.

9. "Reform of the Federal Judiciary: 1937," in Henry Steele Commager, *Documents of American History*, 4th edn. (New York: Appleton-Century-Crofts, 1948), 563.
10. See "The Berger Affair," in F.L. Morton, ed., *Law, Politics and the Judicial Process in Canada*, 2nd edn. (Calgary: University of Calgary, 1992), 147.
11. Article III, sec. 1 of the Constitution of the United States declares, "The judicial Power of the United States, shall be vested in one Supreme Court, and in such inferior courts as the congress may from time to time ordain and establish." In Commager, *Documents*, note 9 at 143.
12. Section 101, Constitution Act, 1867, in Peter W. Hogg, *Constitutional Law of Canada*, 3rd edn. (Toronto: Carswell, 1992), 1326.
13. See W.H. McConnell, "The Judicial Review of Prime Minister Bennett's 'New Deal,'" in (1968), 6 *Osgoode Hall L.J.*, 39.
14. The Committee on the Appointment of Judges in Canada, *The Appointment of Judges in Canada* (Ottawa: The Canadian Bar Foundation, 1985), 66. The writer was research assistant for the Committee.
15. F.L. Morton, "Charter Changed Judges' Role: Their Selection Needs Review," *The Financial Post*, February 20, 1989, 16, reprinted in Morton, *Law, Politics*, 117.
16. Ian Hunter, "Confirmation Hearings for Judges Would Lower Quality of Court," *The Financial Post*, March 27, 1989, 16, reprinted in *ibid.*, 120.
17. Interview of Hon. Allan E. Blakeney with the writer, July 22, 1997.
18. See the discussion about the Supreme Court's disagreement in the *Patriation* case in Chapter 4.
19. Donald Johnston, ed., *Pierre Trudeau Speaks Out on Meech Lake* (Toronto: General, 1990), 130.
20. Guy Laforest, *Trudeau and the End of a Canadian Dream* (Montreal & Kingston: McGill-Queen's University Press, 1995), 140-41.
21. *The Royal Commission of Inquiry on Constitutional Problems*, vols. 1-4 (Quebec: Queen's Printer, 1956), see esp. vol. 2.

22. Laforest, *Trudeau*, 133.
23. *Ibid.*, 134.
24. *Ibid.*, 138.
25. *Ibid.*
26. *Ibid.*
27. *Ibid.*, 145-49.
28. For Trudeau's promise of "constitutional renewal" see Pierre Elliott Trudeau, *Memoirs* (Toronto: McClelland & Stewart), 99, 282, and Richard Gwyn, *The Northern Magus: Pierre Trudeau and Canadians* (Toronto: McClelland & Stewart, 1980), 372-73.
29. The Constitutional Committee of the Quebec Liberal Party, *A New Canadian Federation* (Montreal: The Quebec Liberal Party, 1980), 32.
30. The Canadian Institute of Public Opinion, *The Gallup Report*, "Majority Think Constitution Will Be Good for Canada," June 19, 1982.
31. Blakeney interview, July 22, 1997.
32. *Re: Resolution to Amend the Constitution* [1981] 1 S.C.R. 753 at 869.
33. *Ibid.*, 905.
34. *Reference re A.G. of Quebec and A.G. of Canada* (1982), 134 D.L.R. (3d) 719 (Que. C.A.).
35. *Re A.G. of Quebec and A.G. of Canada* (1982), 140 D.L.R. (3d) 385 (S.C.C.).
36. "Resolution is Unveiled, but Trudeau Bitter at Compromises," *The Globe and Mail* [Toronto], 19 November, 1981, 1.
37. Blakeney interview, July 22, 1997.
38. John D. Whyte, "On Not Standing for Notwithstanding" (1990) 28 *Alberta Law R.*, 348; reprinted in F.L. Morton, "Charter Changed," 467.
39. *The Saskatchewan Human Rights Code*, S.S., c. S-24.1, see, e.g., sections 10 and 11.
40. 198 U.S. 45 (1905).
41. *Re B.C. Motor Vehicle Act* [1985] 2 S.C.R. 486, see below.
42. Blakeney interview, July 22, 1997.
43. *Re B.C. Motor Vehicle Act* [1985] 2 S.C.R. 504-05.
44. *Ibid.*, 504.
45. R.S.B.C. 1979, c. 288.
46. *Re: B.C. Motor Vehicle Act* [1985] 2 S.C.R. 513.

47. *Ibid.*, 531.
48. *Ibid.*, 521-22.
49. *Ibid.*, 508.
50. Archibald Cox, *The Court and the Constitution* (Boston: Houghton Mifflin, 1987), 122.
51. Blakeney interview, July 22, 1997.

VIII

THE SUMMING UP

MCINTYRE RETIRED FROM THE SUPREME COURT in February 1989 with mixed emotions. He could look back with satisfaction on a series of well-crafted judgments, and, as the author of the important interpretation of "equality rights" in the *Andrews* case, he was regarded highly among his fellow jurists. But his restrained approach to Charter interpretation had not commended itself to most of his judicial colleagues. His disagreements on law and policy were never personal, however. He had the friendliest relations with colleagues with whom he disagreed markedly about of the Charter, such as Antonio Lamer and Bertha Wilson.

One factor in his decision to retire before reaching the 75-year age limit was that his wife Mimi was not well, but another was his anxiety about the trend of Court decisions. Expansible Charter interpretations and lengthy, convoluted opinions, often with multiple concurring opinions agreeing with the result but on different grounds, have tended toward legal uncertainty. How can counsel advise clients when it is difficult to say what the law *is*: Judges on lower courts were finding it harder to interpret and apply Supreme Court decisions. The Court's official endorsement of headnotes (sometimes ten pages in length!) was also troublesome, in that it raised the spectre of counsel's citing the law referred to in the headnote when it differed from the law in the text of the judgment itself. In such a case, which would prevail?

Shortly after his retirement, McIntyre was invested with the insignia of Companion of Canada (the highest rank of the Order) at Rideau Hall by a fellow alumnus of the University of Saskatchewan's College of Law, Governor General Ray Hnatyshyn. In 1995 he received an honorary doctor of laws degree from the University of Victoria, whose founding documents he had helped to draft during his legal practice. His sister Barbara, by then a professor at Victoria, proudly bore the mace in the academic procession, and McIntyre was photographed with his grandson Graham wearing the academic cap of an honorary doctor.

McIntyre sadly missed his beloved wife, Mimi, after her death in Vancouver in 1993. Urbane and cosmopolitan, Mimi had nurtured in her family a liberality of outlook and a taste for civilized living — good food, excellent conversation, and community spirit — which enhanced their quality of life. The Reverend J.A. (Jock) Davidson, Bill's fellow resident at St. Andrew's College in Saskatoon more than a half-century earlier, led the funeral service with tactful sensitivity to McIntyre's sceptical attitude to religious dogma. McIntyre bore his loss with fortitude; he continued to live in the apartment on Comox Avenue and commuted daily to the offices of Russell DuMoulin on West Georgia Street in Vancouver, where he served as counsel.

McIntyre now enjoys a quieter life in Vancouver after his busy years on the Court, and has much more time for reading and reflection. Work pressures in Ottawa had for years curbed his passion for outside reading. He considers the workload on the Supreme Court unnecessarily heavy and believes the Court could limit without significant loss the number of cases it considers annually. Only a minuscule fraction of cases can be heard by Canada's highest court. The trick is to choose those (apart from appeals "as-of-right") having significant public import and to rely on provincial courts of appeal (or other courts) to decide the rest.

McIntyre considers, moreover, that Canadians are a litigious people who have been overly served in the past with legal appeals. Countries that do not have comparable avenues of judicial appeal, he adds, get along quite well. To the question of whether another appellate tribunal should be interposed between provincial courts and the Supreme Court of Canada he answers firmly in the negative. He considers that resort to a trial court followed by one appellate review, if necessary, is adequate. A new court of appeal would accomplish nothing. The answer is to limit the number of appeals. Consequently, McIntyre would make it more difficult to appeal. He considers that there should be no vested right to appeal except for a single appeal in criminal cases.

Courts of appeal, he reflects, are of recent origin; the common law managed for five or six centuries without such tribunals. He cites the English humorist A.P. Herbert, who remarked that in most professions error was seen as a matter of regret, but in the legal profession it was seen as a matter of course. He recalls Mr. Justice Kirk Smith of the Supreme Court of British Columbia once making a ruling from the bench dismissing an application but telling the petitioners, "You can go to the Court of Appeal if you wish." As a result of defective plumbing in the courthouse, four or five drops of water then landed on his desk. "It's the result I expected," Judge Smith said, "but I didn't expect it so soon."

In addition to there being too many appeals, McIntyre considers that there is too much law. In a federation, law is enacted on several different levels. There are federal, provincial, and municipal laws as well as a vast number of subordinate regulations enacted under delegated powers, by marketing boards, professional bodies, or other regulatory authorities. Such regulations have the force of law, and severe penalties can be imposed on individual citizens under them, but in many cases they have never been scrutinized by Parliament or any legislative body. There is the potential for loss of liberty in such an ad hoc process. The totality of law, moreover, is becoming so massive that no individual can know more than a small part of it.

The sheer volume of law tends to uncertainty, as tensions and conflicts develop between its various parts, and one law can often be cited against another. This makes it difficult for lawyers to advise clients. Reflecting on the expanding dimensions of law, McIntyre remembers Dean Cronkite's teachings on Jeremy Bentham long ago in Saskatoon. For a utilitarian any law represented "pain," because of the compulsion to obey. On utilitarian premises, if the good and evil consequences produced by a proposed law were equal, it should not be enacted. There is no advantage in producing "pain" in terms of law without a surplus of "utility" or pleasurable consequences. While McIntyre would not describe himself as utilitarian, he at times almost despairs of seeing a reduction in the proportions of enacted law. The regulatory tentacles of the modern state are everywhere.

LEGAL EDUCATION

McIntyre regrets that in this age of increasing legal complexity, aspiring lawyers are not educated, they are simply trained. He predicts that in the future we will be getting uneducated judges. Even now, there are judges sitting on all benches in Canada who simply have no concept of their function as judges. The kind of academic emphasis he would like to see would be a thorough grounding in legal principles, but there is an impression that "principles make you an old fogey." A good legal education results from a union of the academic and the practical.

Law schools should do what they do best, which is to teach legal theory and academic subjects, while more practical training could await a possibly-expanded post-academic phase of bar courses taught by seasoned practitioners, and using articles that emphasize legal techniques. McIntyre considers that it would be more valuable to have subjects like practice, civil procedure, draftsmanship, and evidence taught by experienced lawyers after graduation from law school. He is also unsure whether many academics who teach the subject have the necessary depth of practical experience to teach clinical law effectively.

On the other hand, a thorough academic grounding is vital to a good legal education and should be the aim of the law-teaching profession. Such a fusion of the theoretical and the practical is reminiscent of the philosopher Alfred North Whitehead's idea that, "learning is useless to you till you have lost your textbooks, burnt your lecture notes, and forgotten the minutiae which you learnt by heart for the examination. [T]he function of a University is to shed details in favour of principles."[1] What is truly important in a sound education is that principles remain after details are forgotten. McIntyre thinks that what distinguishes a lawyer from a mere technician is that the former has a good grounding in principle. He also finds that many law graduates can no longer understand literary or Biblical allusions when they are mentioned in court by a judge.

Some of McIntyre's judgments, such as his *Morgentaler* dissent on abortion, have been sharply criticized by academics, and he has some criticisms of his own to direct toward the law teaching profession, particularly its younger members. He finds a depressing homogeneity among them in terms of their equating legal progress with the attainment of particular results in areas such as social policy reform or criminal "due process," regardless of how much the structure of the law must be distorted to achieve those results. They have an agenda, in other words, with as yet few dissentient voices. As legal academics age they are frequently co-opted into better-paying positions in government, industry, or the practising profession, and the leavening effect of experience, which might provide a counterfoil to the program of the younger academics, is lost. What is needed is more adversarial debate within the legal academy.

Here too an understanding of the separation-of-powers is important, for what the judges cannot do, one or another legislature can do by different means. A measure of humility is necessary to recognize that not everything is judicially possible. Younger judges and legal academics must realize that some desired results are simply beyond their jurisdiction or competence. The danger is that if they stretch the norms of the Charter too far, the whole edifice of the law-making will be undermined, and law will become formless and unpredictable.

LENIENCY AND HARSHNESS

McIntyre remembers hearing a younger judge say: "This is a difficult case; I want to do something for this litigant." That is not the right approach, he believes. The judge's function is *not* to do something for *this* person, it is to apply the law to specific human conduct. If the law is arbitrarily varied in an individual case to achieve a specific purpose then there is no law.

In the criminal law process, discretion belongs not to the application of substantive law but to sentencing. Where an accused is charged with both "murder" and "manslaughter," a lenient trial judge might temper his charge to the jury so as to suggest that conviction for manslaughter was more appropriate under the circumstances. The endless variability of fact situations in criminal offences lends itself to such plasticity, but the practice can also lead to distortion by making the boundaries between offences indistinct. For this reason McIntyre does not like fixed or minimum sentences, which tie the judge's hands; in sentencing there should be more room for discretion, so that the sentence can be adjusted to deal with mitigating factors where these exist. If compassion is to be exercised, it should be done in the sentencing.

THE LENGTH OF JUDGMENTS AND HEADNOTES

The increasing length and complexity of Supreme Court of Canada judgments in the era of the Charter, and the growing practice of issuing concurring opinions, both cause McIntyre to doubt whether counsel or lower courts can still clearly determine what the law *is*. In pessimistic moments he is tempted to ask if there will eventually be any "law" at all. His apprehension is shared by many legal practitioners, some of whom have given up reading lengthy legal judgments in despair. "To keep up with the present Supreme Court decisions would be like reading *War and Peace* every two weeks," McIntyre says. In 1992, for instance, there were three bulky volumes of Supreme Court reports published, compared with the two volumes or the single volume that were the standard before. Regardless of the number of annual volumes, the length of cases has greatly increased.

An associated practice, the official endorsation by the Supreme Court itself of headnotes that purport to summarize the main legal issues and findings in a given case, McIntyre also sees as mischievous. Formerly such headnotes were drafted by a court functionary and had no official status. The new practice was established in the late 1980s, in part to encourage journalists to write more accurate news reports of current cases. The headnotes themselves, however, are sometimes so lengthy and convoluted that they defeat their own purpose — journalists do not read them. It is only a matter of time before a disparity arises between the headnote and the text of a case, and counsel cites the former against the latter; the court will be in the embarrassing position of having to choose one of two divergent summations of the same case, both of which it officially endorsed.

THE RULE OF LAW

Counsel who are advising clients or arguing before various courts and tribunals lament that as time passes the very comprehension of law is becoming more difficult. Although one should not overstate the problem, in its worst form such lack of clarity raises questions about the rule of law itself. A system of effective and enforceable laws must be intelligible to lawyers who have to advise clients. Where the law is obscure, basic communication between lawyers and clients becomes less effective and there is a danger that lower courts will misinterpret Supreme Court opinions. Obscurity at the top filters down throughout the system.

The general application of the common law without privilege or favour to individuals or classes developed slowly from its inception in twelfth-century England. McIntyre views common law principles, such as the liberty of a person to do what is not expressly forbidden by law, and the equality of all citizens before the law, as cornerstones of the legal system. He sees the common law and the Charter in a continuum, not as representative of different legal systems or impulses, and many of the rights in the Charter, particularly the legal rights (sections 7 to 14), as essentially incorporating prior common law rights. The rights to liberty (section 7) and equality (section 15), the presumption of innocence, and the privilege against self-incrimination (section 11), were all proclaimed by the antecedent common law. When so viewed, there is a working harmony between the common law and the Charter.

In a reflective mood, McIntyre will relate to visitors to his Vancouver law office the long heritage of the common law in protecting civil liberties before the advent of the Charter of Rights. In many cases common law principles have performed yeoman service in vindicating civil liberties, as in *Entick v. Carrington*,[2] where it was held that neither a search warrant nor the doctrine of "state necessity" authorized the Crown to enter the plaintiff's premises and confiscate his papers. In *Somersett's Case*,[3] decided by Lord Mansfield in 1771, a case much admired by McIntyre, it was held that slavery no longer existed in England in any form, and that once a slave set foot on English soil he had all the legal rights of a free-born person and could employ all the resources of the law to resist removal from the country. An implied bill of rights was articulated by Chief Justice Sir Lyman Duff in a 1938 Supreme Court case, *Re Alberta Statutes*.[4] The Social Credit government of Alberta, which had little or no media support, passed a statute requiring that it be given a right of reply in the same newspapers where criticism had been levelled. Duff found that the Canadian Constitution and parliamentary system, patterned on that of Britain, by implication forbade restrictions on freedom of speech, which the statute had violated. This basic right to freedom of expression was later enshrined in the Charter as section 2(b).

In 1957, in *Switzman v. Elbling*,[5] the Court decided that the Quebec government could not "padlock" premises used to disseminate Communism. In *Switzman*, Abbott, J, said that "Parliament itself could not abrogate this right of discussion and debate."[6] If Abbott's *obiter dictum* was correct, freedom of political expression was virtually entrenched before the arrival of the Charter. In *A.-G. Can. and Dupond v. Montreal*,[7] however, Beetz, J, said for a slender 5-4 majority, that no fundamental freedom inherited from Britain was beyond repeal by competent legislation. The question, essentially, was which legislature under the division of powers could take rights away. *Dupond* gave support to those advocating entrenchment by demonstrating the vulnerability of "implied rights" to legislation. This 1978 decision provided momentum for the adoption of the Charter four years later by emphasizing the fragility of the common law as a guarantor of rights: no unentrenched right was beyond repeal by the competent legislature.

In the Canadian case of *Roncarelli v. Duplessis*,[8] the appellant was a Montreal restaurateur who had irritated the Quebec government by serving as bondsman for his co-religionists, who were charged with distributing religious tracts without a licence. Those charged were members of the Jehovah's Witnesses sect, whose uncompromising denunciation of the Roman Catholic Church made them an unpopular minority in the province and a target for official repression. In retaliation for Roncarelli's action, Premier Duplessis instructed the chief commissioner of the Quebec Liquor Commission to revoke his liquor licence. This meant commercial ruin. A distinguished poet, civil libertarian, and McGill law professor, Frank Scott, represented Roncarelli in the Supreme Court, which found against the premier. The Court held that the legal authority to revoke liquor licences belonged only to the chief commissioner, and was to be exercised by him for proper cause. There was no statutory or other authority empowering the premier to so act. It is an important principle of the rule of law that whenever an official divests persons of their rights, it must be done pursuant to valid legal authority and for valid reasons cognizable by law. Unfortunately, by the time the Roncarelli's case had finally been disposed of in the Supreme Court of Canada, his business had gone bankrupt and he was ruined.

THE LAW OF THE CHARTER

Any enumeration of rights is subject to limitations under exceptional circumstances; as McIntyre says, no right or freedom is absolute in practice. "Freedom of expression" is an ideal, but it does not in practice justify a citizen in a combatant state who discloses troop movements to the enemy in wartime. Nor would "freedom of religion" excuse from criminal sanction a member of a religious sect who, on scriptural grounds, handled poisonous snakes as a test of faith, however sincere. Assuming that the government had enacted statutes prohibiting the exercise of the above "freedoms," a court, pursuant to section 1 of the Charter, would uphold the nullifying statutes which forbade or circumscribed the exercise of these freedoms as a "reasonable limit" on the conduct otherwise protected. Generally, inconsistencies or discrepancies between the rights and freedoms expounded in the Charter and those inhering in common law will be decided in accordance with the Charter. In unusual situations courts may preserve a law that technically conflicts with Charter norms.

While the Charter is a measure of legal validity, courts must not usurp the power of Parliament. The Charter should be used sparingly and in tandem with common law precepts. McIntyre recognizes that this approach to judicial decision-making is considered to be ultraconservative by most legal academics in Canada. His admiration for the common law and his disinclination to apply Charter norms in a sweeping fashion have led to this characterization, but he sees no disgrace in the label if it connotes a desire to preserve common law and a partiality for ordered liberty. On the other hand, McIntyre argues that he could provide a critic with fifty of his own judicial decisions that would compare in liberality of spirit with anything produced by his "free-thinking" colleagues. Like many other judges McIntyre is difficult to classify under such rubrics. He has elements of both conservatism and liberalism in his attitude and approach to the law.

McIntyre reflects that Canadians lived a long time without a Charter and that the protection of citizens' rights was relatively secure. He feels it was not necessary to entrench the Charter, and other countries without entrenched rights, such as the U.K. or Australia, have legal systems in which rights flourish. He regards the Charter as an abrupt departure from the Canadian legal tradition. The Americans entrenched a Bill of Rights, but in some cases their Supreme Court makes rulings that hamstring executive and legislative action, and their more rigid system of separation of powers engenders day-to-day conflicts between rival branches of government which can lead to paralysis. Also, if a national consensus develops against a Supreme Court decision it can only be changed by constitutional amendment — a difficult process. However, in a parliamentary system predicated on working harmony between cabinet and legislature, more decisive action is possible. Governments in Canada usually encounter little difficulty in enacting their legislative programs.

McIntyre now regards Diefenbaker's Canadian Bill of Rights as a step in the right direction, one that defined rights aptly and sufficiently. When it was first passed he thought of it as window-dressing but he has now changed his mind. It was, of course, a statute, and applied only on the national level, but it was essentially correct in its elaboration of a scheme of rights. It complemented later provincial human rights codes. By contrast, McIntyre feels that the Charter will not be numbered among Prime Minister Trudeau's main achievements.

THE CHARTER AND THE COMMON LAW

In an era of rapid legal change ushered in by the Charter of Rights and Freedoms, McIntyre has sought to achieve a synthesis between the Charter and more traditional common law principles. His judicial approach turns on the fact that he did not view the Charter as an abrupt a shift in legal norms, while many of his contemporaries did.

The common law had protected life, liberty, and property, and the legal rights enumerated in sections 7-14 of the Charter had, for the most part, common law precursors. The essential difference was that while the common law declared such rights, the Charter entrenched and guaranteed them. In that both systems had common goals, he saw less conflict between them than did his judicial colleagues, or the growing number of academics who saw in the Charter a panacea for all social and legal ills. As time passed, instead of the creative synthesis between Charter and common law that McIntyre had hoped for, he saw Canadian courts, including the Supreme Court of Canada, invoking the Charter to dismantle the common law. Overexpansive interpretations of Charter norms were being used to strike down laws worth preserving. McIntyre considered the short-term effects of Charter interpretation to be bad for the law in many ways. Through time, with a more positive approach, the Charter might yet serve a beneficial, if less ambitious, role in Canadian law.

In an insightful article Michael J. Bryant suggests that "the ghost of William McIntyre" may yet return to dominate much of the decision-making of the court,[9] in terms of re-emphasizing the correlation between rights and duties in the furtherance of a well-ordered community. Cases cited to document the shift in orientation include *Rodriguez v. British Columbia (A.-G.)*,[10] in which the Court assessed both rights and duties when it rejected a dying woman's plea for physician-assisted suicide, and the *Creighton* quartet,[11] written by Chief Justice Lamer, which "seemed concerned with deterring socially unacceptable acts that threaten the community."[12] It will take more time, certainly, to ascertain whether the above prediction proves true.

McIntyre is situated better, Bryant contends, in a theoretical configuration that "borrows substantially from natural law principles, and ... views rights and responsibilities as fused together."[13] While he carefully qualifies this assessment by declaring that no judge "falls neatly into either of these two broad philosophical categories" (natural law and positivism), and that they "rarely adopt a tradition or philosophy explicitly,"[14] the framework is a thoughtful perspective on McIntyre's jurisprudence. It would be an error, however, to place McIntyre squarely within the natural law tradition. His method is not one of deduction from over-arching principles, but one of careful, detailed, case-by-case decision making which employs the techniques of the common lawyer. Right, duty, and the welfare of the larger community are elements in his approach, but McIntyre's judicial reasoning is tentative, progressive, revisionist, and relativistic, rather than following from a larger metaphysical whole. His approach is typically inductive rather than deductive.

In a case like *Morgentaler*,[15] a natural law jurist might emphasize the value of life as an absolute first principle that proscribes abortion. In his dissent McIntyre said nothing about ultimate values but asked, rather, if Parliament had the constitutional jurisdiction to enact a law providing for therapeutic abortion as defined in section 251 of the Criminal Code. For him that was the decisive question. He has said, moreover, that while in his own mind he is unsure about the rights and wrongs of abortion, he can still address the issue as one of statutory interpretation and parliamentary competence under the constitutional division of powers. Similarly, while considering the validity of capital punishment in *Miller and Cockriell*,[16] he was essentially addressing the issue of whether the death penalty constituted "cruel and unusual punishment," a question that arose directly from section 2(b) of the Canadian Bill of Rights. In neither of these judgments did he approach the issue of "life" as an ultimate value. His approach reflected deference to Parliament and a positivist emphasis on the intention of the legislature enacting the law more than it did any particular philosophical orientation.

Both natural law (and natural rights) and the common law protect life, liberty, and property; it is the reasoning process and the method of vindicating such rights when they are violated that differ in the two systems. For a natural lawyer, a law contrary to "nature" may be absolutely void and not binding in conscience; a common lawyer sees it in a broader context in which the supremacy of Parliament, the intention of the legislature, and statutory interpretation all play a larger part.

"READING DOWN" AND "READING IN"

Another case where McIntyre considers that the Supreme Court blurred the lines between the legislative and the judicial function is *Schachter v. Canada*,[17] decided three years after his departure. It sanctioned the practice of judges "reading in" a "missing provision" in a legislative scheme in order to render it compatible with, for example, equality rights in the Charter. In *Schachter*, Chief Justice Lamer, for the Court majority, considered that by legislative oversight paternity benefits under the Unemployment Insurance Act, 1971,[18] had been given to adoptive parents but not to natural parents. Rather than have the whole scheme founder on a question of constitutional validity, with the result that many adoptive parents would lose existing benefits, the Court's remedy was to "read in" such benefits for natural parents. The "equality rights" standard in section 15 would not be violated by conferring different entitlements on two classes, both of which deserved benefits. Here the judges were acting as quasi-legislators but the judicial technique of "reading in" was mandated by section 52 of the Constitution Act, 1982, which allowed the striking down of laws conflicting "to the extent of inconsistency" with the Constitution. Was this a direction intended to eliminate existing if repugnant provisions, or could judges add new provisions to render a defective legislative scheme constitutionally valid?

"Reading down" was not as controversial as "reading in," and had been resorted to long before the advent of the Charter. If the broad reading of a law results in a statute's invalidation (unless it can be "severed" from the remaining text), while a permissible but narrower reading might preserve it, the latter course should be adopted.[19] This approach accords with the presumption of constitutionality. The technique is used most often where a provincial law, under a broad reading, encroaches on federal jurisdiction; an example would be a provincial debt adjustment measure that could be construed as trespassing on Parliament's exclusive bankruptcy power. If the words of the provincial law, are capable of a narrower reading that will preserve its validity, the court will so interpret them.

The distinction between "reading down" and "reading in" is that in the former case the provision has been enacted by the legislature and already exists. In the latter case the court endeavours to impute a purpose to the legislature that it has failed, through error or negligence, to execute. By assuming the legislative role itself, the court supplies the missing statutory provision that restores constitutional validity.

In a concurring opinion, Justice La Forest (speaking also for L'Heureux-Dubé), declared that he agreed with the result, but introduced a note of caution: "[I]t is for Parliament and the legislature to make laws. It is the duty of the courts to see that those laws conform to constitutional norms and declare them invalid if they do not. This imposes pressure on legislative bodies to stay within the confines of their legislative powers from the outset. Reliance should not be placed on the courts to repair invalid laws."[20] In this case, La Forest thought of "reading in" as similar to "reading down" in other cases and left it at that, although the results of "reading in" can be far-reaching.

McIntyre objects to the judicial technique of "reading in" because it invites the Court to impute a particular intention to the legislature where such intentions are often inscrutable. When the Court tries to divine legislative intention it ignores the fact that a large collective body engages in bargaining and compromise while framing legislation, and a number of disparate intentions may be present. Yet another factor, which the Court in *Schacter* recognized, is that a supposedly missing category, though logically necessary to a coherent and constitutional result, may have been omitted intentionally by the legislature because of prohibitive cost. Accordingly, the court can "read in" the missing provision but suspend operation of the reconstituted law for, say, six months, in order to give the legislature time to amend or repeal the law if the court-supplied alteration results in prohibitive cost.

The filling in of legislative gaps discerned by courts, or "reading in," is inescapably political. A defender of the technique could say that judges often make law interstitially, that is, by amplifying existing interpretations to cover new cases. To amplify, or to extend, however, assumes the existence of a law open to such interpretation. In "reading in," the judiciary are actually framing new law. They are assuming the mantle of legislator, and the implications for the system of checks and balances and separation of powers are dangerous. That is why McIntyre is critical of the innovation.

THE REFERENCE ON QUEBEC SOVEREIGNTY

The very flexibility of the reference device can lead at times to disconcerting predicaments for the Supreme Court. In 1996 the federal cabinet submitted to the Court a constitutional reference concerning the goal of the Parti Québécois government hold another referendum on the separation of Quebec from Canada. In the reference the government asked three questions: (1) Can Quebec unilaterally declare independence under domestic law? (2) Does international law give the province a right to secede?, and (3) If domestic and international law conflict, which takes precedence?[21]

What McIntyre dislikes about these questions is that although they are legal in form they relate to a context so intensely political in nature that they inevitably thrust the Court into the forefront of politics and undermine its credibility as an impartial arbiter of Canadian federalism. Is the Chrétien government using the court for political ends? Quebec rejected the federal initiative from the start, declaring that it would take no part in the reference process, nor would it name counsel. Its position was that the questions were intrinsically political, were to be decided through negotiations in due course, and that a reference to the Supreme Court — with predictable results — would not be helpful. When the federal government, by default, named a "pro-sovereignty" Quebec City lawyer, André Joli-Coeur, to argue that Quebec can unilaterally declare independence, he was appointed over the province's vehement objections.[22]

There is a perception in Quebec that the Supreme Court is a centralist institution that tends to side with Ottawa in constitutional disputes against the provinces. Though difficult to document by surveying the cases decided by the Court since its inception in 1875, the perception is strongest among separatists and, of course, perception is a driving factor in politics.

When the federal Liberals in the late 1930s decided to seek a reference on whether Parliament could discontinue appeals to the Privy Council and make the Supreme Court of Canada the final court for all questions of law in the federation, Quebec, Ontario, New Brunswick, and British Columbia argued that the continuation of provincial appeals was a vested provincial right. The Privy Council disagreed, graciously acceding to its own demise. It decided that under the peace, order, and good government clause and section 101 of the Constitution Act, 1867, Parliament had jurisdiction to establish a final court of appeal in Canada for questions of both federal and provincial law.[23] What concerned politicians and jurists in Quebec and in some other provinces was that the decision had a highly centralist thrust. The reconstituted nine-member Supreme Court would be set up under federal law and would have centrally-appointed judges. In the Duplessis era and later it was feared that Ottawa would consistently appoint federally-biased judges to the Court, jurists who would be partial to the "centralists" in federal-provincial disputes. Probably partly for that reason, during the debate on the Meech Lake Accord, Premier Robert Bourassa of Quebec refused to have the Charter applied to the Quebec "distinct society" clause in the Accord. Indeed, the *Allaire Report* recommended the setting up of a separate Supreme Court in Quebec having final jurisdiction over all civil matters.[24]

Bourassa's refusal may have been based on his chagrin at the decision of the Supreme Court in *A.-G. Quebec v. Quebec Protestant School Board*.[25] In that case the court gave priority to section 23(1)(b) of the Charter, which, unlike Quebec's Bill 101, allowed out-of-province parents to send their children to English schools in Quebec. Education, language, and culture, all key elements in the "distinct society" clause, had proven vulnerable to the Charter, and the Charter could plainly jeopardize a "distinct society" clause. Premier Bourassa's action was not unreasonable, and may even have been eminently politic.

Certainly the use of the Charter by special interest groups to promote particular, even narrow, values is fraught with potential for intergroup conflict. Conflicts in court where there are classes of winners and losers may cause rifts and alienation within the larger society. Moreover, by invoking the Charter an unpopular minority may be able to secure rights that it could not otherwise obtain. For other groups, comparable rights could be achieved only by governmental lobbying. And once an appeal to the Charter is made, the court's decision may make future conflict resolution between different groups less manageable. Resort to courts can also be much more costly than compromise through negotiation in a political forum. There are advantages to both modes of dispute settlement, but McIntyre feels the disadvantages of resort to the Charter will become increasingly apparent.

Given Quebec's adamant refusal to participate in a reference on the constitutional validity of a unilateral declaration of independence, why did Ottawa confide such a politically sensitive task to the Supreme Court? It was done so that in the eventuality of a referendum endorsing separation, federal negotiators could go to the bargaining table armed with a favourable constitutional precedent. Quebec's rejection of the reference initiative was also predictable; the issue was too political to be consigned to a federal court. Ironically, the "unilateral declaration of independence" position is now associated more with former Premier Jacques Parizeau than with his successor Premier Lucien Bouchard, who appears to prefer negotiations prior to leaving, once a referendum endorsing separation succeeds.

It is difficult to disagree with McIntyre that this constitutional reference centred on an issue that is inherently political, and that in retrospect the exercise appears almost pointless. There is something bizarre about this most adversarial of "non-adversarial" processes, in which the most determined political foe of the Quebec government is making provision for appointing Quebec's counsel, and there is not a single separatist jurist on the bench to arbitrate between separatists and federalists. The U.S. Supreme Court would never accept such a reference, because it does not present a genuine "case or controversy" between parties.[26]

THE CHARTER AND THE SUPREMACY OF PARLIAMENT

Taking a long historical perspective on constitutional development, McIntyre sees the emergence of British and Canadian Parliaments as the supreme law-making institutions in the state as a victory for liberal democracy. Universal suffrage, the right to petition legislatures for redress of grievances, the convention of responsible government, and a multi-party system, all carried some assurance that rights will be protected. A vigilant press and a court system responsive to the protection of rights are also critically important. However, one problem remaining is that Parliament and the provincial legislatures reflect majority will, and are not always observant of minority rights, especially in times of crisis. Influential thinkers such as Alexis de Tocqueville[27] and John Stuart Mill[28] warned long ago of the coming "tyranny of the majority" in the United States and Britain, and when Trudeau advanced the Charter in 1980 it was partly to ensure that the rights of minorities would not be trampled upon by legislative majority. McIntyre has argued that despite the fact that the United States has limited government that features an entrenched Bill of Rights, and Britain has a doctrine of parliamentary supremacy without entrenchment, basic rights receive similar protection in both countries. Other factors, such as supportive social attitudes, a court system enforcing traditional common law rights, a free press, and an enlightened citizenry, create a positive milieu for basic rights in Britain, even in the absence of express legal guarantees. By contrast, the 1936 Constitution of the U.S.S.R. contained admirable rights guarantees but because the necessary infrastructure of political and social attitudes and institutional support was lacking, such expressed rights were much less meaningful.

The Charter, with its overarching standards for ordinary law, may lead to inappropriate social policy making and undue rigidity. Why should nine middle-aged lawyers, often from elite law firms, and in many ways unrepresentative of Canadian society, make social policy for Canada in the twenty-first century? If the Supreme Court were to make an insupportable decision in terms of democratic rights, mobility rights, or language rights, that decision could only be changed by means of a difficult, even onerous, constitutional amendment. In areas where the "notwithstanding clause" in section 33 applied (fundamental freedoms, legal rights, and equality rights), Parliament or the provincial legislatures could countervail an unpopular decision by invoking the clause, but might have to pay a heavy political price for doing so. There is much more latitude when legislators are working in a common law environment. The question now is whether the legal regime will remain as fair, equitable, and workable as before the introduction of the Charter.

Even where laws are not struck down on Charter grounds, its prescriptions may require legislative draftsmen and parliamentarians embarking on new legislative programs to be wary of transgressing Charter norms. A number of questions will inevitably arise: Do courts interpreting the Charter make the proper balance between the legal rights of the accused and the protection of the community? Would a progression from equality of opportunity to equal results in equality rights cases, especially if the latter brought employment quotas with it, be acceptable? In the area of freedom of expression in section 2, what is the standard, if any, that will be applied in future to the prohibition of hard-core pornographic literature and films? Answers to these questions would require time and resources entirely beyond the budget and capability of a court. In legislatures, backbenchers working in committee, assisted by expert staff and with funding for outside help, can give them longer and closer scrutiny.

There is also a question of focus. In an adversarial legal system issues are ordinarily defined in the factums of opposing counsel. Compared to the "global" view that a legislature takes, the polarization of views presented to a court may be unduly argumentative, narrow, and legalistic. The aim of counsel is not to advance the public interest but to urge on the court the particular claims on behalf of their clients. A court may occasionally go beyond the adversarial positions of opposing counsel to decide the issue on other legal grounds, but here again the court would be operating, in questions of social policy, without adequate empirical data. Another difficulty in what has sometimes been called "the judicialization of politics" is that what a legislature would consider relevant, and as bearing on social policy issues, would often be excluded as inadmissible "hearsay" evidence in court.

Does the "supremacy of Parliament" remain intact despite patriation and the advent of the Charter in 1982? When a court finds a clear conflict between a Charter provision and a statute, "to the extent of inconsistency," the statute becomes a dead letter. In certain areas of the Charter (*viz.* sections 2 and 7-15), legislatures who consider the finding of the court to be sufficiently obnoxious can overcome it by using the override or "notwithstanding clause" in section 33(1). This device preserves a vestige of parliamentary supremacy. For example, if a court were to rule that the medicare system, as set out in the Canada Health Act, violated a physician's "liberty" to practise his profession, as set out in section 7, Parliament could pass a short statute declaring, "The Canada Health Act shall operate notwithstanding the provisions of section 7 of the Constitution Act, 1982." Any future judicial decision to the contrary would be overridden and Parliament would have the final word. However, pursuant to section 33(3) of the Charter, this override would remain in effect for only five years, and if Parliament thereafter wanted the medicare system to continue it would have to re-enact the override at five-year intervals. The reason for this "sunset clause" provision was that the authors of the Charter wanted to emphasize that their system of rights and freedoms was the ordinary and natural course of events, and that any departure from it by way of override was an extraordinary measure, and an exception from the rule.

Some see the notwithstanding clause as antidemocratic in tendency because it can nullify the operation of rights and freedoms in highly significant areas and, if applied on the provincial level, it can create a kind of libertarian patchwork quilt. Certain rights may exist in one province, but, because of the use of the override, not in a neighbouring province. Yet, according to Professor Peter Russell, the notwithstanding clause has a very useful purpose:

In a nutshell, the argument about the substance of decision-making is as follows. Judges are not infallible. They may make decisions about the limits and nature of rights and freedoms which are extremely questionable. There should be some process, more reasoned than court packing and more accessible than constitutional amendment, through which the justice and wisdom of these decisions can be publicly discussed and possibly rejected. A legislative override clause provides such a process.[29]

His point that the use of the notwithstanding clause generates public discussion is an important one. Before a government invoked the notwithstanding clause, it would have to defend the policy of setting aside the judicial decision, pilot the statute embodying the override through three readings in the legislature, and field all the attendant media publicity and public debate. The voters could exact a heavy price at the next election for a use of the override they disapproved of.

Since its adoption as a part of the Charter, the override provision has been used sparingly by legislatures. There has been little controversy about its application, except for a sweeping declaration by the Parti

Québécois government, assented to on June 23, 1982, which re-enacted each of the Acts of the legislature passed before 17 April, 1982, adding to each, as a separate section at the end, the words, "This Act shall operate notwithstanding the provisions of sections 2 and 7 to 15 of the Constitution Act, 1982."[30] This exercise was partly symbolic, emphasizing indirectly that Quebec was not bound by a constitutional instrument to which it had not assented. Despite the fact that Quebec law applied all the Charter sections susceptible to override to all existing provincial statutes, this broad use of the notwithstanding clause was upheld by the Supreme Court in *Ford v. Quebec A.-G.*[31] In this case the Supreme Court held, essentially, that if an override could be used against a single statute, it could be used against all statutes. This one case seems to defeat Professor Russell's contention that the use of the override is a spur to public debate; there could hardly be a real debate if it were applied in relation to *all* statutes. However, there was protracted debate in Quebec and elsewhere about the provincial government's universal invocation of the notwithstanding clause, and *Ford* was not a typical case. Russell's point would apply to all the other cases. In 1985 the succeeding Bourassa government of Quebec rejected this "global" use of the override, committing itself to use the device only in individual cases, which it proceeded to do by Bill 178 of 1988, to override the *Ford* decision on the use of the English and the French language on Quebec commercial signs.[32]

Another provision modifying the application of the Charter is section 1, the "reasonable limits" clause. This enables courts to uphold statutes that violate one or other substantive section of the Charter if the law enacted is a "reasonable limit" of the right affected. The provision emphasizes that virtually no right or freedom is absolute, and all should be subject to some limitation by the legislature in the public interest. Even in constitutions that do not contain such a provision, courts have generally held that rights are not absolute and are subject to limitation by law. Although section 1 does not always apply, and while the evidentiary burden that the offending statute should be maintained rests on the party affirming its validity (often the government that enacted the statute), by virtue of its purpose the "reasonable limits" is sometimes also known as the "legislative supremacy" clause. When one considers the psychological and political constraints on legislators who are contemplating an override of "rights and freedoms," and the paucity of cases where rights have been overridden by government, the last word on legislative policy appears now to belong to the judges. McIntyre is not an enemy of the Charter. However, his deep attachment to common law principles leads him to view its influence over the Canadian body politic with some sadness.

MCINTYRE IN RETIREMENT

Living in active retirement in Vancouver, McIntyre acknowledges that he misses the days that he spent on the Supreme Court in Ottawa. He also greatly misses Mimi, his wife and lifelong companion. He has many happy associations with the nation's capital, and counts Chief Justice "Tony" Lamer and Madam Justice Bertha Wilson — with whom he differed strongly on Charter matters — among his closest friends.

Justice McIntyre commutes daily from his home on Comox Avenue to his office in the 24th floor suite of the Russell DuMoulin law firm at 1075 West Georgia Street in Vancouver. As counsel he advises the firm (one of the largest in Canada) on complex constitutional and other legal problems, and occasionally presides at seminars on law for the large number of articling students and younger lawyers employed there. He also maintains cordial contact with former law clerks.

He often enjoys a meal at a restaurant and quaffing a bottle of Piesporter with old friends such as his former law partner Lloyd George McKenzie, a distinguished retired judge, and Mr. Justice D.M.M. Goldie, who argued as British Columbia counsel before him in the 1981 *Patriation* case. In relaxed moments he gives play to his wry wit, which was rarely evident on the bench, where his somewhat reserved manner made him very hard to read. He now has more time to read history, biography, and law than he did during his busy years on the bench.

Looking back on McIntyre's distinguished judicial career, comprising over two decades on three different courts, Justice McKenzie reflects, "Bill has always enjoyed the admiration and respect of his peers — lawyers and judges — on every forum on which he sat. That is a considerable compliment in itself and a mark of his accomplishment." On McIntyre's long journey from the Moose Jaw of his boyhood to his rewarding legal career in Victoria, Vancouver, and Ottawa, many who have known him warmly endorse this sentiment.

NOTES

1. A.N. Whitehead, *The Aims of Education* (London: Macmillan, 1929).
2. (1765) 95 E.R. 807 (K.B.).
3. (1771) 20 How. St. Tr. 1 (K.B.).
4. [1938] S.C.R. 100.
5. [1957] S.C.R. 285
6. *Ibid.*, 328.
7. [1978] 2 S.C.R. 770.
8. (1959) S.C.R. 121.
9. Michael J. Bryant, "Criminal Fault as *Per* the Lamer Court and the Ghost of William McIntyre" (1995) 33 *Osgoode Hall L.J.*, 79 at 83-85.
10. [1993] 3 S.C.R. 519.
11. *R. v. Creighton* [1993] 3 S.C.R. 3; *R. v. Gossett*, [1993] 3 S.C.R. 76; *R. v. Finlay* [1993] 3 S.C.R. 103; *R. v. Naglik* [1993] 3 S.C.R. 122.
12. Bryant, "Criminal Fault," 96.
13. *Ibid.*, 85.
14. *Ibid.*, 86.
15. [1988] 1 S.C.R. 30.
16. (1976) 63 D.L.R. (3d) 193 (B.C.C.A.).
17. [1992] 2 S.C.R. 679, 93 D.L.R. (4th) 1 (S.C.C.).
18. Stat. Can., 1970-71-72, c. 48, ss. 30, 32(i).
19. Cf. *McKay v. The Queen* [1965] S.C.R. 798.
20. *Schacter* (1992) 93 D.L.R. (4th), 35.
21. Sean Fine, "Court Role Goes to PQ Stalwart," *The Globe and Mail* [Toronto], Tuesday, July 15, 1997, A1, A3.
22. *Ibid.*, at A4, and see Sean Fine and Tu Tranh Ha, "Quebec Gets Advocate It Feared," *The Globe and Mail* [Toronto], Wednesday, July 16, 1997.
23. *A.-G. Ontario v. A.-G. Canada* [1947] A.C. 127 at 153 (J.C.P.C.).
24. See M. Bowker, *Canada's Constitutional Crisis: Making Sense of It All* (Edmonton: Lone Pine Publishing, 1991), 49.
25. [1984] 2 S.C.R. 66.
26. Cf. *Muskrat v. U.S.*, 219 U.S. 346 (1911).
27. Alexis de Tocqueville, *Democracy in America*, ed. Richard D. Heffner (New York: Mentor, 1956).

28. John Stuart Mill, *On Liberty* (Englewood Cliffs, NJ: Prentice Hall, 1956).
29. Peter H. Russell, "Standing Up for Notwithstanding," in F.L. Morton, ed., *Law, Politics and the Judicial Process in Canada*, 2nd edn. (Calgary: University of Calgary Press, 1992), 476.
30. *An Act Respecting the Constitution Act, 1982*, S.Q. 1982, c. 21.
31. [1988] 2 S.C.R. 712.
32. Gérald-A. Beaudoin, *La Constitution du Canada* (Montreal: Wilson & Lafleur, 1990), 788-89.

BIBLIOGRAPHY

Banting, K.G. and R.E.B. Simeon, eds., *And No One Cheered* (Agincourt, ON: Methuen, 1983).
Batten, Jack, *Robinette, The Dean of Canadian Lawyers* (Toronto: Macmillan, 1984).
Bayefsky, A.F. and M. Eberts, eds., *Equality Rights and the Canadian Charter of Rights and Freedoms* (Toronto: Carswell, 1985).
Beatty, David, *Constitutional Law in Theory and Practice* (Toronto: University of Toronto Press, 1995).
Beaudoin, G.A., *La Constitution du Canada, institutions, partage des pouvoirs, droits et libertés* (Montreal: Wilson & Lafleur, 1990).
———, ed., *The Supreme Court of Canada* (Cowansville, QC: Yvan Blais, 1986).
———, and Errol Mendes, *The Canadian Charter of Rights and Freedoms*, 3rd edn. (Toronto: Carswell, 1996).
Bilson, Beth, "'Prudence Rather Than Valor': Legal Education in Saskatchewan, 1908-23," (1998) 61 *Saskatchewan Law Review*, 341.
Blackstone, William, *Commentaries on the Laws of England*, facs. edn. [1765-69], 4 vols. (Chicago & London: University of Chicago Press, 1979).
British Columbia Aural Legal History Project (Victoria, BC: University of Victoria).
Brooks, Stephen, *Canadian Democracy: An Introduction*, 2nd edn. (Toronto: Oxford, 1996).
Bryant, Michael J., "Criminal Fault as Per the Lamer Court and the Ghost of William McIntyre" (1995) 33 *Osgoode Hall Law Journal*, 79.
Bushnell, Ian, *The Captive Court: A Study of the Supreme Court of Canada* (Montreal & Kingston: McGill-Queen's Press, 1992).
Cairns, Alan C., *Charter versus Federalism: The Dilemmas of Constitutional Reform* (Montreal & Kingston: McGill-Queen's Press, 1992).

Cairns, Alan C., *Disruptions: Constitutional Struggles from the Charter to Meech Lake*, Douglas E. Williams, ed. (Toronto: McClelland & Stewart, 1991).
The Canadian Encyclopedia, 2nd edn. (Edmonton: Hurtig, 1988).
Cantor, Norman F., *Imagining the Law: Common Law and the Foundations of the American Legal System* (New York: HarperCollins, 1997).
The Committee on the Appointment of Judges in Canada, *The Appointment of Judges in Canada* (Ottawa: The Canadian Bar Foundation, 1985).
Constitutional Committee on the Quebec Liberal Party, *A New Canadian Federation* [The Beige Report], (Montreal: Quebec Liberal Party, 1980).
Countryman, Vern, ed., *The Douglas Opinions* (New York: Berkley, 1978).
Cox, Archibald, *The Court and the Constitution* (Boston: Houghton Mifflin, 1987).
Dawson, R.M., *Constitutional Issues in Canada, 1900-1931* (London: Oxford University Press, 1933).
De Tocqueville, Alexis, *Democracy in America*, Richard D. Heffner, ed. (New York: Mentor, 1956).
Forsey, E.A., *The Royal Power of Dissolution of Parliament in the British Commonwealth* (Toronto: Oxford University Press, 1943; rp. 1968).
Gérin-Lajoie, P., *Constitutional Amendment in Canada* (Toronto: University of Toronto Press, 1950).
Gibson, Dale, and W.W. Pue, eds., *Glimpses of Canadian Legal History* (Winnipeg: Legal Research Institute of the University of Manitoba, 1991).
Greene, Ian, *The Charter of Rights* (Toronto: Lorimer, 1989).
Greschner, Donna, and Ken Norman, "The Courts and Section 33," (1987) 12 *Queen's Law Journal*, 155.
Gruending, Dennis, *Promises to Keep: A Political Biography of Allan Blakeney* (Saskatoon: Western Producer Prairie Books, 1990).
Gwyn, Richard, *The Northern Magus: Pierre Trudeau and Canadians* (Toronto: McClelland & Stewart, 1980).
Heard, Andrew, *Canadian Constitutional Conventions* (Toronto: Oxford University Press, 1991).
Hogg, Peter W., *Constitutional Law of Canada*, 3rd edn. (Toronto: Carswell, 1992).

Holdsworth, William, *A History of English Law* (London: Methuen & Sweet and Maxwell, 1938; rp. 1966).
Johnston, Donald, ed., *Pierre Trudeau Speaks Out on Meech Lake* (Toronto: General Publishing, 1990).
Karp, Cecil, and Carl Rosner, *When Justice Fails: The David Milgaard Story* (Toronto: McClelland & Stewart, 1991).
Keir, D.L., *The Constitutional History of Modern Britain Since 1485*, 8th edn. (New York: Norton, 1966).
Knopff, Rainer and F.L. Morton, *Charter Politics* (Toronto: Nelson, 1989).
Laforest, Guy, *Trudeau and the End of a Canadian Dream* (Montreal and Kingston: McGill-Queen's Press, 1995).
Lang, O.E., ed., *Contemporary Problems of Public Law in Canada* (Essays in Honour of Dean F.C. Cronkite) (Toronto: McClelland & Stewart, 1964).
Lederman, W.R., ed., *The Courts and the Canadian Constitution* (Toronto: McClelland & Stewart, 1964).
Lederman, W.R., *Continuing Canadian Constitutional Dilemmas* (Toronto: Butterworths, 1981).
Mandel, Michael, *The Charter of Rights and the Legalization of Politics in Canada* (Toronto: Wall & Thompson, 1989).
Manfredi, C.P., *Judicial Power and the Charter: Canada and the Paradox of Liberal Constitutionalism* (Toronto: McClelland & Stewart, 1993).
McCloskey, R.G., *The American Supreme Court* (Chicago: University of Chicago Press, 1960).
McConnell, W.H., *Commentary on the British North America Act* (Toronto: Macmillan, 1977).
———, *Prairie Justice* (Calgary: Burroughs, 1980).
———, "The Judicial Review of Prime Minister R.B. Bennett's 'New Deal,'" (1968) 6 *Osgoode Hall Law Journal*, 39.
———, "Some Comparisons of the Roosevelt and Bennet 'New Deals,'" (1971) 9 *Osgoode Hall Law Journal*, 221.
McCormick, Peter, *Canada's Courts* (Toronto: Lorimer, 1994).
———, and Ian Greene, *Judges and Judging* (Toronto: Lorimer, 1990).
McWhinney, Edward, *Judicial Review in the English-Speaking World*, 2nd edn. (Toronto: University of Toronto Press, 1960).
———, *Quebec and the Constitution, 1960-1978* (Toronto: University of Toronto Press, 1979).

McWhinney, Edward, *Constitution-Making Principles, Powers, Practices* (Toronto: University of Toronto Press, 1981).
Mill, J.S., *On Liberty* (Englewood Cliffs, NJ: Prentice Hall, 1956).
Monahan, Patrick J., *Politics and the Constitution* (Toronto: Carswell, 1987).
———, *Constitutional Law* (Concord, ON: Irwin Law, 1997).
Moore, Vincent, *Angelo Branca: Gladiator of the Courts* (Vancouver: Douglas & McIntyre, 1981).
Morton, F.L., *Morgentaler v. Borowski, Abortion, the Charter and the Courts* (Toronto: McClelland & Stewart, 1992).
———, ed., *Law, Politics and the Judicial Process in Canada*, 2nd edn. (Calgary: University of Calgary Press, 1992).
O'Brien, David M., *Storm Center: The Supreme Court in American Politics* (New York: W.W. Norton, 1990).
Pickersgill, J.W., *Seeing Canada Whole: A Memoir* (Markham, ON: Fitzhenry & Whiteside, 1994).
Pound, Roscoe, *The Spirit of the Common Law* (Boston: Marshall Jones, 1921).
Pue, W.W., "Common Law Legal Education in Canada's Age of Light, Soap and Water," (1996) 23 *Manitoba Law Journal*, 654.
Romanow, R., J. Whyte, and H. Leeson, *Canada.... Notwithstanding* (Toronto: Carswell/Methuen, 1984).
Royal Commission on Dominion Provincial Relations, *Report* [Rowell-Sirois Report], (Ottawa: King's Printer, 1940).
Russell, Peter H., *Constitutional Odyssey: Can Canadians Become A Sovereign People?* (Toronto: University of Toronto Press, 1993).
———, *The Judiciary in Canada: The Third Branch of Government* (Toronto: McGraw Hill-Ryerson, 1987).
———, *Leading Constitutional Decisions*, 4th edn. (Ottawa: Carleton University Press, 1987).
———, *The Supreme Court of Canada as a Bilingual and Bicultural Institution*. Documents of the Royal Commission on Bilingualism and Biculturalism (Ottawa: Queen's Printer, 1969).
Scott, Stephen A., "Entrenchment by Executive Action: A Partial Solution to Legislative Override," (1982) 4 *Supreme Court Law Review*, 303.
———, "The Canadian Constitutional Amendment Process: Mechanisms and Prospects," in Clare Beckton and A. Wayne MacKay, eds., *Recurring Issues in Canadian Federalism* (Ottawa: The Royal Commission on the Economic Union and Development Prospects for Canada, 1986), 77.

Snell, James G., and Frederick Vaughan, *The Supreme Court of Canada: History of the Institution* (Toronto: University of Toronto Press, 1985).

Strayer, B.L., *The Patriation and Legitimacy of the Canadian Constitution* (Cronkite Memorial Lectures: College of Law, University of Saskatchewan, 1982).

———, *The Canadian Constitution and the Courts*, 3rd edn. (Toronto: Butterworths, 1988).

Swinton, K., *The Supreme Court and Canadian Federalism: The Laskin-Dickson Years* (Scarborough, ON: Carswell, 1990).

[Tremblay Report], *Royal Commission on Inquiry on Constitutional Problems* (Quebec: Queen's Printer, 1956).

Trudeau, P.E., *Federalism and the French Canadians* (Toronto: Macmillan, 1968).

———, *Memoirs* (Toronto: McClelland & Stewart, 1993).

———, and Gérard Pelletier, eds., *Against the Current: Selected Writings, 1939-1996* (Toronto: Carswell, 1965).

Varcoe, F.P. *The Constitution of Canada*, 2nd edn. (Toronto: Carswell, 1965).

Waite, P.B., *Lord of Point Grey: Larry MacKenzie of U.B.C.* (Vancouver: University of British Columbia Press, 1987).

Wheare, K.C., *Federal Government*, 4th edn. (London: Oxford University Press, 1963).

———, *The Statute of Westminster and Dominion Status*, 5th edn. (London: Oxford University Press, 1953).

Whitehead, A.N., *The Aims of Education* (London: Macmillan, 1929).

Williams, David R., *Duff: A Life in the Law* (Toronto and Vancouver: Osgoode Society and the University of British Columbia Press, 1984).

———, *Just Lawyers, Seven Portraits* (Toronto: Osgoode Society and the University of Toronto Press, 1995).

Whyte, J.D., and W.R. Lederman, *Canadian Constitutional Law*, 2nd edn. (Toronto: Butterworths, 1977).

INDEX

A

Abbott, Justice Douglas 221
Aboriginal Rights 187, 189
"Abortion rights" 117-23, 187, 218
Abusive process 47, 186
"Adverse Effect" discrimination 139-44
A.G. Can. and Dupond v. Montreal 221
A.G. Que. v. Irwin Toy 134-36
Alberta Statutes, Re 221
Allaire Report, the 228
Ancio, R. v. 154-55
Anderson government (Saskatchewan) 3
Anderson, T.M. 7
Anglin, Chief Justice 66
Arnup, Justice 18, 179
Arthurs, Harry 9

B

Bacon, Sir Francis, 33
Bagnall, R. v. 44
Basford, Ron 195
B.C. Government Employees Union v. AGBC 132-34
Beetz, Justice Jean 66, 69, 75, 83-89, 119, 135
"Beige Paper," Quebec Liberal Party 201
Bennett, Prime Minister R.B. 190
Best v. Samuel Fox & Co. Ltd. 173
Bhinder v. C.N.R. Co., Re 142-44, 186
Biden, Senator Joseph 193
Big M. Drug Mart, R. v. 118
Bilingualism on the prairies 168-72
Bird, Chief Justice 34
Black, Justice Hugo 192, 195
Blackstone, Sir William 172-73
Blair, Justice 175
Blakeney, Premier Allan ix, 185, 196, 198, 202, 203-10
Booth, General Bramwell 26
Bork, Judge Robert F. 193, 208
Bouchard, Premier Lucien, 116, 229
Boucher v. The King, 130
Bourassa, Henri 102
Bourassa, Premier Robert 85, 228
Bracton, Henry 163
Brennan, Justice William 192
Britnell, Dr. George 6
Brooke Enterprises Ltd. v. Wilding and Jones 45
Bryant, Michael J. 224
Burger, Chief Justice Warren 193
Byng, Lord, 113

C

Cahan, C.H. 191
Cairns, Alan C. ix, 185, 200
Caldwell et al., Re 177-80, 186
Canadian Bill of Rights, The 48-52, 67, 136-38, 164, 223, 225

Canadian Charter of Rights and
    Freedoms 63-64, 165, 168,
    170, chapter 7, 218-19, 222ff.
Cantell, Edward ix, 24
Capital punishment 47ff.
Carswell, Judge Harrold 193
"Categorical Imperative," The 10
Catholic school teachers, doctrinal
    requirements 177-80
Charlottetown Accord 72, 202
Chouinard, Justice Julien 69, 82,
    84-85, 88, 89
Chrétien, Prime Minister Jean 102,
    122, 197, 227
Chromiak, R. v. 163-64
Churchill Falls Reversion Act, Re 115-
    17
Clark, Prime Minister Joe 198
Coady, Justice James 28
commercial speech 134-36
common law, the 128, 129, 163,
    176, 180, 187, 188, 199, 220ff.
"Comprehensive Examination," the
    12
Consortium, loss of 172-74
Constructive murder 126-29
Consumer Protection 134-36
Corry, J.A. 8
Cory, Justice Peter 138
Court system 37-38
"*Creighton quartet*," the 224
Cronkite, Frederick C. 8-10, 88,
    217
Curtis, Dr. George F. ix, 3, 8, 10

D

Daniels v. The Queen 48-49
Davidson, Rev. J.A. ix, 67, 216
Dawson, R. MacGregor 8
Depression in Saskatchewan 4-5,
    19-20
De Tocqueville, Alexis 185, 230

Diamond, Elizabeth (McIntyre) 2,
    15, 17, 24, 35, 38
Dickson, Chief Justice Brian viii, 63,
    65, 66, 69, 72, 73, 77, 78, 82,
    91, 100, 117, 118, 133-34,
    143, 160, 168, 180, 192
Diefenbaker, Prime Minister John 2,
    7, 83, 197
Dobson v. Dobson 3, 22-23
Dole, Senator Robert 193
Douglas, Justice William O. 54
Driedger, Elmer A. 7
Drury, Ken 28
Duff, Chief Justice Sir Lyman P. 66,
    67
Dunlop, Professor Bruce 138
Duplessis, Premier Maurice 102,
    199, 222, 228

E

"Equality Rights," in Charter 220,
    226, 231
Estey, Justice W.Z. ("Bud") 7, 12,
    64, 65, 69, 83-84, 88, 89, 104,
    119, 165, 171-72, 177, 203
Exclusion of evidence pursuant to
    Charter 163-66

F

Farris, J.W. de B. 28
Farris, Chief Justice John L. 41, 51
Fauteux, Chief Justice Gerald 66
Ferguson, Premier G. Howard 102
Forsey, Senator Eugene A. 114
Fortas, Justice Abe 193
Frankfurter, Justice Felix 192
Freedom of Speech 129-31, 134-36,
    231
"Fundamental Justice," in s. 7 of the
    Charter 205-09

G

Gilmour, Fred J. 17, 19

Goldie, Justice D.M.M. viii, 105, 110, 134
Gouzenko, Igor 29
Grant, Justice William ix, 91
Gregory, George 31

H
Haldane, William H.M. 28
Hall, Justice E.M. 8
Harman, J. Howard 30
Harman, Robert H.G. 30
Harry v. Kreutzinger 55
Hatch, Senator Orrin 193
Haynesworth, Judge Clement 193
Head v. R. 155-57
Headnotes; McIntyre's criticism 89ff., 219-20
Herbert, A.P., 217
"Heritage Property" 176-77
Hill, Anita, 193
Hnatyshyn, Ray 7, 8, 215
Hogg, Peter W. 73, 124, 136-37
Holmes, Justice Oliver Wendell 51, 123, 163, 192
Hopkins, E. Russell 7, 11
Horback, R. v. 44
Hrabinsky, Justice Paul 155-57
Hugessen, Justice 125
Hughes, Chief Justice Charles Evans 189
Hunter, Ian 196
Hutchison, Bruce 38
Hutt v. The Queen 166

I-J
Iacobucci, Justice Frank 88, 145
Jackett, Chief Justice Wilber R. 7
Jebsens v. Lambert 55-56
"Joint Address" procedure, constitutional 102-03, 106, 108, 113, 115
Judges, appointment of 65ff., 185, 193ff.

Judiciary and Navigation Acts, in re 80

K
Kant, Immanuel 10
Keate, Stuart 26
King, Dr. Carlyle ix, 6
King, Prime Minister W.L. Mackenzie 191

L
La Forest, Justice Gerard V. viii, 8, 75, 83, 87, 169-72, 226
Laforest, Guy 185, 199-207
Lajoie, R. v. 154
Lalonde, Marc ix, 63, 67
Lamer, Chief Justice Antonio viii, 69, 70, 78, 82, 88, 91 ff., 106, 118, 126, 127-28, 143, 155, 160, 180, 192, 207-08, 215, 224, 225, 234
Lang, Otto E. 6, 7, 46, 47
Laski, Harold 197
Laskin, Chief Justice Bora 58, 63, 64, 65, 66, 69, 81, 100, 104, 106, 117, 189, 203
Law v. Canada 145
Law Society of British Columbia v. Andrews 89, 123-26, 186
Le Dain, Justice Gerald 82, 86-87, 89, 164-65
Lederman, William R. 114
Legal Education 217-19
Lewis, Douglas 209
L'Heureux-Dubé, Justice Claire 85-86, 88, 90, 226
Length of Supreme Court Judgments: McIntyre's criticism 89ff., 219ff.
Lévesque, Premier René 102, 197-98
Lochner v. New York 205
Loreburn, Lord Chancellor 79
Lougheed, Premier Peter 72, 203

INDEX

Lyon, Premier Stirling 203, 204

M

MacDonald, Vincent 8
Macfarlane, Allan 34
MacKay v. The Queen 136-38
MacMinn, George ix, 24
MacPherson, Justice D.K. 204
MacPherson, M.A. 5, 19
MacPherson, Justice M.A. "Sandy" ix, 8
McAllister, George A. 8
McAlpine, Claude 47
McCulloch v. Maryland 169-70
McDonald, Justice James 56
McEachern, Chief Justice 132-33
McIlree, John N. 30
McIlree, John Raymond 19, 22, 25, 30
McIntyre, Barbara 1, 3, 215
McIntyre, Charles Sidney 1ff., 24, 35
McIntyre, Eleanor 1
McIntyre, Hermione ("Mimi"), née Reeves 15, 215-16, 234
McIntyre, Hugh 1, 15, 16-17
McIntyre, Jean 1
McIntyre, John Duncan ("Jack") 1
McIntyre, John Stuart viii, 18, 24, 25, 35, 38
McIntyre, Pauline May 1, 24, 35
McIntyre, Justice William Rogers
Appointment to British Columbia Supreme Court 34; Appointment to British Columbia Court of Appeal 46; Appointment to Supreme Court of Canada 63; Austers (flight instruction) 14-15; Bencher of the Law Society 33-34; Canadian Officers Training Corps. 13; Companion of Canada, investment 215;

(McIntyre, W.R. *cont'd*)
honourary LLD, University of Victoria 215; marriage 16-17; Moose Jaw, Saskatchewan, life in 3ff.; musical interests 15; Ortona, Battle of 14; retirement from the Supreme Court of Canada 93-94; University of Saskatchewan, legal education at 5-13; Victoria, British Columbia, move to 18-20, 21ff.; Victory Bond tour 14; war service 5, 13ff.
McKay, Robert M. 30
McKay, Professor R.S. 138
McKenzie, Justice Lloyd George ix, 24, 27, 29, 30, 57, 187, 234
McLachlin, Justice Beverley 88, 124-25
Maksymiuk, J.P. 123
Mandatory minimum sentences 159-61
Manson, Justice A.M. 29-30
Mantha, Leo Anthony 31
Marshall, Chief Justice John 169-70
Marshall, Justice Thurgood 192
Martin, Gordon, 27
Martland, Justice Ronald 10, 65, 66, 67, 69, 83, 88, 107
Medical treatment, provision of to children 161-63
Meech Lake Accord 72, 202
Mercure, R. v. 168-72
Mercure, Father André 169
Mifflin, Chief Justice Arthur S. 75
Mile, Edward 7
Milgaard, David 59
Military Justice 136-38
Mill, John Stuart 230
Miller and Cockriell, R. v. 25, 47ff., 186, 225
Miranda v. Arizona 165
Monroe, Justice Craig 29
Morgentaler, Dr. Henry 117-23

INDEX   247

Morgentaler, R. v. 117-23, 186, 187, 218, 225
Morton, F.L. 144, 195
Moxon, Arthur 8
Mundell, David 7
Murphy, Kenneth 30
Muskrat v. United States 229
Myers v. Peel County Board of Education 174-76

N-O

Negligence, standard of care 174-76
Nemetz, Chief Justice Nathan 34, 133
"New Deals," Canadian and American 75, 78, 187, 190-91
Nicholson, John R. 34, 38
Nixon, President Richard M. 193
Norris, Tom 19
"Notwithstanding Clause," in Charter of Rights 231ff.
Odgers, Graham 24
O'Malley v. Simpson Sears 139-41, 186
Ontario Human Rights Commission v. Etobicoke 138-39, 141, 143, 179

P-Q

Parizeau, Premier Jacques, 229
Passchendaele, Battle of 38
Patriation of the Constitution 69, 101 ff.
Pickersgill, J.W. 7
Pierlet, Roger 48
Pigeon, Justice Louis-Philippe 53-54, 66, 198
Pound, Roscoe, 9, 210
Powell, Justice Lewis F. 192
Privy Council, overseas appeals to 47, 228
"Property," entrenchment of in Charter 204-05
Prostitution, legislation relating to 166-68
Pybus v. Pybus 45
Pym, Sir Francis 70, 110
Quebec v. Quebec Protestant School Board 228
Quebec, Province of, constitutional position of 101-03, 232-33
Quebec, Re Secession of 227-29

R

Rankin, Harry ix, 25, 48
Ratushny, Edward J. 140
"Reading Down" and "Reading In," judicial techniques of 138, 225-27
Reagan, President Ronald 193
"Reasonable Limits" clause 233
Reeves, Hermione (see, Mrs. Hermione "Mimi" McIntyre)
Ritchie, Justice Roland A. 65, 66, 69, 82, 83, 88, 107
Robertson, Justice A.B. 48, 51
Robinette, J.J. 105-06
Robinson, Svend, M.P. 195
Roethke, Theodore 26
Romanow, Ray 102, 197
Roncarelli v. Duplessis 221
Roosevelt, President Franklin D. 187-89
Rourke, R. v. 47, 186
Rushton v. Rushton 45
Ruttan, Justice Jack 31, 34, 57
RWDSU v. Dolphin Delivery 129-34
Ryan, Claude 102, 197
Ryan, William F. 8

S

St. Laurent, Louis S. 7, 81
St. Peter's Evangelical Lutheran Church v. Ottawa 176-77
Schachter v. R. 225-27
School Law 177-80
Schumpeter, Joseph 197

Scott, Frank 222
Scott-Harston, J.C. 25-26
Seaton, Peter 34
Second World War 13ff.
Senate reference, the 114-15
Sifton, family, 1
Smallwood, Joseph 115
Smith, Brian, 93
Smith, R. v. 159-61
Sommersett's case 221
Stevens, Geoffrey 67
Stratton, Chief Justice 87
Strayer, Barry 7, 112
Stubbe Estate, Re 45
"Substantive Due Process" 205ff.
"Supremacy of Parliament," the Charter and 230ff.
Supreme Court of Canada chapter 4, *passim*
Switzman v. Elbling 221

T

Tallis, Justice Calvin E. 156
Tarnopolsky, Justice Walter 160
Taschereau, Premier L.A. 102
Thatcher, Prime Minister Margaret 70, 110
Therens, R. v. 163-66
Thomas, Judge Clarence 193
Tobin, Brian, 116
Tollefson, E.A. 7
Tremblay Report 199
Tremblay v. Daigle 43
Trudeau, Pierre Elliott 11, 38, 64, 66, 69, 73, 102, 114, 185ff., 197
Tupper, Reginald 27
Turgeon, Gray 39
Tutton, R. v. 161-63
Tyrwhitt-Drake, Justice Montague 26, 57

U-V

United States Supreme Court 188ff.
University of Saskatchewan 5-13
University of Victoria 31
Vaillancourt, R. v. 126-29
Vancise, Justice William J. 156
Victoria, B.C. chapter 2
Volenti non fit injuria 175

W-Z

Wade, H.W.R. 103
Waite, P.B. 7
Warren, Chief Justice Earl 192
Whitehead, Alfred North 218
Whitmore, Ernie F. 11
Whittaker, Norman 19, 22, 26
Whitter, R. v. 166-68
Williams, David Ricardo ix, 40
Willis, John 8
Wilson, Justice Bertha viii, 16, 18, 24, 34, 65, 68, 75, 76, 85, 88, 89, 93, 119-21, 168, 180, 192, 207, 215, 234
Wilson, Chief Justice J.O. 23, 38-40, 46, 57, 185, 191
Woelk v. Halvorson 172-74
Wood, Josiah 48
Workload on the Supreme Court: McIntyre's criticism 89-90
Yebes, R. v. 157-59